A SCOTTISH FOOTBA

This book is dedicated to my father
TOM CAIRNEY
(1908–63)
who took me to my first football match

And this was the very ticket!

MAINSTREAM / SPORT

A SCOTTISH FOOTBALL HALL OF FAME

JOHN CAIRNEY

MAINSTREAM
PUBLISHING
EDINBURGH AND LONDON

This edition revised & updated, 2004

First published in Great Britain in 1998 by
MAINSTREAM PUBLISHING COMPANY
(EDINBURGH) LTD
7 Albany Street
Edinburgh
EH1 3UG

ISBN 1 84018 920 7

A CIP catalogue record for this book is available
from
the British Library

Typeset in Sabon
Printed in Great Britain by Cox & Wyman Ltd

Match Programme

Acknowledgements

The author's deep gratitude is owed to the following, who replied to my incessant letters, answered my telephone calls, e-mail messages and faxes, gave their time, the use of their laptops, beds for the night, meals at all times and the benefit of their libraries, scrapbooks and football memories. For all the long discussions, agreements and disagreements, good ideas and suggestions made, the decisions arrived at, for better or worse, I have to thank this group of people. They come from all over the world, from Scotland, England, Ireland, Canada, the United States, Australia and New Zealand, but they all have in common a real love of football and all who have played it. Every person mentioned will know what they have done in helping me make this book possible, and I sincerely thank them all.

Bob Adams, Mary Adams, Moira Anderson, Graham Bean, Bert Bell, the late Alan Bold, Alison Bowden, Ronnie Browne, Ron Caird, Alison Cairney, Jim Cairney, Jonathan Cairney, Philip Cairney, Andy Cameron, Bill Campbell, Jimmy Chalmers, Margaret Chalmers, John H. Clay, Elizabeth Craig, Jim Craig, Bob Crampsey, Judy Diamond, Tommy Docherty, John Donald, Elizabeth Donaldson, Brian Farquhar, Russell Galbraith, Bill Gilmour, Alan Gordon, Hugh Grant, Joan Grant, Derek Hill, Billy Hunter, John Hutchinson, Tony Irvine, Lorraine Kemp, Andrew Laycock, David Letham, Iain Livingstone, Jane Livingstone, Allan Lugton, Eugene MacBride, Stuart Marshall, Robert Matteo, Tony Matteo, Peter Matthews, John F. McBeth, Jack McGinn, Gerald McGrath, Frank McGuire, Paul McGuire, Peter MacKenzie, the late Jack McLay, Peter McLean, Andrew Miller, Andy Mitchell, Allan Moyes, Bobby Murdoch, Bill Murray, Jack Murray, Ged O'Brien, Martin O'Connor, R. Campbell Ogilvie, Kara Ogilvie, Alannah O'Sullivan, Alan Pattullo, R.W. Reid, Austin Reilly, Trevor Royle, Alan Sharpe, the late Ronnie Simpson, Grant Sword, Tom Wharton and Pat Woods.

A special acknowledgement is due to David Clarkson and the staff of Clarkson Car Hire of Baillieston who provided the car which allowed me to travel round Scotland and England in pursuit of updates.

My brother Jim playing for Portsmouth

A Personal Preface

Matt Busby might have been my father. I must hurriedly explain that there is no doubt whatsoever that Tom Cairney was my father, but before she married Tom in 1929, Mary Coyle had been walked home by the young Matt Busby from the Saturday night dancing at the Miners' Institute in Baillieston. Considering that that is a fair old walk, one is tempted to concede that anything might have happened in the country mile or two that separated rural Lanarkshire from the eastern outskirts of Glasgow, but my mother insisted that Sir Matt was always a gentleman. However, Tom Cairney was the better dancer. She said that, anyway, Matt was three weeks older than my father and that made a difference. Besides, he was going away to England to work and she didn't want to live in England. She never knew till February 1958, with the news of the Munich air crash, just what sort of work the once and future knight, the much-loved Matt Busby, went away to England to do. All my mother knew about football was that every other Saturday she had a houseful of men in our Parkhead room and kitchen and that meant extra soup plates and having drink in the house. As it happened, my father only had a passing interest in the game, After all, who could compete with Matt Busby? There is a story that my father kept goal for a Baillieston team but he gave it away as soon as he could and took up with the banjo and the bagpipes. He was in heavy demand playing at dances around Lanarkshire, that bedrock of Scottish football, but at the same time he was in just as heavy demand by my mother. When they got married in Baillieston he gave up the banjo and dance dates and concentrated on the local pipe band.

His younger brother, Phil, was said to have been a great player and Middlesbrough were all set to sign him just as war broke out in 1939. However, when he came back, invalided out of the army in 1943, his football days were over before they had even begun. This happened to a lot of promising players in that era. Nevertheless, Uncle Phil was influential in the development of my own young brother Jim as a footballer. Jim was good right from the beginning, and it was rather demoralising for me struggling to get into any team at St Mungo's Academy to find that my brother was right half in their very good third eleven while still in his second year. The trouble was that I was a sweeper before such a position was fashionable and my progress was hindered also by the fact that I would steal a cigarette while play was up at the other end. My only claim to football fame was that I was picked to kick Tommy Docherty whenever he kicked brother Jim when our respective Boys' Guild teams hacked it out on Shettleston Hill.

To further my own football ends around fourteen I organised our excellent little ad hoc Williamson Street team into a regular outfit we called the Springfield Rangers – a daring move for a collection of Parkhead boys, but since Jim and I, and little Felix McKenna, were the only Catholics, we had no option but to side with the majority who were all Rangers supporters. Anyway, it turned out to be quite a good team by street standards. We even had our own referee, a big boy for his age, who lived in a better kind of tenement in the next street. He couldn't play much, so we let him be referee. He wasn't bad at it at all and took it all very seriously. He even bought his own whistle. His name was Tom Wharton – or Tiny as he is known today to the world of international football referees. I couldn't play either. Well, certainly not as well as Jim or wee Felix. I started out in goal and made my way through most of the outfield positions as my inadequacies were discovered and eventually, when I got to outside left, I was unanimously promoted to match secretary. I took my revenge by disbanding the team soon afterwards and selling our Aston Villa jerseys at a nice little profit to another street team who went on to play in the Juvenile League with some success. It was the jerseys that did it.

There had been a couple of good players in the Springfield Rangers but only a few continued playing beyond their teens. Felix McKenna and Tom Gibson played Junior and Bill Murray had a good left foot, as they say, but my young brother Jim had class. Even then he had that calm in his play that all good players have. He was a footballing centre-half in the Willie Woodburn, Willie Corbett-style and before long he had moved from the street team to the school team to Tollcross Clydesdale as a juvenile then to Strathclyde Juniors, gathering Scottish caps at every level until he was asked to train across the road with Celtic. It looked as if he would follow the well-known path trodden by every Catholic football hopeful in the west of Scotland but a scout called Hugh Bone suddenly appeared around 1949 and enticed Jim to Portsmouth. He had been keeping an eye on his progress and rightly thought he was a hot property. Why not come and see what Pompey had to offer? He could bring his mother and father with him. It would be a nice wee holiday for them – all expenses paid. Well, when you live in Parkhead and you survived the awful winter of 1947 and somebody offers you a week in the sun on the south coast of England, you take it. So, Jim went down, and our parents went too. I was doing my National Service with the RAF in Germany or I daresay I might have gone as well.

Celtic, in the person of Jimmy McGrory, their affable but somewhat unimaginative manager (who proved that very few great players make great managers), had warned Jim not to sign anything. McGrory was little more than Chairman Kelly's man at the club, yet no one had made a move to sign Jim beforehand. In the manner of the management at that time, they took it for granted that they had a divine right to every boy in Glasgow who went to a Catholic school. When Jim returned from his week in the south, he resumed training at Celtic Park and was met immediately by Mr McGrory.

'Well, how did it go with Pompey?' he asked.

'Great,' replied Jim.

'You didn't sign anything then?' laughed the manager.

'Well, yes. In a way, you might say –' began Jim.

'Whit's that?'

'I signed a –'

'I thought I told you –'

'But I only –' said Jim again but he wasn't allowed any explanation and the upshot was that he was asked to collect his boots from the dressing-room. What he couldn't explain to the obtuse McGrory was that all he had signed was a receipt for the hotel expenses, not a playing contract. So Jim didn't sign for Celtic and instead went south to begin a career with Portsmouth, York City and teams in New York and Toronto that would keep him playing football until he was forty. He made a good life out of the game, yet he never fulfilled that high promise his early skills suggested because he had the bad luck at Portsmouth to be in reserve to the impregnable half-back line of Scoular, Flewen and Dickinson – who went out to set a record of 764 consecutive match appearances. Jim did manage to get a game against Arsenal at Highbury, and according to Charlie Buchan, the sports commentator, played a blinder, but he never got the chance again. He had few complaints, however. He was twenty and in his heaven. Well-paid, well-fed by a loving landlady (not to mention the landlady's daughter), well-thought-of by the board and by supporters alike, he drifted easily along, amassing a large Frank Sinatra collection, an immoral number of suits and changing his car every season. He was having a good time. At least it was better than working. He made good friends like Jackie Henderson (who was in the first team and played for Scotland) but Jim was happy to play as selected and take home his paypacket. He enjoyed his football and when he stopped enjoying it, he simply stopped playing.

Jim's is a more typical football story than might be guessed. Not all footballers make the banner headlines on the back page just as not all actors make the gossip columns. In both fields, the vast majority plug away quite contentedly, doing quite good work, picking up a decent wage, and ending their careers as placidly as they had begun them. In many ways these players are lucky. If they have never known the heights, they have similarly never plumbed the depths. Theirs is the middle course, the reward of a solid professionalism which is never dull because it is doing the same job as the big boys and they wouldn't be able to do it if the supporting players weren't there to help them. Football, like acting, is a team game after all. There are a lot of stars in the sky but there is a lot more sky than stars.

My cousin Philip (Uncle Phil's son) also played professionally but he did it later in a posher sort of way. He kept goal for Clyde while training to be a PT teacher and clearly he had a better perspective on life outside the dressing-room than many young players have at the start of their hoped-for careers. Another cousin (on my mother's side), Peter McNamee, enjoyed a full sporting life as outside-left for Peterborough United. Peter of Peterborough was his full title. My own son Jonathan was an enthusiastic footballer until he had to wear glasses. He remains enthusiastic about football but I honestly think his sister Jane was the better ball-player. Jonathan went up to Cambridge (where football as we know it began) but, like his grandfather, he has taken to playing pop music rather than any sport. Or is he really only playing for time? Football is hardly a bankable career option. However talented a boy can be, one harsh tackle can see the end of it all in a moment. Injury put paid to the brilliant Brian McLaughlan's promising career with Celtic. He is only one instance of good young players who never make it beyond the colt's stage for one reason or other. The attrition rate in talent is almost as high as it in the theatre yet thousands of boys at the start of every season look to it for glory and fame instead of being content – and lucky enough – to make a good job of it for life as my young brother did. It is such a ludicrously short life – you are a veteran at thirty. Small wonder the professional footballer, particularly when he has had his share of success at a good level, has problems in adjusting to reality when his playing days are finished. The main trouble is that what he is dealing with while playing is not reality. It's a dream world he inhabits, albeit of kicks and bruises and sometimes broken limbs, but the footballer knows he is working out the fantasies of thousands of his supporters. He is caught up in the temporary delirium they call football fever and there is no antidote for it. Once you catch it, you've got it for life and though the effects may diminish with age, you can never quite shake it off.

Is there a life after playing? Will the players of today return to the pavilions of their youth, to chat at the bar of the hospitality suite with old team-mates? Score old goals again, and net in hindsight all the sitters they missed. There is a place for extended truth in everyone's rosy memories, for sentiment and warm imagination. When we can give ourselves a pat on the back and take time to do the same for the up-and-coming youngsters to whom the great football names are just that – only names.

The Cairney name has certainly not made its mark on Scottish football. Brother Jim played all his senior football outside Scotland and even though Chic Cairney figured in the Celtic team-sheets after the Second World War and a Jimmy Cairney featured before it, neither could be said to have made a lasting impression. It was another Jimmy Cairney, from Paisley I believe, that charged wee Jimmy Johnstone with assault in 1974, but that is, admittedly, a rather tenuous football connection. Harry Cairney is a seasoned professional of the present day, and although he too is no relation, I am glad that he is taking the name into the game, even if at a sturdy rather than a distinctive level. For my own part, I never rose beyond the dizzy heights of player-manager for the Springfield Rangers, although I was once ordered off in a show business game at Tynecastle for kissing the goalkeeper. She was a blonde, I must hastily add.

Nevertheless, sixty years after seeing my first game, I am still football crazy and hope to stay that way for the remainder of my pensionable years. Meantime, as a professional actor, I only ask the reader to bear in mind Hamlet's injunction to Polonius:

'Will you see the players well-bestowed? . . .
for they are the abstracts and brief chronicles of the time . . .'

Introduction

In the seven years since the first edition of this book, Scotland has gained a Parliament but seems to have lost the place as far as football is concerned. According to FIFA we are ranked at 56 in their ratings, sandwiched between Latvia and Qatar, hardly the position one would expect of a nation that helped to give the sport to the world nearly a hundred and fifty years ago. We are now down among the minnows in a game where we were once quite big fish. What happened? Did the world end with the passing of Jim Baxter or the retiral of King Kenny Dalglish? It can't really be as simple as that, though those two great talents will never be easily replaced. Have the players lost the passion that marked the likes of Billy Bremner or the flair that belonged to Denis Law? Surely not. These were men of our yesterdays who, themselves, had to follow after older players like big George Young, Matt Busby and Jimmy Delaney, who, likewise, in their generation, followed the decade that gave us the Wembley Wizards. This is the football pedigree we in Scotland have inherited and it goes all the way back to men with long beards and big moustaches – the precursors of the 'Scotch professors', with gold guineas in their boots, who passed on their soccer skills to countries that are themselves now considered the giants of the contemporary game. It is a very Scottish irony.

But one question remains; why with our long history in the game, why have we not produced a Pele? Although with Jimmy Johnstone, still of recent playing memory, we have come close. And Bobby Templeton from another age had his many admirers, so had Bobby Walker from earlier still, but none quite attained Pele's peerless position. Why? If the answer can't be found in our past players, can it be deduced from our present squads? Many of our present Scotland players are there because they have come through the coaching system rather than any blazing performances on the field. At the moment, we are producing worthy professional tradesmen, when we ought to be searching for the artists.

It may only be the fault of the times we live in, where the bottom line is money and any other consideration is irrelevant. A lot of fun has gone out of the game and the emphasis appears to be in not losing at any cost. This is only because there is so much money at stake. One lost match can make the difference between make or break for a team for the whole season, so who can blame the players. They play *frightened*. As a consequence, the approach is negative and a lot of the old exhilaration has gone. There is little sense of playing the game, but rather of two teams working at it. This is a real pity because the essential appeal of a football match is the excitement it generates at the prospect of a goal, not in the stolid preventing of one. We seem to have got it back to front in some way and it may take time to get the game back to its green grass roots.

Who would have thought, when this book was first published in 1998, that seven years later, football institutions like Heart of Midlothian would be facing bankruptcy and the possible sale of their Tynecastle ground. Even as I write, the threat of what is now called 'administration' is sweeping through Scottish football like the Black Death. 'Administration' is the euphemism for the old-fashioned bank foreclosing but any other word would smell as sour. All it means is that the lawyers and accountants have moved in and the books are on the table. The clubs can't be run from a biscuit tin any more – it is PLC where FC used to suffice. The roll of Scottish League members in 2004 reads like a war memorial with its list of the fallen. Dundee and Motherwell are already being 'administered', the old Airdrieonians have gone the way of Clydebank and Dumbarton died just as the invincible Renton did all those years ago. Albion Rovers are teetering on the edge and Falkirk, too, is clinging on thanks mainly to their supporters. And how ludicrous to see Partick Thistle trying to play out their season in the courtroom. It's all so sad, but it's the way of the football world today.

It's a sign of our corporate times. Big bucks is the only language spoken by the new princes of the market-place, like Roman Abramovitch, whose oil roubles have bought Chelsea as if it were a toy to play with, but football clubs are not toys. They are flesh and blood organisms whose existence matters to thousands of people who resent being toyed with. Then there are the players' agents, the new boys on the street, who operate stealthily behind a whole alphabet of initials and at the end of expensive mobiles. The late, great Jock Stein was one of the far-sighted who prophesied that the coming of the agent would theatricalise the sport and bring it to an end as a seasonal, competitive entity. He was right. The ubiquitous and iniquitous, if inevitable, activities of middlemen are a mixed blessing to say the least. The game will have to be wrested from their hands, and those of the other various entrepreneurs who have descended on football from their tax havens like so many locusts.

Football is now a virtual, year-round, publicity-bound adjunct of the entertainment industry forever tied to its inexorable demands. Television is the name of the game and if the cameras don't get you, the bailiffs will. Which is why we have breakfast-time kick-offs and logos with everything. The referee must take his cue to start the game from the television director as if he were an actor in the studio. Yet what is an actor, after all, but a player too. As Macbeth puts it – 'a poor player, that struts and frets his hour upon the stage, and then is heard no more'. The same might be said of the footballer. His is a short life and the rest of his days often stretch to an increasing anonymity – so who can blame him for making hay while the floodlights shine?

But someone has to pay for this particular harvest and it is always the punter, the ordinary supporter. In Scotland's case, the foot soldiers of the Tartan Army. In the end it all comes down to one man and his boy – or girl – at the turnstiles. The supporter is the real payer of the wages and it is the cost of these wages that is crippling the clubs and bringing them down. Why can't wages come down, or at least be better dispersed? It is surely iniquitous that at one end of the spectrum a player can earn ten thousand pounds a day while at the other a whole club can't bring that sum in through the gate. This is why the smaller clubs are folding. It is this kind of pressure that inhibits any kind of experiment and leaves everyone clinging to a stale status quo that has already outlived its day. What is needed now in Scottish football is not further evolution, but revolution. Barricades must come down and old anomalies exposed. Dying clubs should be put out of their misery. Ailing clubs should amalgamate. Time-serving directors with long-standing egos should be dispatched to the golf club and energetic executives brought in to steer football's survivors into the 22nd century.

Rangers and Celtic have outgrown Scotland. They lumber through their Scottish League fixtures like a couple of sixth-formers in a kindergarten. It's too one-sided to be fair sport any longer. They should be playing in England – or at least as part of a new British league – or even the Super-European League that will surely one day come. Yet, even Rangers and Celtic are in debt to the tune of millions. In what other way of business could a firm, even the 'Old Firm', continue to trade while trailing such monumental deficits behind them? Yet both go blithely on bolstered by their legions of fans, immune from the strictures of business practice that would put a plumber in jeopardy were he to follow their working example. The Old Firm is so obviously far above the rest, but surely they are not above the law? If these two titans have to operate while on overdraft, what chance have the little clubs who survive on a shoestring anyway? Money has become so unreal in football that reality itself begins to seem the fiction. The truth here is that something has got to change and change quickly and who better to give the lead than the two biggest clubs in Scotland?

In this post-Bosman era, freedom of contract has brought many much-needed benefits to the status of the professional player but its side effects have had a near fatal effect on the game as a whole. Traditional loyalties now appear to mean nothing and there is little incentive for the minor clubs to find and groom their own players as once they did. It would seem time to find a new system – or revert to the old one. I think the only answer in the long run is to revert to amateurism at the lower levels of the game and let the youngsters play for nothing and for the love of it. If he is good enough he will attract the notice of the bigger clubs and both he and his club will benefit from any transfer fee and even a share of later transfers. Queen's Park have worked this way from the beginning and they are still around.

A modern professional game should be run in a modern manner but at its heart should still be all the passion and enthusiasm that typified its development. Players once played for the jersey and they should be allowed to do so again. Only in this way would a proper attitude be rekindled and steps taken to retrieve our former status as a football nation. The game for the game's sake should be the rallying cry at the basic level. Money should come into it as the apprentice rises in his trade, and when he has served his time he can take full financial advantage of his talent. In the meantime, both he and his club would have breathing space to survive – and even prosper. This is a difficult proposition to accept on a day when a 14-year-old boy in American soccer, Freddy Adu, can sign a contract that will net him half a million dollars in his first year. But that is America and we are Scotland. We have to cut our tartan cloth to more severe standards.

Good players, like good entertainers, appear in every generation and there's no reason to suppose that the supply of either will suddenly dry up. It is harder, however, to get started in the professional game today. Young boys are glued to their computers and are not easily tempted to come out and play as they once were. Schoolteachers are not encouraged to organise the school matches on a Saturday morning the way they used to, and most of the juvenile and junior clubs, once such valuable stepping-stones to higher things, have gone the way of their senior counterparts. The way to the top was once a measured, deliberate way up the slope, learning where to put your feet and building up your stamina with your skill as you went along. Watching your step and listening to the older players on the park and off. Nowadays, if a boy shows some promise at ten, he is immediately shunted off to some football academy where he is treated as a professional player and hurried up the ladder towards a place in the big team. Small wonder the youngster arrives at the top breathless and can't last the pace. Not all of us can be a Wayne Rooney.

The Wayne Rooneys and the Freddy Adus are the Mozarts of their profession. They are unique, genuine prodigies, and are out of the norm. Who knows, 16-year-old James McCluskey of Hibs could be the same for us one day, but young professionals in their apprentice years shouldn't be hurried. They should be encouraged to play much as they might have done in the streets when jackets were thrown down on any available open space. They might still have the company of old seniors on their way down who would be able to pass on to the youngsters all the tricks of the trade they themselves had learned on their own way up. In this way, a valuable experience is passed on, and that can do nothing but good. Freed from the burden of an overweight wage bill, clubs would be able to pay their way from week to week and consequently survive from season to season.

Meantime, lessons will have to be learned from the contemporary exploitation by mercenaries on all sides. And *in* all sides. Only recently, Rangers fielded a team in a Scottish league game, which did not boast a single Scot. The fans don't mind this, but they object to subsidising these gilded imports, who enjoy their season in the sun before going off to serve the next paymaster. The foreign influx is a comparatively recent phenomenon but it was foreseen before the First World War. Even then, some were demanding native-only teams, which provoked a quick response in football circles of the time. As Jack Alexander reported in his excellent *McCrae's Battalion* (Mainstream 2003), John McCartney, manager of Heart of Midlothian, writing to the Edinburgh *Evening News* in 1911, said quite bluntly:

'If an albino piccaninny with one leg shorter than the other can play the game better than any of the men already here, then I will sign him. If he comes from Bacup rather than Newtongrange, it will not make one jot of difference.'

He went on:

'One of these days, when the game has developed more in some of the Continental countries, we will have Danes and Belgians, Germans and Frenchmen, Hungarians and Russians, and Turks and Bulgarians coming over to take part in our football. It may still be a long way off, but a day may come when an effort will be made in that direction, and even those who may be inclined to laugh at the idea as fantastical will surely admit that it would be a good thing if it could be carried out.

There are many who are still not so sure, but there is no denying the presence of at least one Continental player in every team in the country. What Mr McCartney could never have foreseen, however, no matter his prescience in this respect, was the impact that Africa and the Far East have made on the present-day game. This is a presence that can only grow as the power of the agents grows. The sport must be returned to its proper balance, acknowledging only three main components – the clubs, the players and the supporters. The first, who want to stay in business, the second, who want to play, and the third, who only want to watch them. It's really all very simple. Which is why Mr Thring called it *The Simplest Game* in 1862. In 2004, it has become very complicated. There is a new meaning today in playing for the jersey. It indicates that the player is the property of the sponsor. Corporate demands rule – OK? Since there is no obvious other way ahead, as good a way of any is to try and put us back on course. The question remains – 'Stands Scotland where she did?' Perhaps the best thing for football to do would be to look back to its beginnings for the answer.

It's hard to believe that in football there was life before Bosman. There was a time when agents were unknown and money wasn't everything. It was *nearly* everything but players did play for the jersey when it didn't have a number or a logo on it and although winning was important, playing the game for its own sake was still possible. And watching it, as it grew over the century, and before the advent of cheap cinema, it was often the only solace the poorer people had. It was an escape, an opiate in the hard times, the only colour in a drab week. Footballers became accessible as immediate heroes, they were hailed as gods even though they were in fact, as everyone knew, mere ordinary working-class men themselves, who smoked and drank, swore fulsomely, put bets on horses and had women on the side when they could. That may have been, but to the grey caps on the terracing they were from Olympia via the Garngad and Govan.

Football is more than a mere game in Scotland; it is a part of the Scottish psyche whatever team the individual Scot may support.

The founding fathers of the game could never have foreseen the enormous impact this sport cum commercial operation would have on modern life. Across the world, thanks to FIFA, it has a financial turnover of more than two hundred billion dollars, greater than any multinational company but that is almost the least of its effects on society as we know it. It is now the accepted secular pan-religion, the new coinage of prestige among nations and it joins whisky, haggis and bagpipes as something that Scotland is, or was, especially known for. We are such a wee country yet we once produced big football players. Not great teams, perhaps (we are too thrawn and self-destructive to do that), but there is no denying that in every decade we produce great players. This is why football matters in Scotland, because it matters *to* Scotland. This is why it is important to remember our past in this respect and why the history of the great men who played football for Scotland is meaningful in the context of our more complicated times. They have supplied us with a football heritage we must try to remember and treasure.

Association Football might owe its name to the manner of its emergence in 1848, but it is also an association of memory, place, colour, event and personal meaning that makes the sport both mythic and mysterious. It is not only a matter of results and statistics, medals and silverware and reports in the newspapers. It is a metaphysical phenomenon woven into the very fabric of our lives and to try and tear it out would rip us apart. Football is often more real than real life because we live it in our heads and it's there all the time. We go to sleep on it and waken up on it and we regulate our reaction to everyday events by how they related to a game we saw that day – or night – and very often we know more about our team's players than we do about our next-door neighbours. Football to the fanatic is family. It is flesh and blood. It is also a malaise, a fever, a drug and the recovery rate is not high. You can die from it, but it takes years – well a few seasons at least – but during a match you can experience a lifetime's sensation of abandoned joy, dragging despair, hot anger, and cold disgust. This is football as therapy, and a lot to ask of a mere game.

Lest we forget altogether where our football roots lay, it is good to remember the best of the past. Deep down, it is still the same game and deep down it is still the same players, but one cannot help wonder who of today's heroes will still be remembered a hundred years from now?

Football memories are more than souvenirs of supreme athleticism, mental tokens of a big occasion, they are etchings on the subconscious that sear to the very heart of our indefinable Scottishness, a deep part of our national pride. Yet the creators of this meaningful resource were only footballers playing for money – but they were much more than that. They were us. And still are. Which is why we remember them still and keep them close to us, near the heart and always available. We can take them out now and again and look at them fondly. They are still pristine and young. And for that moment, so are we. This is the joy of nostalgia. This is why, more than ever, we need our heroes.

One Hundred Footballers for Scotland

(with teams played for and date of first appearance)

1. **A.F. Kinnaird** (*Old Etonians and the Wanderers*) 1870
2. **W.M. McKinnon** (*Queen's Park*) 1872
3. **H. McNeil** (*Third Lanark and Queen's Park*) 1874
4. **J.J. Lang** (*Clydesdale, Third Lanark and Sheffield Wednesday*) 1876
5. **W. Arnott** (*Queen's Park, Corinthians, Kilmarnock, Linfield Athletic, Third Lanark, St Bernard's, Celtic and Notts County*) 1883
6. **J.E. Doig** (*Arbroath, Blackburn Rovers, Sunderland and Liverpool*) 1886
7. **J. Kelly** (*Renton and Celtic*) 1888
8. **H. Wilson** (*Newmilns, Sunderland, Bristol City and Third Lanark*) 1890
9. **J. Bell** (*Dumbarton, Everton, Celtic, New Brighton and Preston North End*) 1890
10. **A. McMahon** (*Hibernian, Burnley, Celtic, Partick Thistle*) 1892
11. **D. Doyle** (*East Stirlingshire, Newcastle East End, Grimsby Town, Everton and Celtic*) 1892
12. **J. Drummond** (*Falkirk and Rangers*) 1898
13. **J. Madden** (*Dumbarton, Celtic, Dundee and Tottenham Hotspur*) 1893
14. **N. Gibson** (*Rangers and Partick Thistle*) 1895
15. **R.S. McColl** (*Queen's Park, Newcastle, Rangers and Queen's Park*) 1896
16. **J. Cowan** (*Vale of Leven, Aston Villa and Queen's Park Rangers*) 1896
17. **N. Smith** (*Rangers*) 1897
18. **J.T. Robertson** (*Morton, Everton, Southampton, Rangers and Chelsea*) 1898
19. **A. Smith** (*Rangers*) 1898
20. **R.C. Hamilton** (*Elgin City, Queen's Park, Rangers, Fulham, Hearts and Dundee*) 1899
21. **A.G. Raisbeck** (*Hibernian, Stoke City, Liverpool, Partick Thistle and Hamilton Academical*) 1900
22. **H.G. Rennie** (*Morton, Hearts, Hibernian, Rangers and Kilmarnock*) 1900
23. **R. Walker** (*Hearts*) 1900
24. **A.T. Buick** (*Arbroath, Hearts and Portsmouth*) 1902
25. **R.B. Templeton** (*Hibernian, Aston Villa, Newcastle, Arsenal, Celtic, Kilmarnock and Fulham*) 1902
26. **C.B. Thomson** (*Hearts and Sunderland*) 1904
27. **J. Quinn** (*Celtic*) 1905
28. **J. McMenemy** (*Celtic, Stenhousemuir and Partick Thistle*) 1905
29. **A. McNair** (*Stenhousemuir and Celtic*) 1906

30. J. Brownlie (*Third Lanark and Dundee United*) 1909
31. A.L. Morton (*Queen's Park and Rangers*) 1920
32. J. McMullan (*Third Lanark, Partick Thistle, Maidstone United and Manchester City*) 1920
33. A. Cunningham (*Kilmarnock, Rangers and Newcastle United*) 1920
34. A.N. Wilson (*Middlesbrough, Hearts, Dunfermline, Chelsea, Queen's Park Rangers and Nîmes*) 1920
35. D.D. Meiklejohn (*Rangers*) 1922
36. H.K. Gallacher (*Queen of the South, Airdrie, Newcastle United, Chelsea, Derby County, Notts County, Grimsby and Gateshead*) 1924
37. A.S. Jackson (*Dumbarton, Aberdeen, Huddersfield Town, Chelsea, Ashton, Margate and Nice*) 1925
38. A.W. James (*Raith Rovers, Preston North End and Arsenal*) 1926
39. J.D. Harkness (*Queen's Park and Hearts*) 1927
40. R.L. McPhail (*Airdrieonians, Rangers and St Mirren*) 1927
41. J.E. McGrory (*Celtic*) 1928
42. J. Thomson (*Celtic*) 1930
43. D. Duncan (*Hull City, Derby County and Luton Town*) 1933
44. M.W. Busby (*Manchester City, Liverpool and Hibernian*) 1933
45. T. Walker (*Hearts and Chelsea*) 1934
46. J.M. Simpson (*Dundee United and Rangers*) 1934
47. J. Dawson (*Rangers and Falkirk*) 1934
48. J. Delaney (*Celtic, Manchester United, Aberdeen, Falkirk, Derry City, Cork Celtic and Elgin City*) 1935
49. J. Carabine (*Third Lanark*) 1938
50. W. Shankly (*Carlisle United, Preston North End and Partick Thistle*) 1939
51. W.B. Liddell (*Liverpool*) 1947
52. W. Miller (*Celtic, Clyde and Hibernian*) 1946
53. W. Waddell (*Rangers*) 1947
54. W.A. Woodburn (*Rangers*) 1947
55. G.L. Young (*Rangers*) 1947
56. G. Smith (*Hibernian, Hearts, Dundee and Drumcondra*) 1947
57. W. Steel (*Leicester City, St Mirren, Morton, Derby County, Dundee and in USA*) 1947
58. J.C. Cowan (*St Mirren, Morton, Sunderland and Third Lanark*) 1948
59. R. Evans (*Celtic, Chelsea, Newport County, Morton, Third Lanark and Raith Rovers*) 1948
60. L. Reilly (*Hibernian*) 1948
61. J. Mason (*Third Lanark*) 1948
62. W.R.L. Bauld (*Hearts*) 1950
63. R. Auld (*Celtic, Birmingham City and Hibernian*) 1950
64. W. McNaught (*Raith Rovers*) 1951
65. R.Y. Collins (*Celtic, Everton, Leeds United, Bury, Morton, Oldham Athletic, Shamrock Rovers and in Australia*) 1951
66. R. Johnstone (*Hibernian, Manchester City and Oldham Athletic*) 1951
67. T.H. Docherty (*Celtic, Preston North End and Arsenal*) 1952
68. W.E. Ormond (*Stenhousemuir, Hibernian and Falkirk*) 1954

69. T. Younger (*Hibernian, Liverpool, Falkirk, Stoke City and Leeds United*) 1955

70. E. Caldow (*Rangers, Stirling Albion and Corby Town*) 1957

71. D.C. Mackay (*Hearts, Tottenham Hotspur, Derby County and Swindon*) 1957

72. W.D.F. Brown (*Dundee, Tottenham Hotspur, Northampton Town and Toronto Falcons*) 1958

73. J.A. White (*Alloa Athletic, Falkirk and Tottenham Hotspur*) 1959

74. D. Law (*Huddersfield Town, Manchester City, Torino, Manchester United and Manchester City*) 1959

75. A. Young (*Hearts, Everton, Glentoran and Stockport County*) 1960

76. J.C. Baxter (*Raith Rovers, Rangers, Sunderland and Nottingham Forest*) 1960

77. W. McNeill (*Celtic*) 1961

78. W. Henderson (*Rangers, Sheffield Wednesday, Hong Kong Rangers and Airdrie*) 1963

79. J. Greig (*Rangers*) 1964

80. W.M. Hamilton (*Sheffield United, Middlesbrough, Hearts, Hibernian, Aston Villa and Ross County*) 1965

81. W.J. Bremner (*Leeds United and Hull City*) 1965

82. J. Johnstone (*Celtic, San Jose Earthquakes, Sheffield United, Dundee, Shelbourne and Elgin City*) 1965

83. R. Murdoch (*Celtic and Middlesbrough*) 1966

84. C. Cooke (*Aberdeen, Dundee, Chelsea and in USA*) 1966

85. R.C. Simpson (*Queen's Park, Third Lanark, Newcastle, Hibernian and Celtic*) 1967

86. J. Smith (*Aberdeen, Newcastle and Whitley Bay*) 1968

87. A. Gemmill (*St Mirren, Preston North End, Derby County, Nottingham Forest, Birmingham City, Wigan and Jacksonville*) 1971

88. R.A. Hartford (*West Bromwich Albion, Manchester City, Nottingham Forest, Everton, Norwich City and Bolton Wanderers*) 1972

89. K.M. Dalglish (*Celtic and Liverpool*) 1972

90. D.F. McGrain (*Celtic, Hamilton Academical and Rochdale Rovers, Brisbane*) 1973

91. J. Jordan (*Morton, Leeds United, Manchester United, AC Milan, Verona, Southampton and Bristol City*) 1973

92. G.J. Souness (*Tottenham Hotspur, Middlesbrough, Liverpool, Sampdoria and Rangers*) 1975

93. A.R. Rough (*Partick Thistle, Hamilton Academical, Hibernian, Celtic, Ayr United and Orlando Lions, USA*) 1976

94. J.N. Robertson (*Nottingham Forest, Derby County, Nottingham Forest, Corby and Grantham*) 1978

95. D. Cooper (*Clydebank, Rangers and Motherwell*) 1980

96. G.D. Strachan (*Dundee, Aberdeen, Manchester United and Coventry City*) 1980

97. J. Leighton (*Aberdeen, Manchester United and Hibernian*) 1983

98. C. Nicholas (*Celtic, Arsenal, Aberdeen and Clyde*) 1983

99. P.M.L. McStay (*Celtic*) 1984

100. A.M. McCoist (*St Johnstone, Sunderland, Rangers and Kilmarnock*) 1986 and

101. A.N. Other

Chapter One

Specious Origins

If Adam had been a Scot he would've trapped the apple as it fell, slipped it forward to Eve, run forward to receive the return and banged it past the devil as he came out to cut down the angle. God would have blown for a goal and the world might have been a totally different place. At least for all Scots who loved football. That fanciful image of a supposed original paradise in the garden of Eden is just as acceptable as any when one considers the origins of this game of football. Despite the scholarly zeal of such as Professor H.A. Giles of Cambridge, and the work of later writers like Geoffrey Green and Brian Glanville, nobody is really sure how it all began. Bill Murray, author of the comprehensive *Football: A World Game* (Scolar Press, 1994), is adamant that there is no specific origin. According to all authorities there was a form of football in China more than 2,000 years ago during the Han dynasty. It was called *tsu chu* and consisted of shooting a leather ball with the foot at a small aperture in a silk screen hung between two bamboo poles about thirty feet high. The two teams assembled more or less in the manner of a penalty shoot-out today and whoever got the ball through the hole the most times was the winner. The winning team was treated to wine and gifts, but the captain of the losing team was flogged. In Japan, some fourteen centuries ago, their version was called *kemari* and it was played on a stretch of level ground between four trees – a pine tree at one corner, a cherry tree at another and at the other end, about fourteen metres away, a willow and a maple. Such an arboreal demand wouldn't make for the widespread development of this form, one would think. There were eight players in each side, four at each tree and the game was to kick the ball, ceremoniously and artistically, to your opponents and they were to return it if possible and with the same degree of ceremony. It was almost a more decorous form of a pre-match kickabout, with perhaps a finer display of ball control.

Thus, the beginnings of the game came out of the East and re-emerged as a much less formal ball game known to the Greeks as *episkyros* and to the Romans as *harpastum*, a word which derived from the Greek word for handball. The Romans may have brought this game to Britain, for a form of it was played at Chester where the two teams or bands attempted to get the ball past the other's line by any means possible. This game became so violent that it was banned and replaced by foot races, but a form of it still continued to be played annually on Shrove Tuesday right up to the Middle Ages. In the absence of a ball, teams of soldiers would use an enemy's head. So serious did these early games become that commanders complained that people did not give proper attention to archery, so obsessed were they by their various football rivalries. In Midlothian, Scotland, when the men were away at war, the married women would play the spinsters. The married women always won. As the Romans spread through Europe so did their games. In Italy, the rough and ready battle of citizens in the streets was refined somewhat as the medieval game of *calcio* played on feast-days in Florence. By this time, two sides of twenty-one young men faced each other across the piazza, which was covered with sand for the occasion. No doubt to absorb the blood which was spilt. It is difficult to describe such strenuous recreations as *playing*.

Nevertheless, this primitive form of football allowed the common people to have their day and its history could be written in terms of the constant attempts to suppress it. Royal edicts, parliamentary proclamations, magisterial pronouncements all sought at various times over several hundred years to prevent, or at least control, the riotous assembly of youths who met to vie with each other in the search for a ball through city streets and country fields from first light to last. Some were killed in the process, many were seriously wounded but many, many more saw it as a chance for fun, an opportunity for looting and a way of letting off steam within – and often without – legal limits. From the first century, the Irish had taken the Roman game and made it their own in a code they called *hurling* – which they still play today. A mixture of football, rugby and hockey which could reasonably be described as manslaughter. In Scotland, the old Handsel Monday football match played on the Roman camp at Callander was held to be 'a custom of immemorial usage'. The same crude form still exists in the famous Ba' Game in Jedburgh. On Candlemas Day, in every parish, the married men played the bachelors, the ball being thrown up at noon and the game was carried on till sunset. A contemporary report describes it as follows:

> Brissit, brawnis, and broken banis,
> Strife, discord wastie wanis,
> Crukit in eild, syne halt withal,
> Thir are the bewties of the fute-ball.

Such was the mass of involvement in what might be called folk football across the land that the authorities were powerless to prevent it – but they tried. The first Parliament of James the First, held at Perth in 1424, ordained that:

> na man play at the fute-ball, under the paine of fiftie schillings, to be raised to the Lord of the land, als often as he be tainted or the Schireffe of the land of his ministers . . .

The Parliament of James the Second, held in Edinburgh in 1457, also ordained that 'the fute-ball and the golfe be utterly criet doon . . .' And in 1491, James the Fourth decreed 'that in na place of the Kinge's realme there be usit fute-baws, golfe, or other such unprofitable sportes.'

In the late eighteenth century, a Shrovetide football match was held at Scone, in Perthshire.

> The game was this: he who at any time got the ball into his hands ran with it until overtaken by the opposite party and then, if he could shake himself loose from those on the opposite side who seized him, he ran on. If not, he threw the ball from him, unless it was wrested from him by the other party. The object of the married men was to hang it, or put it three times into a small hole in the moor, which was the dool, or limit, on the one hand; that of the bachelors was to drown it or dip it three times in a deep place in the river, the limit on the other. The party who could effect either of these objects won the game.

This can be seen to be more handball than football, but at this stage it was anything goes in football and rules could be made up by those taking part, often as they went along. Sufficient to say that before any game, the children were taken indoors and windows were boarded up. Not much has changed in a few hundred years. In the early nineteenth century the men of Ettrick, sponsored by Sir Walter Scott, met the men of Yarrow, backed by the Earl of Home. One result was a song by Sir Walter, 'Lifting the Banner of the House of Buccleuch'. This could be described as the first football song.

I spy the Furies of the Football War:
The Prentice quits his Shop, to join the Crew,
Increasing crouds the flying Game pursue.

Football was obviously an excuse for more than just scoring a goal but it could no longer be limited to feast-days and holidays, and the increasing alarm felt by the populace made itself evident by the growing concern of the authorities. Social forces were being released here that could be dangerous. In the pre-industrial society unrest was easily precipitated and football passions could spark off even wider disturbances. The games were played on a Sunday and this attracted a vehement reaction from the churches. Yet ironically it was from the Church, or at least Christianity, that the first move came to create some kind of order from the general mayhem that passed for football before the early decades of the nineteenth century. Until that time, football had never been accepted by people of influence or property. With the growing industrialisation of the country and the movement of large sections of the population into the towns, the game no longer had the space that it had enjoyed. It had to adapt to the changing times but the rules were in such a state of flux it was difficult to know where to begin.

The British game had never attained the discipline and control of the Italian *calcio* and as long as it remained a threat to public order it could not have the support of the landed classes. It had been played but frowned on at the two universities but it was from these same universities, or rather the public schools that fed them, that the decisive lead finally came. Meanwhile, football at this time, *circa* 1837 (when Victoria ascended the British throne), was beginning to pull itself together and tighten up. Mob rule ceased to apply but the general aim of the game remained the same – to score a goal.

James Walvin quotes this report in his *The People's Game* (Mainstream, 1994):

> When a match of foot-ball is made, two parties each containing an equal number of competitors, take the field, and stand between two goals, placed at a distance of eighty or a hundred yards the one from the other. The goal is usually made with two sticks driven into the ground, about two or three feet apart. The ball which is commonly made of a blown bladder, and cased with leather, is delivered in the midst of the ground, and the object of each is to drive it through the goal of the antagonists, which object being achieved, the game is won. The abilities of the performers

are best displayed in attacking and defending the goals; and hence the pastime was more frequently called a goal at football than a game at football. When the pastime becomes exceeding violent, the players kick each other's shins without the least ceremony, and some of them are overthrown at the hazard of their limbs.

Samuel Butler, head of Shrewsbury School until 1836, dismissed the game as 'fit only for butcher boys' and Eton could not consider the game of football 'at all gentlemanly'. Yet it was Dr Thomas Arnold, Headmaster of Rugby, who initiated, however unwittingly, the movement that eventually reformed the whole playing of football. There is yet another irony. Myth has it that it was at this same school, in 1823, that William Webb Ellis, 'with a fine disregard for the rules of football as played in his time, *first* took the ball in his arms and ran with it, thus originating the distinctive feature of the Rugby game'. One wonders how Ellis, a future clergyman in the Church of England, would have fared playing against the married men of Scone.

Dr Arnold inaugurated the doctrine of Muscular Christianity, and it was this creed, assisted by the fictions of such writers as Charles Kingsley and Tom Hughes, which created a movement which, like St George, slew the old dragon of mob-football and gave it rule, order and discipline. Muscular Christianity was the belief that glory might be given to God through organised games. The new public schools now springing up throughout England needed to find a means of *tiring* the several hundred young boys under their charge so it was a case of *mens sana in corpore sano* and games, especially football, were introduced as part of the curriculum. However, the football played could not be the plebeian game. There was not the space for it, or for the numbers involved, in the quadrangles, closes and enclosed playgrounds of many of the public schools. Only those in the rural areas, such as Rugby, Shrewsbury, Lancing, etc., had playing fields. Others, like Eton, Harrow, Westminster and Charterhouse, had to accommodate the game in their respective premises and for the most part each school had its own rules – but the one thing they all had in common was that the ball was propelled forward *by kicking it with the foot*. This allowed for a greater containment in limited areas. It was this rule that Webb Ellis contravened. One could catch the ball but it must be put to the ground and kicked forward. There were mauls and rucks but only the feet must be used. Some *scragging* or *rucking* was permitted, *tripping* and *hacking* were allowed, but the emphasis was on dribbling the ball between the feet. A one-handed throw-in was permitted from the side if the ball went out of play.

Lancing introduced the goalkeeper as the only one who could use his hands and two backs were there to assist him with their feet. No one as yet thought to head the ball. The other eight players were used as an attacking pack of dribblers.

This was the way that the game was played in the public schools up till 1846 but because there were so many variants in the rules it was difficult for the schools to play each other. A common code was obviously needed and it was in order to arrive at this that two Shrewsbury old boys met with several old Etonians while they were at Cambridge and formed a football club to play at Parker's Piece, a playing field available to Trinity College. Unfortunately, they couldn't agree about if and when to handle the ball, whether to ruck or not and if a goal were scored above or through the goal posts. A general meeting was called by a Mr Thring and fourteen schools sent representatives with spokesmen for Oxford and Cambridge. They met after Hall and from around 5 p.m. till midnight they deliberated in an attempt to arrive at a playable compromise.

The results of their discussions were The Cambridge Rules, the first attempt to codify the rules of football and drawn up by an association of public school men within a university and that is why it came to be called Association Football, which is its proper title to this day. A copy of the ten simple rules agreed upon was pinned to a tree on Parker's Piece and the delegates dispersed to their different schools. The piece of paper was soon blown away and nothing remains at this spot in Cambridge to acknowledge where the worldwide game known as Association Football or soccer began. Soccer is a spurious term, although it is the name now gaining most currency due to its usage in the United States. There are two versions of its origins. One is semantic, in that it came from a corruption of Assoc. used as an abbreviation of Association in correspondence between the clubs. The other version is entirely anecdotal. It would seem that Charles Wreford Brown, a famous Corinthian and England footballer, when an undergraduate at Oxford, was having breakfast in Hall, when a friend invited him to come and join a game of *rugger* after *brekkers*.

Wreford Brown is reported to have replied: 'No, thank you, John. I'm going to have a game of soccer.'

Wreford was being jocular of course, and he may have had his long stockings already worn outside his trouser legs in the manner of footballers then, which also might've suggested *sock* to him. Indeed, it was printed as *socker* in 1906. Whichever the way of it, we were landed with soccer and now we are stuck with it.

J.C. Thring, who had called the first meeting at Cambridge, became a master at Uppingham, and in 1862 he published the ten rules arrived at then as *The Simplest Game* in 1862. By this time, word had spread about the new code and the first club outside the public schools had been formed at Sheffield in 1855 under the influence of Old Harrovians, and other clubs, like Notts County, followed in 1862. In October 1963 a further meeting was held at Cambridge to consolidate the original decalogue and introduce fresh points which might include both dribbling and handling in a new acceptable single game under the *Cambridge University Football Rules*. These then were discussed at some length by the Football Association which was inaugurated on 23 October 1863 – a week after the second Cambridge meeting. Association Football was now formally recognised as such but it could not agree a definitive ruling about handling, hacking and tripping in the new code. Finally, hacking was the only matter which divided the two sides and neither would give way to the other. One group thought it crude and the other considered it manly. An irreconcilable *impasse* had been reached.

So it was that, at 7 p.m. on Tuesday, 8 December 1863, in a top room of the Freemason's Tavern, Great Queen's Street, Lincoln's Inn Fields, lit by oil lamps, thick with smoke from the fireplace and the cigars and pipes of bearded men, whose top hats stood upside down on the polished table before them, an amendment was proposed by Messrs Campbell and Gordon of the Blackheath Club retaining hacking and handling in the laws of Association Football. It was defeated by thirteen votes to four. Blackheath walked out, taking Charterhouse (there as observers) with them. They were resolved to found a separate code, which they did eight years later in 1871, calling themselves the Rugby Union after the school where the first handling of the ball is reputed to have taken place. The new Football Association, at its very outset, had missed a chance to keep everyone in the one fold. It was not to be the first time the FA was to turn its back on a once-in-a-lifetime opportunity but now at least the air had been cleared – if only of tobacco smoke.

The two factions were to become more and more disparate as the years went on. Association rapidly became the poor man's game, and Rugby the preserve of the rich for no other reason than that the public schools reverted to the handling code entirely and even changed the shape of the ball so it might be carried more easily. The handling code, while still a relative of its senior kicking cousin, spawned further offshoots of its own which were to develop in the future, into Rugby League, American Football, Gaelic Football and into the family black sheep called Australian Rules. They were all from the one stem nonetheless, that is the ancient football in the old order, and Association Football is a legitimate offshoot. It also retained the traditional round ball, shaped like a globe. This was not altogether inapt, as the new footballer stood for the moment with the world at his feet. The actual football itself came in all shapes and sizes at first; but gradually, with increased manufacture by machinery, a standard size was attained – i.e. not more than 28 inches in diameter, not less than 27; weighing not more than 16 ounces, not less than 14; and at a pressure of 10 pounds 7 ounces at sea level.

The game in its new form first took root in Scotland on the playing fields of the Queen's Park recreation ground on the south side of the Glasgow. In the beginning, the young men there, drawn largely from local Presbyterian churches, the YMCA and some caber-tossing Highlanders, played football among themselves for amusement although the only thing that was laughable was their absolute ignorance of the rules as they now applied. Fortunately, there was no obvious use for a caber. Their football was described as 'vigorous, if not exact; and the enjoyment true, if not scientific'. Some of them met at 3 Eglinton Terrace (moving on later to White's Public House in the Victoria Road) on 9 July 1867 for the purpose of forming a football club but they weren't very sure how to go about it. Thirteen committee members were elected and someone was deputed to write to the *Sportsman* for a copy of the Rules of Football. Edinburgh Academicals did bring out a copy of the rules for Scotland but that wasn't to be until a year later. Eventually, a reply was received from the Notts County cricketer, James Lillywhite, and the Queen's Park committee adapted the new rules to their liking. They tried them out in matches among themselves at first, Married *v* Singles, Smokers *v* Non-smokers, etc., until they were ready to face other teams in the west of Scotland like Glasgow Thistle, Cowlairs and Lugar Boswell or anyone else who could raise a team, like Hamilton Gymnasium for instance. Their first official match was against Thistle in August 1868 and it was played by Queen's Park rules – twenty a side and an hour each half. Thistle were also asked to bring their own ball. Queen's won by two goals to nil.

In this way was the famous Queen's Park Football Club begun and they were to go on from there, via a series of ad hoc challenge matches, until 1872 before a single goal was scored against them and until 1876 before they suffered their first defeat, and that was by the London Wanderers in the English FA Cup. They might have done more in England but the players couldn't afford the time off from their jobs or the continual rail fares, although they did contribute a guinea towards the cost of the first Football Association Cup suggested by Charles W. Alcock. They twice reached the final (in 1884 and 1885) and were beaten by Blackburn Rovers each time but there was no denying that in this period they were not only the first team in Scotland but also in England. Not bad for a bunch of YMCA members who didn't know the rules in 1867.

One must bear in mind that in those early days the game was an uneasy mixture of the two codes – Association and Rugby – and scoring was done by goals *and* touchdowns. The rules tended to overlap from time to time, much to the consternation of the spectators – not to mention the players. Gradually however, things sorted themselves out and, in this, Queen's Park were to the fore. They had been born in the glorious age of the amateur sportsman and they were to remain true to that noble, if rather tattered, ethos. They belonged to an age when professional men played football as a game and not as a means of earning a living and they have held to that ideal from the start. Nevertheless, as a club, they had the foresight in due course to build the finest football stadium in Britain, Hampden Park, which recently underwent its fourth rebuilding as Scotland's national football arena. Scotland as a country, as much as Scottish football, owes much to those Victorian gentlemen who met so casually in 1867. We may have become, in Jim Sillar's biting phrase, merely 'ninety-minute patriots', but football has done much to focus the aspirations of the nation at times when its self-esteem was low and when its energies were denied national expression. Football is culture in Scotland, occasionally it is high art, but it is never other than at the very front of Scottish concerns and Queen's Park have had much to do with that by their efforts in establishing the game in Scotland. The story of Scottish football is in effect the story of three great clubs – Rangers, Celtic and Queen's Park – and Queen's Park was the first of these. That is this great club's place in football history and it belongs by right.

It is important at this stage to see football in its Victorian perspective. The players were whiskered if not bearded. They wore long trousers and caps. The crossbar was a tape and a goal was scored by kicking under it, not over it. And every time a goal was scored the ends were changed. As mentioned earlier, touchdowns at either side of the goal were still allowed and throw-ins were one-handed. It was the golden age of the dribbler – 'To see some players guide and steer a ball through a circle of opposing legs, turning and twisting, as occasion requires, is a sight not to be forgotten.' Play allowed for eight forwards and three defenders but as time went on players were withdrawn from the front pack to create extra defenders in midfield. However, it was not until 1883 that Cambridge University experimented with five forwards, three half-backs and three defenders, one of whom became the goalkeeper. This spread of players over the field was taken up by other clubs and it was from this basis that the modern team formation duly arrived. Once again, Cambridge had made a signal contribution to the development of football in Britain.

In 1870 however, the gentleman-amateur ruled and the transplant to the working classes had not yet begun to any extent. Although the game had gone north and clubs like Notts County and Sheffield Wednesday were in existence, the focal energy for the spread of the game radiated from London and no one was more zealous in its propagation than Charles W. Alcock, the acting secretary for the infant Football Association, while playing robustly as centre and captain for the Wanderers. In 1870, he wrote to the *Glasgow Herald* challenging the Scots to a game of football at the Oval in London later that year:

> In Scotland, once essentially the land of football, there should still be a spark left of the old fire, and I confidently appeal to all Scotsmen to aid to their utmost the efforts of the committee to confer success on what London hopes to found, an annual trial of skill between the champions of England and Scotland.

Known as the 'Alcock Internationals', there were five such encounters at the Oval in London, for each of which Alcock selected both teams, and none of which 'Scotland' won. The matches had no official status and do not figure in the record books but they are of importance in the indication they give of the latent commercial promise in such fixtures. Queen's Park, of course, ought to have represented Scotland (as they were later to do in 1872) but once again, because of costs and the work commitments of their players, they were unable to travel. So they nominated one of their members, Robert Smith, who had moved to London, to represent them and he played on the left wing. However, the handful of matches between March 1870 and February 1872, were significant in introducing players on to the 'international' football scene who were unlikely to grace it again but who, nonetheless, were fine players of the game in their day. There were some notable names among them, none more so than Lord Kinnaird, who was the first of Scottish blood to make his mark in the new game and therefore becomes the first of the hundred names to grace this Scottish Football Hall of Fame.

Arthur, LORD KINNAIRD (1847–1923)

Right half-back for Old Etonians and the Wanderers

1

The Honourable, later Sir, Arthur Fitzgerald, and finally Lord Kinnaird was a born gentleman and the only aristocrat known to have given the best part of his life to the game of football. Ostensibly the perfect English gentleman, he was a Scot, born in 1847, the only son of the tenth baron of Kinnaird of Rossie Priory, Inchture in Perthshire. His selection for the first 'Scottish' teams in 1870–72 was due entirely to his being a Scottish landowner. Thus, the Kensington-born, Eton-educated Kinnaird, fresh from an MA at Trinity, found himself among an assortment of London-Scots, near-Scots and blatant Englishmen with Scottish-sounding names who comprised the so-called 'Scotch' teams that played against an English select in the series of friendly games from 1870. Both teams were in fact selected by Charles Alcock.

From this very casual beginning was to come the first international fixture between two countries, and the future Lord Kinnaird was as much a part of that beginning as he was of that triumvirate which, with Alcock and Sir Francis Marindin, created the fabric of Association Football in England. He did not win his only official cap till 1873, but he is given first place here because he represents in himself all those influences that came together around that time to make the first Scotland team of 1873 possible.

The redoubtable Kinnaird, of the long, white trousers and red beard, of the quartered cap and boundless energy (he once stood on his head in front of goal after winning the cup against Blackburn Rovers in 1882), was the first of the game's great characters and such was his stamina and enthusiasm that he continued playing until he was forty-six years of age and still full of running. He lost in his only official game for Scotland at the Oval in 1873, but went on to play in a record nine FA Cup finals with Crusaders, Old Etonians and the Wanderers and was in the winning side in five of them. He played every game to the hilt. When Lady Kinnaird protested to Marindin that her husband would come back one day with a broken leg he replied, 'Quite possibly, my dear Lady Kinnaird – but don't be alarmed, if he does it will not be his own.' On another occasion when captaining Old Etonians, Alcock, captaining Old Harrovians, asked him: 'Look here, Kinnaird, are we going to play the game or are we going to have hacking?' Kinnaird beamed in reply: 'Oh, let us have hacking by all means.'

When he finally stopped playing, his Lordship became a formidable administrator of the fledgling Football Association and did much to bring the various regional groups into the one national fold. In recognition of his lifetime contribution to football in Britain, he was awarded his very own FA Cup in 1911. He was President of the FA at the time of his death in 1923, aged seventy-five. Arthur Kinnaird was the first of the game's heroes, a superb Victorian athlete, who was also, in the new Edwardian age, a respected administrator, merchant banker, member of parliament and His Majesty's Lord High Commissioner to the General Assembly of the Church of Scotland. He remained to the end true to his class. Although to all intents and purposes English, Lord Kinnaird was technically the first great football Scot, and the last of Scotland's very few gentleman-players.

It is hard to remember that Lord Kinnaird was a merchant banker. He gave so much of his life to football that it didn't seem possible to fit anything else in. He genuinely loved the game and thanks to his influence many of the best aspects of it were retained as it developed from a leisure pursuit to a full-time professional occupation. By the time he died he had seen the first Cup Final at Wembley before a record crowd, FIFA had been formed, the first competition had taken place in South America, promotion and relegation had been introduced to the Football League and the first four-figure transfer had been agreed when Alf Common moved from Sunderland to Middlesbrough. In short, his Lordship had seen football grow up.

It had in fact shot up, the way boys do in their early teens, and Kinnaird knew that the best of football was boyish. At heart, it must keep its sporting innocence, no matter how many commercial scars it may suffer in the present hard world. He also recognised its classlessness and firmly believed that football united all strata of society and had nothing but a beneficial effect on society as a whole. He spoke, of course, from a position of great privilege. He could afford to be altruistic, but there was no denying his sincerity and goodwill and this was recognised wherever he went in football circles. When he was a player, the crowd had taken the horses from his carriage and pulled him to the pavilion. When he was an administrator, the officials at the Football Association would rise to a man as he entered the room. He had won their love, respect and admiration and he deserves ours. In two generations he had seen the whole face of football change and he remained optimistic to the last:

> I believe that all right-minded people have good reason to thank
> God for the great progress of this popular national game.

No better words could close this first chapter of the Scottish football story.

Chapter Two

Beginning with the End

The end of the century marked the beginning of football's second phase when the rules fracas had sufficiently settled to allow progress to be made among the leading clubs in organisation and method. In Scotland, this could only mean Queen's Park. In 1872 they challenged England to come to them in Scotland and the resulting game, played in Glasgow on Saturday, 30 November (St Andrew's Day), marks the official start of international football. This time, it was a much more realistic Scotland team, as it was made up entirely of Queen's Park players, including the two Smith brothers who travelled up from London with Lord Kinnaird and Alcock. The last two, who had been originally chosen to play for their respective countries, stood down in favour of younger men.

The venue was the West of Scotland Cricket Ground in Partick which was hired for ten pounds with a further ten to be paid if receipts exceeded fifty. In fact, they were to be well over the hundred and Queen's Park made a handy little profit. So in the end everyone was delighted. Glasgow, it would seem, was agog about the game:

> The match was a topic of conversation at every luncheon bar. Business in the city being then as usual on Saturday afternoons, was almost entirely suspended in legal offices and commercial houses. There was great demand for locomotion to Partick, and the home of the West of Scotland Cricket Club. Every tram car which reached Jamaica St *en route* to Whiteinch was besieged by young men. The outside seats were crammed in a second, and the patience of the guards was sorely tried. By three o'clock the ground at Hamilton Crescent was much crowded, and on all four sides the ropes were strained by the masses. Soon the road and streets were crammed and even the windows overlooking. The Scotland team was Mr Gardner at the goal, Mr Ker and Mr Taylor at the back, and Mr Thomson and Mr Smith at half. Forward, Mr Leckie, Mr Rhind, Mr Weir, the other Mr Smith, Mr McKinnon and Mr Wotherspoon.

It is to be noticed that the report did not favour the readers with the result of the game. Mr Weir was J.B. Weir, known as the Prince of Dribblers and Billy McKinnon was beginning what was to be an auspicious run in the Scottish team. One young attender at the game was to make his name with both Queen's Park and Scotland, full-back Walter Arnott, and at that time he was ten years old. He remembers:

> We started off in the forenoon to walk to the ground – a distance of nearly five miles; but after reaching our destination found that there was no chance of getting inside the ground unless we paid at the gate. What few coppers we had among us were gone by this time; and how disappointed we felt, after such a weary walk, at the poor prospect of our getting a view of the game. Just when we had given up all hope, we earnestly begged a cabman to accommodate us on the top of his cab, and it was from that perch I witnessed the first encounter between the two nations.

The Queen's Park officials had hoped for a crowd sufficient to meet the expenses but nearly four thousand people, paying a shilling each, crowded into the neat little ground nestling among the tenements, and on a wet, miserable day saw a goalless draw in which, according to reports, Scotland had had all the play.

> Individual skill was generally on England's side, but the Southrons did not play to each other as well as their opponents who seemed to be adept at passing the ball . . .

This was the vital strategy that Queen's had developed – the passing game. It was the result of playing together and thinking about the game. They threw the English team into confusion by their tactics but their finishing on the day was not equal to their outfield play – something that was to be the bugbear of so many Scottish international teams. One goal was disallowed because the ball was adjudged to have gone above the English tape, but the moral victory was Scotland's, if only for the first display of the passing game. Football had divided itself into handlers and dribblers, now the dribblers would divide themselves by those who could give and take a pass. What they had made into an art form could now also be considered as a science. One good pass could do the work of a whole pack of dribblers. The game had many more ramifications yet.

The Scotland team wore a red lion rampant badge sewn on their Queen's Park jerseys of blue and white hoops and the lion has remained a Scottish emblem to this day. A photographer was arranged but the Scottish players would not promise to buy the prints, so the photographer took his camera away. However, a print of the 1874 Queen's Park team is still extant and several of the players may be seen in that. The six Scottish forwards in 1872 had all been chosen for their dribbling skills but what had taken the eye was their skill in passing the ball between each other and this was to become the hallmark of so many Scottish teams in the immediate years to follow. It was a style of playing that was to be much copied later and not always to Scotland's advantage, but there was no denying that while England had given the world football, Scotland had added the pass. This tactic, though small in itself, was to add much to the game as a spectacle, and when used well by a team, transformed the sport into an art form. It was not an inconsiderable contribution, and it would have its repercussions for some time to come. For the moment, however, it was time to build on the Queen's Park initiative. From the *North British Daily Mail*, 24 February 1873:

> Thus, football was begun in Scotland by the Queen's Park Football Club, whose true sporting spirit aimed right at elevating the game to a higher platform than pounds, shillings and pence, to purify and ennoble, to rear and produce, not procure and pay. Always, and at all times, even till our own day, to play the game, and play it for the game's sake.

On Monday, 3 March 1873, the following notice appeared in the Scottish newspapers:

> It has been proposed by the committee of the Queen's Park Club that Scotch clubs playing Association rules should subscribe for a cup to be played for annually, and retained for the year by the winning team, the competition to begin next season. Scotch clubs who may wish to join this movement are invited to send two representatives to a meeting to be held to consider this matter in Dewar's Hotel, 11 Bridge Street, Glasgow on the evening of 13th inst. at eight o'clock.

By coincidence, in the very same newspapers, an adjoining notice invited all those interested in forming a Rugby Football Union to meet at Elmbank School that day. The handlers were wasting no time in distancing themselves from the dribblers.

On the 13th, seven clubs attended at Dewar's Hotel – Queen's Park,

Clydesdale, Vale of Leven, Dumbreck, Third Lanarkshire Volunteer Reserves, Glasgow Eastern and Granville. Kilmarnock sent a letter stating that they would join if the others did, and so these eight clubs formed the original Scottish Football Association. In this way, the first order was brought to the Scottish game and a gesture made towards not only a club's but a nation's need for recreation and amusement. One club's policy had become a country's requirement.

For the bulk of the people, urban Scotland was not a pretty place to live in at this time and Glasgow in particular was badly affected by overcrowding and under-employment. Public football as a spectacle couldn't have come at a better time for the vast majority of working-class people who lived at a level never more than a slice of unbuttered bread away from poverty. In the cities, tramlines had now been laid and their tentacles spread in every direction, giving cheap access to the new football grounds being hurriedly constructed wherever space could be found among the tenements and factories. Football had always been a town sport and now it was returning to the towns-people as a cheap entertainment. Municipalisation was the current fashion in local government and Glasgow in particular was ahead in this method of citizen service. Loch Katrine had just been munici-palised to provide the best drinking water in Britain. From the new craze to municipalise came municipal baths, laundries, gas lighting, refuse collection, art galleries, libraries and telephones. There was even a municipal farm on the north-western outskirts. One wonders why no one suggested a municipal football team. After all, these services were not intended to make a profit. They were organised to function for the good of the citizens and Victorian Glasgow was a surprising leader in this field. Queen's Park was to all intents and purposes a gentlemen's private club. A municipal club for all of greater Glasgow might have been a good idea. Think what a force a combined Rangers and Celtic would be; but that is in the realms of the impossible dream.

Whatever one's local football loyalties, it has to be admitted that Glasgow Rangers (formed in 1872 although the public record says 1873) constitute the most important contribution ever made to Scottish football. Even from their first days, they were a force in the land and, from then, they have gone on to win more titles, trophies and competitions than any other club and to have provided more players for the Scotland team than any other. They were to become rich, powerful and well-nigh invulnerable on the pitch and to attract the largest support of any club in Britain, but their main strength was their dour and relentless consistency. Right from the beginning, they favoured big, strong players who were fast on the ball and had unquestioned stamina. They were never to be renowned for their ball-players, but they were never to lack for results. They laid a heavy hand on Scottish football and rarely slackened that grip. Their day was yet to come, however, and Queen's Park were still synonymous with football in Scotland. Although the sport wasn't finding it all that easy to take root in the land of the mountain and the flood. The *North British Daily Mail* of 24 February 1873 reports:

> A match was played on Saturday between Queen's Park and East Kilbride on the ground of the latter. The field was rather narrow for the game and had been symmetrically divided, with an incorruptible fidelity to proportion, into 15 foot furrows, which, by introducing alternate hill and dale, no doubt lent a charm to the landscape, but while giving the place a poetic beauty, rather spoilt it for the stern prose of football . . .

Another match reported at the time involved a lesser football journey for QP players, this time to the Glasgow Green to play Eastern. They walked to the match, but the game ended prematurely when the watching crowd broke on to the field to start a *mêlée* suspiciously near where the Queen's Park players had piled their jackets. The players also had to put up with unexpected initiatives on the part of the host club. When the new Rangers played Jordanhill at Jordanhill they found that no lines had been marked off. Jordanhill promptly borrowed a horse and plough and marked off the playing area by a series of deep ditches. It was said that some of the Rangers players got nasty wrenches from repeated falls. These were extreme instances, however, and for the most part the grounds were playable – just. Things were improving. The *Scottish Umpire* of 21 August 1884 was later to write:

> Take any club that has come to the front and the onward strides will be found to date from the hour when the rough and tumble gave place to swift accurate passing and attending to the leather rather than the degraded desire merely to coup an opponent.

In that pithy sentence, so typical of its period, we have the perfect answer to hacking. Queen's Park's football colours of narrow black and white horizontal stripes had given them the nickname of the 'Spiders' and it led one writer to call them 'weavers of lovely webs on the field'. The Spiders provided the first Scottish team to gain a victory over England. In the second match at Hamilton Crescent, played on 7 March 1874, Queen's Park aka Scotland beat England 2–1 and 'Spider' Harry McNeil was carried shoulder-high from the field by the crowd as the hero of the day. It was the start of a remarkable run for Scotland in internationals. They were only to be beaten once (by England) in a series of thirty-one games until 1888. Queen's Park won the first Scottish Cup by beating Clydesdale in the final with Billy McKinnon, the hero on this occasion, scoring the first-ever goal in a final. Scottish football at home had already found its first two heroes – McKinnon and McNeil.

William Muir McKINNON (1852–1942)
Forward for Queen's Park   2

Billy McKinnon (or MacKinnon), a mercantile clerk by profession, played in the first-ever official Scottish international team in 1872 and in the next six games which followed. He therefore deserves his place as the forerunner of the many Scots forwards who were later to make their mark on the rapidly emerging game and in doing so endear themselves to the hundreds and later thousands who gathered to admire their prowess. McKinnon was the ideal footballer of the time, an ace dribbler in an age of dribblers. His mastery of close possession, a lost art except to the greats in today's game, allowed him to score five goals for Scotland in nine games and a lot more for Queen's Park in a comparatively short career of not much more than ten years from 1870. In addition, his staying power, astonishing for so slight a figure, was remarkable in the rough and tumble of the early years and anticipated the later type of Scottish footballer who used his brain not his brawn. McKinnon captained the Queen's Park Strollers as early as 1871 at the age of eighteen, and three years later he was not only a fixture in the first team but a member of the Queen's Park committee as well. It was as such that he further distinguished himself by scoring the very first goal in a Challenge Cup Final (later the Scottish Cup) at Hampden against Clydesdale, when Queen's Park won 2–0 in 1874. It was said of him at the time: 'He cannot be surpassed as a forward. One of the most brilliant dribblers and dodgers on the field, and has great endurance.'

He must have had, he lived to be ninety.

Henry McNEIL (1853–1924) 3
Winger, inside-forward and half-back for Third Lanark and Queen's Park

Harry McNeil was one of seven brothers from the Gareloch, four of whom (William, Peter, Moses and Harry) rowed with a group who had their boat-shed on the Clyde at Glasgow Green. It was here, on a piece of ground known as the Flesher's Haugh, that they saw the Glasgow Eastern play the new game of Association Football. Impressed, the brothers decided to form their own football team, and joining with other young men like Tom Vallance, also from the Gareloch area, they became the Argyle, which in turn became, on the suggestion of Moses McNeil, the Glasgow Rangers Association Football Club in 1873. While Moses, William and Peter McNeil went on to play with them, Harry joined the Third Lanarkshire Volunteer Reserves (an army team) before transferring to Queen's Park. Harry and Moses formed the left wing for Scotland in the 4–0 victory over Wales at Hamilton Crescent in 1876, Harry being one of the scorers. Moses played once more for Scotland, but his two caps did not compare to his big brother's ten, but then Harry McNeil was a formidable comparison on any terms. He was a born leader of men and a natural captain. He greatly influenced the development of the passing game to counter the dribblers of the day and this aspect of play became a hallmark of the Scottish game in the years to come, while at the same time allowing Queen's Park to remain well-nigh invincible during football's first decade. Although he began on the left wing, he moved back as his experience increased and it was as a playmaker just behind the forwards that he made his mark. He was at inside left in the team which beat England 6–1 at the Kennington Oval in 1881 (still the highest defeat suffered by England in internationals in England). McNeil retired from the international scene in 1883 to coach the younger players at Queen's Park and eventually became mine host of the Royal Hotel in Bangor, north Wales, where no doubt he regaled his patrons with tall tales of those halcyon amateur days when both he and football were young and innocent.

In addition to the passing game, the Scottish clubs introduced what came to be called the 'Scotch Throw', that is, when the ball went out of play at the touchline, it was returned using two hands behind the head instead of the old one-handed hurl in any direction. Now that the scope and speed of the game were increasing, so it was improving as a spectacle. Crowds were increasing all the time and attendances of ten thousand were not unknown at the new Hampden Park. Rules for goalkicks and corners were regularised and free kicks were allowed for infringements. Only the goalkeeper could handle now. With this new conformity, new clubs sprang up all over Scotland – Renton, Dumbarton, Vale of Leven, Glasgow Eastern, Clydesdale, Glasgow Oxford, Aberdeen Bon-Accord, etc. – but it was also at this time, around 1875, that the first rumblings about hidden payments to star players began to be heard in the all-amateur world of football.

Working-class teams emerged and the cloth cap vied with the bowler in striving for supremacy in the sport. The top hat, for the moment, remained aloof, still convinced that the game was properly theirs and they could still manage it from the armchairs of the better clubs in Mayfair and St James's, but the tide was slowly turning. In Cambridge, the originating seat of the new football, an unnamed Chancellor succinctly summed up the current football situation by observing that, 'Football is a gentleman's game played by hooligans, and rugby a hooligan's game played by gentlemen.' The Wildean paradox is too neat, although Wilde himself said, 'Football is all very well for rough girls but it is hardly suitable for delicate boys.' The clichés of the great divide were already forming. At the same time, the Scottish and English Associations were drifting further apart and the Scots were already resenting the gradual increase of the number of players crossing the border, ostensibly to find employment in England, yet many of these tradesmen found a place in English football teams amazingly quickly. Darwen, Preston North End, Newcastle, Blackburn Rovers and Accrington Stanley were only some of the English teams to be comprised almost entirely of Scotsmen.

Queen's Park were unperturbed by this professional groundswell and continued their winning way with excellent cup runs in Scotland and England, although they lost to the emerging Vale of Leven in 1876, a team who also beat the mighty Wanderers at the Oval in the same year. Charles Campbell, the later President of the young SFA, became a stalwart in defence as well as attack and became noted for his heading skills. One Irish spectator is reputed to have remarked at one match: 'Sure, that man kicks well with his head.' (Little was known then of the later damage excessive heading of the heavy leather ball would cause professional footballers.) Dr John Smith was another famous Spider of this time. Standing six foot three inches and weighing more than fifteen stone, he played rugby at Edinburgh University before converting to the Association code. After his time with Queen's Park, he played for the famous Corinthians in a match against the professional Bolton Wanderers and for this he was banned by the SFA. So he toured Australia with the Scottish rugby team and returned to become a doctor in Kirkcaldy. Rangers too were beginning to make their presence felt but they also lost to the Vale of Leven in the final of 1877. The same two teams contested the final of 1879 and the crowd was so large that it caused the collapse of part of the pavilion. It was the first of the sad scenes of crowd accidents that were to dog the Ibrox team. In the meanwhile, the trickle of 'sham-ateurs' into the English game had become a flood and the SFA pompously declared them to be football exiles, thus depriving Scotland of some of its best football talent. Players like Third Lanark's J.J. Lang, who had begun in the game with Clydesdale and Glasgow Eastern, and was now a much sought-after forward by clubs in England.

James J. LANG (b. 1851)   4
Forward for Clydesdale, Third Lanark and Sheffield Wednesday

Described as 'a muscular little bundle of energy, captivating to watch. First rate at dribbling', Jimmy Lang, nicknamed 'Reddie' on account of his red hair, was almost the archetypal Glasgow footballer and he has good claim to be recognised as the first-ever professional footballer. Born in Clydebank, he worked in the shipyards while playing in Scotland but soon found that his soccer services were in greater demand than his shipbuilding skills. Despite the fact that he was blind in one eye, due to an injury in the yards, more than one club was happy to take a Nelsonian attitude to this handicap and in 1876 Lang moved into England to play for Sheffield Wednesday for money. That this was illegal at the time (professionalism in the sport was only recognised in England in 1885 and reluctantly accepted in Scotland eight years later) did not deter Lang, nor many more of his fellow countrymen. At first, their professionalism was disguised in the effort made by the English clubs to find work for the players in their respective trades, or to repay them for 'broken time' off work, but it was no secret that the greater part of their earnings were found in their boots after the match. Wilson of Vale of Leven went in this way to Blackburn Rovers, as did Peter Andrews of Glasgow Eastern when he joined Sheffield Heeley. Oswald of Third Lanark was offered a fully stocked tobacconist's shop by Notts County and when Partick Thistle came down to play a friendly with Darwen they left their two best players, Fergus Soutar and James Love, behind to help Darwen thrash Old Etonians in the FA Cup. The Scotland team of 1891 was even waylaid on the train journey back from Wales by agents for English clubs – eager to pay for Scottish skills. Not every Scot, however, could be so induced. James Kelly stayed with Celtic when he found himself the owner of a pub and Frank Shaw, a Pollokshaws forward, turned down Accrington Stanley because he was sailing his yacht around the Western Isles. There were still a few gentlemen playing the game, but players like Kelly and Shaw and Willie Groves of Hibernian, whose stonemason's wages were suspiciously well above the average, were the exceptions. Most of the better Scottish players travelled south. As the game spread, so did they. Altogether, more than three hundred players had succumbed to 'English gold' by the time the SFA recognised the inevitability of the professional game. Reddie Lang had seen this long before and though some might dispute his claim to be football's first professional, he was the first to admit that he played football for money. It was his example that converted the 'Scotch Professors', as the early Scottish footballers were called, into the soccer missionaries they became. Men like Madden, Harley, Dick, Cameron and the rest who carried the Scottish passing game around the world and laid the basis for the world game as we know it today. There is no doubt that this one-eyed ex-shipyard worker certainly started something before he retired to Glasgow to become a ground steward at Ibrox Stadium. His other claim to fame is that he is the only known professional footballer to be officially registered as blind.

More than Scottish players were imported south. William McGregor, a Perthshire draper, had opened a shop in Birmingham and it was there in 1887 that he had the idea of a Football League. Though not a player himself ('I tried it once when I was very young and had to take to my bed for a week'), he saw the need for the forward planning of fixtures, as friendly matches were becoming more and more difficult to arrange. From a local beginning in the Midlands it spread until the idea took root nationwide and the first League Championship took place in 1888. It was won by the Preston North End team, which contained the one token Englishman, Goodall, and even he had been brought up in Kilmarnock. The first-ever League goal was scored by a Scotsman, Jack Gordon, and 'The Invincibles', as Preston were called, went on to make it a League and Cup double, then came north to beat Queen's Park convincingly in Glasgow. The writing was on the wall for the gentleman amateur. Queen's Park were still a force to be reckoned with, however. They still won more games than they lost and they still produced players of class – the latest in the line being full-back Walter Arnott.

Walter ARNOTT (1863–1931)
Right full-back for Queen's Park, Corinthians, Kilmarnock, Linfield
Athletic, Third Lanark, St Bernard's, Celtic and Notts County

5

Walter Arnott was a tough customer. He always played in bare legs, despite the fact that shinguards had been invented (by an Englishman, Sam Widdowson of Nottingham Forest, after a single experience of playing against the Scots in 1884). Wattie didn't even bother with the long, coloured socks so favoured by C. Wreford Brown and the Corinthians. No, full-back Arnott was content to appear in the field as God made him, in boots, shorts and jersey, convinced that any other apparel would, in his own words, 'spoil the springiness of the limbs'. Although he made occasional guest appearances for many clubs, the Corinthians among them, Walter Arnott was essentially a Queen's Park and Scotland man. He grew up determined to play for both, and did. He played for his country on nine successive occasions and not till his final game (in 1888) was he ever on the losing side. He was below par in that rare 5–0 defeat, and as a result so was Scotland. Soon afterwards, he retired to coach the Hampden youngsters and to spend more time on the bowling green where he also excelled. The secret of his athleticism on the football park was perhaps the whipped eggs and milk he had before every game. Or it might have been the superb artistry he allied with high technical skills. Wattie would play for anyone at any time, with or without official permission. In his time, he turned out for Kilmarnock (1884), Linfield Athletic (1891), Third Lanark (1892), St Bernard's (1893), Celtic (1894) and Notts County (1895). The game was the thing for Wattie. He was famous for his pivot kick on the run which he called his screw-kick. Indeed, the SFA Annual for 1884–85 acknowledged this in its ambivalent comment: 'Arnott has never been equalled for screwing.'

Renton won the Scottish Cup in 1888 and this entitled them to play West Bromwich Albion, who had surprisingly beaten Preston North End in the English Cup final, for the title 'Champions of the World'. Renton won in a snowstorm and the little Dunbartonshire village team, who reputedly trained on chicken bree (or broth), proudly claimed the title. The star of the Renton team was their centre-half-back, James Kelly. Hibernian had beaten Preston the previous year in the same match but there had been no mention of a World Championship then. All the talk was of Willie Groves's wonder goal when he waltzed through the Preston defence on his own in the manner of the famous Archie Hunter of Aston Villa (see page 231). Two thousand people waited at Waverley

Station to welcome Hibernian home. It was no surprise, however, when both stars were invited to join the new club which had sprung up in the East – the East End of Glasgow. It was also an Irish club, and it called itself Celtic, on the suggestion of a local Marist schoolteacher, Brother Walfrid. Catholics in Glasgow were delighted to have a team to call their own but their brethren in Dundee and Edinburgh were not so pleased. Both Hibernians there were sectarian teams (before that term was pejorative) and they found that the Glasgow Celtic now openly poached their best players. The game in Scotland was supposedly amateur but everyone knew that players like Groves and Kelly could not be got by the mere recital of a Hail Mary – however sincere.

With the arrival of the Celtic on the scene in 1888, the Great Trium-virate was now in place. The Glasgow Irish joined the Govan Protestants and the Mount Florida gentlemen in a friendly rivalry, as it was at the beginning, to create the trinity that was to dominate Scottish football till the '20s when Queen's Park would field their last great team. The old order passeth, giving way to the new.

Only some players, like Ned Doig, who went to Sunderland and became a landlord and James Kelly, who signed for Celtic and became a publican, seemed to be aware of what the realities were. As always, like all pros, they were away ahead of the game – literally.

John Edward DOIG (1866–1919)
Goalkeeper for Arbroath, Blackburn Rovers, Sunderland and Liverpool

6

Ned Doig was an early football exile to England. However, he had his international acknowledgement while with his native Arbroath in season 1886–87, before making a complete commitment to a life and career south of the border. He was a colourful character and one of the first goalkeepers to take command in the penalty area. So authoritative was he in this respect that he usurped the great McAuley of Dumbarton, a fellow goalkeeper, who had captained Scotland on several occasions. Unfortunately, Ned Doig fell victim to the bias against Anglo-Scots and earned only a handful of caps in a long career. However, he kept the best till the last. In 1903, he made his final appearance (against England again), this time at Sheffield, and had the best game of his career, his heroics in goal allowing Scotland to win by the odd goal in three. He retired in 1908 but continued to play for St Helen's Recreation until he was forty-three. He and his wife opened a boarding house for young footballers in Liverpool.

James KELLY (1865–1932)
Centre half-back for Renton and Celtic

7

James Kelly was captain and mainstay of the Renton football club in 1888 when they won the Scottish Cup and successfully challenged West Bromwich Albion for the 'Championship of the World'. That same year, he joined the very first Celtic team, which had been founded in the year before, although they played their first competitive game in 1888. In those days, the centre-back was always the best player in the side and the pivot of the team. Kelly's skill was in being able to blend with attack and defence. The *Scottish Referee* of 21 January 1889 reported:

> There are many people who believe that when Scotland adopted the centre half-back position she sacrificed much of her power in the game . . . If the players who fill this position in other clubs were men of Mr Kelly's calibre . . . we would have no cause to regret having followed England in adding to the defensive parts of our elevens.

James Kelly could be said to be the first total footballer in the modern sense and the last great Scottish pivot, that is, one who controlled play from the centre of the park, playing both in defence and attack. He spent the rest of his career at Parkhead, becoming first a coach to the younger players, then a committee man, and finally a director in 1897. He was chairman 1909–14 and died in 1931. His son, Sir Robert Kelly, was chairman in the Jock Stein years and Dr Michael Kelly and Kevin Kelly kept the family connection with the club until recent times.

The officials in the early years, like all officials in any sport, tended to be officious. Some have office thrust upon them, others grow into office but the real official is born to it. He is conservative by nature and says 'No' to everything by sheer instinct. Football officials were no different and already clung to a code that was already beginning to look old-fashioned. Not that they didn't have a case. Like Queen's Park, many of them saw that giving in to the new professionalism meant that prestige, local loyalty and pride in the jersey would begin to mean less and less and that if money was the only criterion then football would become nothing more than a gladiatorial exchange between paid mercenaries. Tradition would be meaningless, only results would matter and players would move from club to club at the whim of the highest bidder. Already, however, there was a steady and growing movement of players between clubs in Scotland, although it must be said that Doig and Kelly were instances of players with a predominant one-club loyalty in their careers. Players could, and did, play for the jersey, especially the international jersey. Caps had been awarded for international appearances since 1886 and they were much prized by the players. What a shame therefore, that because of the Scottish Association's continued obduracy, they were not given to players who had moved into England.

This was why Scotland lost the services of such as Sandy Tait, Nick Ross and Archie Hunter, each a quality player of the period and proved in the new English league. Results against England reflected the narrowness of the selective mind, Scotland began to be beaten, but the SFA was adamant – only Scottish players playing in Scotland could play for Scotland. It was the age of the Tartan Bias, and it seemed as if kilts were mandatory in the dressing room. English players were just as resentful of the number of 'Scotch Professors' in their local teams, but in Scotland there were other just as pressing concerns in the game. It was obvious now that a Scottish League would soon be required to cope with the demands of new clubs anxious for games and established clubs keen on continuing fixtures – and on making money. The *Scottish Sport* announced: 'The entire rules (of the proposed Scottish Football League) stink of finance – money-making and money-grabbing.'

As Bob Crampsey wrote, in his *The First 100 Years of the Scottish Football League*:

> *Scottish Sport* showed its usual ability to disregard the way things were going. The adoption of professionalism in England in 1885 had made it impossible for Scottish clubs to hope to retain their best players. The top English sides recruited them mercilessly through the means of agents whom they employed in Scotland. These agents were hated, feared, and not infrequently assaulted . . . Taking the highest possible moral ground *Scottish Sport* had thundered in December 1888: 'What Scot worthy of the name would be so base as to deliver a fellow-countryman into abject relations of humiliation and subservancy?' The answer, of course, was that quite a few Scots would. Those who went south to play shut their ears to the departing censures of the papers. The dyer, Wilson, who had gone to play certainly for Blackburn Rovers and dye possibly, was urged in the same newspaper to 'weigh against

tempting gold the moral and physical shipwreck inseparable from life of a professional football player.' No future career was envisaged for the ex-professional other than ownership of a dramshop . . .

But the tide could not be turned, and as John McLaughlin of Celtic now pointed out: 'You might as well attempt to stop the flow of Niagara with a kitchen chair as to endeavour to stem the tide of professionalism.'

Queen's Park held the leg of the kitchen chair gamely, and marched off with it rather than risk being soaked. This was a mistake. Powerful influences were at work and, as ever, Mammon was to prove irresistible. Queen's might've used the umbrella of their own steadfast amateur tradition, but instead they made their protest by walking out of the new league, and by doing so, almost walked out of football.

Chapter Three

A League Onward

In March 1890, Peter Fairly, secretary of the Renton Football Club, sent the following letter to fourteen clubs in Scotland:

> Gentlemen – You are requested to send two representatives to attend a meeting to be held in Holton's Commercial Hotel, 28 Glassford Street, Glasgow, on Thursday 20th inst. at 7.30 p.m. to consider the question of organising League matches in Scotland.

Eleven teams turned up on the night to join Renton – Abercorn, Cambuslang, Celtic, Cowlairs, Dumbarton, Heart of Midlothian, Rangers, St Bernard, St Mirren, Third Lanark and Vale of Leven. The two absentees were Queen's Park and Clyde – the former because no agenda was published and the latter for no good reason, but it did not take either club long to see that they had to go along with the tide, no matter how murky the waters were becoming with the ever-increasing flood of professionalism. Even if no other future was offered to them at the end of their playing life than the ownership of a 'dramshop', many players considered that what was good enough for Kelly of the Celtic was good enough for them. And the *Scottish Athletic Journal* had asked: 'The working population had to be amused – Is it to be the football field or the dramshop?' Both, it would seem. Both players and public alike wondered why they couldn't have their dram and drink it, although there were murmurings about why so many football players, ostensibly unpaid, suddenly became the owners of pubs. Some of the better minds in football, like Alcock, had seen the end coming. He wrote:

> What has been the recreation of the few is becoming the pursuit of thousands, an athletic exercise carried on under a strict system and in many cases by an enforced term of training, almost magnified into a profession.

He saw no reason why a footballer should not become a professional much as cricketers had done. There was no reason why they should not be able to play with the amateur. This showed how much he underestimated the drawing power that football clubs were to have and the money they turned over in a season. It could not benefit by any example given by cricket, it was to dwarf cricket as it would every other sporting pursuit, except perhaps angling and golf. There was no doubt that a monster was being brought into existence and at this time it had no idea of its own strength.

In the meantime, while the momentous change to the openly paid was drawing nearer and nearer, the game itself was undergoing modifications. The Irish had introduced the penalty kick, the two umpires gave way to a single referee with a whistle and the goal tape had been replaced by the crossbar. The goal itself had been draped in nets because too often the ball had gone into the crowd behind the goal area never to be seen again. In short, football was beginning to look like itself. On 6 August 1890 the first Scottish League programme took place and four matches were held – Celtic were beaten 4–1 by Renton and Rangers beat Heart of Midlothian 5–2 at Ibrox. Some 4,000 spectators turned up at Ibrox and 10,000 at Celtic Park, and new names were coming into the Scottish team from all parts of Scotland. Some won their first caps and then immediately took the low road to England. Two such were Hugh Wilson and Jack Bell.

Hugh WILSON (1869–1940)
Inside-forward, half-back/full-back for Newmilns, Sunderland, Bristol City and Third Lanark

8

Like so many of his generation, 'Lalty' Wilson had a scant international career despite a splendid professional life 'in pursuit of the leather', as the contemporary phrase had it. A big, strong man, he could, and did, play anywhere on the field and even though he began with Scotland as an inside-forward on either flank, he ended his career with Third Lanark playing more often as full-back. He might lay claim to the title of the first utility player. He had amazing vitality and might have played all positions at once if really called on. He had a mighty throw and his shies from the touchline were often worth a free kick to his team. He played for Sunderland when it was a Scottish team with an English name. Hugh never lost his Scottishness and no man was prouder to wear the Scotland jersey. He scored on his debut at left-half and also played at inside- and outside-left in the Scottish team, but one feels that his very versatility was his undoing. A contemporary writer noted: 'Big, lean and muscular, he covered the ground in long strides.' He certainly ran through a long career encompassing several clubs, but he was a valued player in any side for which he played. Hugh was also noted for his singing of Scottish songs in the after-match social.

John BELL (b. 1869)
Winger for Dumbarton, Everton, Celtic, New Brighton and Preston North End

9

Jack Bell started early. He was playing first-class football at fifteen. Tall for a winger and heavier than most, this didn't prevent his speeding down either wing as selected and giving the opposing full-back the problem of first catching him before trying to put in a tackle. Typical press comment said, 'Bell has plenty of weight, runs fast and has a rattling good shot.' Jack saw the game as a man's game and didn't hesitate to use his physique as well as his skill. 'A thrusting winger, a precision passer, and a defence-buster as the mood took him,' said another report. He was certainly robust and tough enough to survive being run over by a taxi-cab on the day of one international – he turned out as if nothing had happened and scored a goal. There is no record of how the taxi fared. Bell was also alert to the new sense of professionalism that pervaded the game in his day and did much to improve conditions for his fellow players. After joining Everton, and scoring for them in the 1897 Cup final, he was appointed chairman of the first professional players' union. He worked very hard for their ideals and often to the detriment of his career. Above all, he hated amateurs. One such Corinthian was C.B. Fry, a good player, who turned out for Portsmouth against Everton in the 1903 Cup final. He was strongly tackled by Jack Bell and soon afterwards retired, not only from the match, but from the game. Jack had shown who was master now. No one can say that that was Mr Bell's intention, but no one can say either that it wasn't. Jack was alive and well in Wallasey as late as 1951.

At this point it is well to remember that the term football *club* meant just that. From the very start the club aspect was as important as the football. Each club was a society, its aims were social as much as sportive, and the Victorian tendency for men to gather together in rooms for smoking, drinking and talk not ideally suited to their wives' parlours was well met in the formation of football clubs whose focus was comfortably male and well-removed from female intrusion. The social element had a visible cultural input too, albeit at a shallow, undemanding level. At the end of each match the two teams, and their respective officials, would get together in the clubroom, or in the nearest hostelry, to salve their bruises with liquid refreshment and entertainment. There were numerous glee clubs within the clubs and the nucleus of a fine male voice choir was often found among the full-backs and forwards. The after-match smoking concert was sometimes better value than the actual match. The players were amateur for the most part, and there were many of a high artistic and performing merit among them. Many players had their signature songs and no night would be complete without their singing their song as usual. How advantageous it might be in our own day if opposing clubs met within the hour to banter jokes and sing songs and entertain each other, instead of climbing into their respective luxury coaches waiting at the door to waft them away to steak and chips or a curry at some hotel hideaway. Who knows what talent other than football may be lurking within the Premier League or in the dark recesses of Division Three? The phrase 'a village Hampden' could take on a whole new significance.

A more cavalier instance of dressing-room histrionic talent, however, was an unlikely looking football player whom his fellows dubbed the 'Duke' and supporters knew as the inimitable Sandy McMahon.

Alexander MᶜMAHON (*circa* 1870–1916)   10
Inside-forward for Hibernian, Burnley, Celtic and Partick Thistle

A Borderer by birth, 'Duke' McMahon went from his native Selkirk to Hibernian and then on to Burnley before joining Celtic in 1891. He signed for Nottingham Forest in 1892 but never kicked a ball for them, as Celtic pursued him into England and talked him into coming back to Parkhead as inside partner to left-winger Johnny Campbell. They made a devastating if often exasperating pairing, as both players loved to dwell on the ball, creating intricate inter-passing patterns and beating an opponent twice where once would do. The crowds loved their antics, especially Sandy McMahon's. 'So deft was he in his manipulation of the ball [that] he patted and pirouetted with it in the manner of a premier danseuse.' Given that he played at a time when fair charging was allowed and that few players had the skill to hold the ball against the rough tactics often used, it says much for the Duke's courage that he indulged in such mazy gyrations on his own or in tandem with the like-minded Campbell. No wonder the crowds loved him. 'Arms held high, spread out like ostrich wings, head down, back bent forward, enormous feet . . . but McMahon could use those feet as other men use their hands.' Willie Maley, the Celtic manager, thought him the best header of a ball he had ever seen, even allowing for the later McGrory. 'He could almost hold a high cross with his head, then direct it with the greatest of ease. He was a terror to defences at corner kicks.' His one weakness, however, was that he was so intent on doing beautiful things with the ball that the scoring of goals was secondary, but he was the first Celtic player to epitomise an era in much the same way as Quinn, Gallagher, Delaney and Jock Stein were later to do. McMahon was hardly prepossessing. He was a big man, as ungainly off the pitch as he was gainly on it. He had thinning hair and a drooping moustache that hid the fact that he had no front teeth. Yet this dental handicap did not stop him from regaling the dressing-room after the match with Shakespearian recitations and impersonations of the famous actor-managers of the day. No reports of the performances are in print, but they are said to have been well received by his fellow players. One wonders who among modern players would dare to offer such elocutary exercises after a match. The Duke had no qualms, it would seem. He was a scholarly and well-read man, as witness his proclamation to the dressing room after they had beaten Rangers 4–0 in the Scottish Cup: 'Gentlemen, we have taken Kruger's advice. We have staggered humanity.' His nickname 'Duke' derived from the French President of the time, the Duc de MacMahon, descended from a Scottish soldier who had seen service with Napoleon. When that distinguished gentleman died, Glasgow news-boys sang out 'MacMahon deid! MacMahon deid!' People flocked to buy the papers, thinking they meant the Celtic star. For a star he was, there was no doubt about that, as the *Daily Record and Mail* of September 1936 vouched when it said 'You who did not see Sandy McMahon play knew nothing of the weaving artistry of our football game; all ease and grace, as if born to make a football answer his will.' That was Alexander McMahon, a Duke without peer. He finished his playing days with Partick Thistle and died soon after at the early age of forty-seven, during the First World War. He was as much a casualty of his times as of the demands of a football life. When he went he took something special away with him. We have not seen it since.

*

Players weren't above showing a little initiative with their inter-national selections. In 1892, Baird of Hearts was selected to play against Wales and Keillor of Montrose was chosen to play against Ireland. The players agreed to swap places as each had played against those respective countries before. In the same year, four Renton players, two of them the McCall brothers, withdrew from the Scottish team to play Ireland. James McCall had been chosen as captain, but their club was suing the SFA at the time. (They were later expelled after only five matches for the sin of professionalism.) On the motion of Celtic, and just in time for the 1893–94 season, the SFA yielded to the inevitable and voted to allow the same dreaded professionalism. Renton returned as Old Renton but they did not last long and the 'Champions of the World' disbanded. The immediate result of the new open attitude and the selection of the professional players (albeit from Scottish teams only) was that Scotland won the Home Championship and that the Scotland–England game at Richmond, won by Scotland 5–2, drew a record attendance of 16,000. Third Lanark played a friendly against Vale of Leven under artificial lights at the first Cathkin Park as early as 1878, but the experiment was not encouraging, although Celtic played an evening match under lights in 1892. It was a whole time of experiment and expansion and football could hardly keep up with all the new ideas. Football had caught on, and in many ways it was a victim of its own success.

The same was true of many of the players. Young men were being paid a lot of money by working-class standards and it had gone to their heads. Some were being given their first glimpse of the good life and they liked what they saw. Now that they could be openly regarded as professional men, they sought to take every advantage of their new social and economic position. Some players couldn't cope. The unexpected pressures gradually told and they fell by the wayside, psychologically drained by trying to play at working or failing to work at what they had previously regarded as playing. It was a difficult situation and there was little understanding at the time of the traumas involved in such occupational changeovers. Certainly there was no counselling available and many would have been insulted or bewildered had it been offered.

To play a game for a living was something very difficult for the Victorian to comprehend, hence the vehement resistance to professionalism in the new football. It was hardly foreseen by anyone then what a huge industry it would become, involving much more than the result of ninety minutes' pursuit of a round ball by twenty-two athletes over a given green rectangle watched by people who had paid to see them. This was not the vision the gentlemen of Cambridge had, still less that of the elegant mandarins of the Football Association in London. And as for the first officials in the Scottish game, all at Queen's Park it must be admitted, it was to be 1900 before they accepted the facts of everyday football life. Given such a lead, it was small wonder so many early clubs and players failed. Only half of the clubs survived the first decade. The attrition rate for players might be even larger. Others, however, did very well in this transition from hobby to trade, from artisan to professional artist, and the better players soon became part of the new sporting bourgeoisie. A good example was Celtic's full-back, Dan Doyle. Dan didn't always let his football duties stand in the way of a good time.

Daniel DOYLE (1864–1918)

Full-back for East Stirlingshire, Newcastle East End,
Grimsby Town, Everton and Celtic   **11**

Dan Doyle, nicknamed Ned, took his time getting to Celtic, but once at Parkhead he served that club well and led them as captain for ten seasons until he retired with every honour the game could give him. Tall, dark and Irish-handsome, Dan came from Paisley and won his first cap against England in 1892, and his last representative game was against the Irish League in 1899. In those seven years he was perhaps the most stylish full-back in the country but was first-call for Scotland on only eight occasions, Arnott, Smith and Drummond being still to the fore. Even when he was capped, he was not always prompt to turn up. For instance, just before the 1895 game against England at Liverpool, there was no sign of Doyle at the pre-match lunch and an hour to go before kick-off, he still hadn't turned up. Bob Foyers of St Bernard's was drafted in at left-back to partner Jock Drummond in Dan's place and was told to change. Then, just before kick-off, he swanned in to Goodison Park with an Everton ex-team-mate with whom he'd stayed the previous night and Foyers put on his suit again. Dan was not in the least put-out and stripped quickly. England won 3–0. His luck was as bad when he went into a whisky business at the end of his playing days. It soon failed and the cheerful Dan ended up as a builder's labourer. At the end, when he was dying of cancer in a Glasgow hospital, he drew aside the blankets to show his emaciated legs to his old manager, Willie Maley. 'Ah well,' he said wryly, 'they made a wee bit o' Celtic history in their time.' The same legs made their mark in other ways. In 1889, when Dan was playing for Grimsby

Town before he came to Celtic, he collided hard with a stavely winger called Cropper. Dan was soon on his feet, but poor Cropper was carried off. He died next day.

Dan Doyle's last club, Celtic, might be said to have been the leading club of the decade that ended the nineteenth century. Queen's Park had diminished to one Scottish Cup win in 1893. Celtic, on the contrary, had gone from strength to strength. Their intricate, close-passing style was based on the play of the Preston North End 'Invincibles', that Scottish-English team which had made such an impression in the English League and only two years before had won the first League and Cup double. Celtic played with the same flair, and to their credit they already had four League Championships and three Scottish Cups. Rangers, already their closest rivals, had won three Leagues, sharing the first with Dumbarton and winning three Cups, but their best was yet to come, winning the League in 1898–99 without losing a game – a feat that has never been repeated anywhere. However, just before the opening of their new stadium at Ibrox in 1899, Rangers had been going through a bad spell and lost half of their matches played. Celtic, in their brand-new Parkhead stadium, took the opportunity to revel in their more cavalier style, while the roundheads were momentarily disorganised. Celtic had come into being, fully grown so to speak, thanks to the Maley brothers, James Kelly and imports like Groves from the Edinburgh Hibernians. They never had to go through any apprentice stages, they were journeymen at once. Many resented this, as well as their obvious Irish, and therefore Catholic, base, and this bias was never really to disperse in Scottish football. The sectarian difference between them and Rangers was not marked at this time. Rangers had begun as a rowing club, not as an adjunct of the Orange Order, but as the years went by, their religious positions appear to have become polarised as both clubs recognised that they could call on a bulwark of support that had definite loyalties to opposite camps, but this was not the case as the century ended. Both clubs were football clubs first and foremost and with the same reliance on good players who were happy to pull on their jerseys.

Rangers could boast such as Jock Drummond, who wore a cap in every match, at the heart of their defence and Celtic could boast such wily forwards as Johnny Madden, who had considerable brains in their feet.

John DRUMMOND (1870–1935)
Left full-back for Falkirk and Rangers

12

Like his international team-mate, Arnott, Jock Drummond believed football to be a man's game and played it accordingly with sleeves rolled up and his cap pulled down to his eyes. The two men only played three times together, but Jock equalled Walter's record fourteen caps for Scotland and was captain in what was his best game, against England in 1896. His last international appearance was against Ireland in 1903 when that country defeated Scotland for the first time. When the best of his career was over, Jock returned to his home team Falkirk (he was born at Alva) where he had served his football apprenticeship. Drummond's partnership with his regular Rangers club-mate, Nicol Smith from Darvel, was legendary although they were rarely in the Scotland team together because of Arnott's continued presence in the right-back slot. All three full-backs shared the same sure-footedness in defence, a tremendous tackle and a robust shoulder-charge, a feature of the game in those early, straightforward days, but the sheer strength of Drummond's game was noted. He was the first of a long line of sturdy full-backs who have played for Rangers on the left flank – typified by the redoubtable Tiger Shaw who held the same position in the famous 'Iron Curtain' defence of the immediate post-Second World War years. Jock Drummond was the last player in first-class football to wear a cap while playing. He said he did so to keep a cool head.

John MADDEN (1865–1948)
Wing and inside-forward for Dumbarton, Celtic, Dundee and Tottenham Hotspur

13

Celtic tried to sign John or Jake Madden, nicknamed the 'Rooter' (because he once uprooted a goalpost with a shot), for the 1888 Exhibition Tourney. In fact, he did turn up to join them at the dressing pavilion, but he was asked outside to meet a friend and wasn't seen again that day. He had been kidnapped by Dumbarton. However, he joined Celtic for the next season and became part of their first great team under James Kelly. He was an unashamed professional, although his trade had been as a boiler-maker in the Clyde shipyards and when he got the chance (through being mistaken for the great Scottish captain, Jackie Robertson), to coach a side called Slavia in Prague, he jumped at it. The fact was that Robertson, who was a close friend despite being a Rangers player, was offered the job but passed it on to Madden. Jake quickly had his photograph taken wearing a Rangers jersey and the Czechs were happy to accept him at face value. It must be said that his command of Slavonic languages was only a little less than his command of English, but he was unperturbed. As he said himself: 'I learnt enough to swear in – and anyhow, it beats boiler-makin' in the yards.' By sheer power of personality, skill in coaching, and tactical innovation, he was an enormous success. He married and settled there, virtually becoming an institution in Prague. By this time, his command of Czech had improved as much as his command of English had deteriorated, but then he always insisted he couldn't speak English anyway. When he died in 1935, he was buried in the Olsanke cemetery like a hero. He had come a long way from Dumbarton Rock, but the football seed he had planted on the continent was to bear ample fruit. Just another wee Scottie on the make maybe, but look at what he made.

While on the subject of Scotland's football missionaries, others that spring to mind are McKean, who played for Allemania-Berlin in 1891 and was dubbed Der Unvergleschliche (The Incomparable) by the locals. Another was Robertson, who coached MTK Budapest in 1911, and everyone knows the place Hungary now has in football history. Alec McNab of Morton trebled his wages by crossing the Atlantic and Tommy Muirhead of Rangers coached the Boston Wonder Workers in 1925 to such effect that the USA reached the semi-finals of the first World Cup in Uruguay in 1930.

Yet what was obvious quite soon was that more than half of the city's football population was taken up with only two clubs, Rangers and Celtic, and by far the greater part of that half followed Rangers. Why this is so has little to do with football, as Celtic were the better team for the first twenty years at least. The religious differences was always there – hardly surprising when one club was formed from a Presbyterian cadre and the other founded to assist Catholic charities. Despite this, Rangers had signed Catholic players – Kivlichen has already been mentioned. There was also Colin Mainds in 1906, Tom Murray in 1908 and 'Punch' Kyle who was signed from Parkhead Juniors in 1908. It was with the coming of the First World War, and the importation of Irish workers from Belfast to cope with the rush of work at the new Harland and Wolff shipyard in Govan, that led to a marked increase in the type of support attracted to the clubs, particularly for Rangers. The Ulstermen brought with them all their Orange traditions and that meant all their historical hatreds, principally of all things Catholic, and Celtic FC, of course, were sitting ducks. Football became a focus for a lot of extraneous bias, which then hardened into bigotry. Soon the walls were set up in Glasgow, brought brick by brick from Belfast, and the slogans raised. There was to be NO SURRENDER. The Celtic followers, for their part, fell back on their Irish roots and built their own peat-bog barriers, so that we had the spectacle of two sets of Scots, two sets of Glaswegians, two sets of football supporters, drawing back into themselves and away from each other to create a divide, a gulf which was wholly artificial, entirely insupportable, and which still exists. A fact that has to be totally deplored by anyone of sense who loves the great game. Are we really to believe that a man's spiritual views are ascertained by his reaction to an inaudible air played on an invisible flute or that a young man's football future can be determined entirely by which school he went to? Danny McGrain of Celtic, a life-long Rangers supporter, was lost to the Ibrox club precisely because of this catholic bias. Yet how does it equate with the import of catholic Italians to Ibrox at the time of writing? Success, it seems, can surmount bigotry.

Partisanship is inevitable in sport. It has been a part of games since the first Olympiad when Euripides aptly described a spectator: 'He is a man of loose tongue and intemperate manner, given to tumult and to leading the populace to mischief with empty words.' He might have been any football fan at any time. So what changes?

The first book on football was called *The Simplest Game* by Mr Thring, the schoolmaster who helped devise the Cambridge Rules. Perhaps he saw, even then, that the simplest game appeared to attract the simplest minds. This, of course, is in itself a simplification, but one is amazed that the nineteenth-century game seemed to lure the publican into management and the sinner onto the new terraces. God appeared to show His face only to the Elect, that is, the players, and only to a very few of them, and then only intermittently. When it appeared, however, no one who saw it ever forgot it. Great players were still rare but good players abounded and the general standard of play was rising all the time. Rangers were a power in the Establishment and they began to build up a management structure, a stadium and a team worthy of that status. During the last season of the old century they won all eighteen matches in the championship, thanks to a last-second penalty at Easter Road against Hibs, but still couldn't win the Scottish Cup, which, for the first time, went out of the west of Scotland when Hearts beat Hibernian in the Logie Road Cup final. Hearts also won the League in that decade, so Glasgow wasn't having it all its own way. A second division of clubs was formed in 1892 and officialdom wrangled in their official-like way about composition and regulations, but to the public the players were still the thing. That's what they came to see in the now-accepted hebdomadal rite called the Saturday match. Everybody had the afternoon off now and no matter what was happening in the outside world the football fans flocked to see their favourites. At Ibrox, one such shyly emerged – Neilly Gibson.

Neil GIBSON (b. 1873)
Wing half-back for Rangers and Partick Thistle   **14**

The slim, fair-haired, boyish Neilly Gibson had class, was undoubtedly one of the footballing stars of his generation and equalled the record for the number of caps at that time shared by Arnott and Drummond – fourteen. Like another Partick Thistle favourite, Alex Raisbeck, who went on to make his name with Liverpool, Gibson learned the game in Larkhall in Lanarkshire, already a prolific nursery for football players, but unlike so many gifted Scottish players, he spent his entire career in Scotland, first with Rangers for ten seasons and then with Partick Thistle, until he retired. Gibson's speciality was his confident way with high balls which he would often volley clear with a back heel – even in his own penalty area. His three sons, Jimmy, Willie and Neil, were all professional footballers and all did well in the game. So they should. They were from good football stock. Jimmy played for Scotland too and told a nice story about his father and what it meant to play for Scotland then. Jimmy Millar was knocked out scoring the winning goal against England in 1897. Neil was the first to him. 'Are you all right?' he asked anxiously. 'Did I score?' gasped Jimmy. 'You did,' Neil told him. 'Then I'm all right,' said Jimmy.

In the reshuffle of clubs during 1899, Queen's Park belatedly accepted the inevitable and applied for full membership of the Scottish League. Ladysmith could not have been more relieved. Scottish football still needed Queen's Park, because Scotland needed Queen's Park players of the calibre of their centre-forward R.S. McColl.

Robert Smyth McCOLL (1876–1959)
Centre-forward for Queen's Park, Newcastle United
and Rangers

15

When young Bob McColl first arrived at Hampden Park as a seventeen-year-old in 1893, the doorman mistook him for one of the hamper boys and wouldn't let him into the players' dressing-room. However, it didn't take long for the slight teenager to be recognised by all in the game as a footballer who had everything – speed, ball control, courage, an amazing swerve and ruthless finishing, with the ability to curl the ball past the opposing goalkeeper by putting 'side' on it so as to bend it, as all good players do today. He was a Scottish international at nineteen and went on to score three hat-tricks in five games, the first of these in the famous 4–1 victory over England at Celtic Park on 7 April 1900, when Scotland played in Lord Rosebery's racing colours (primrose and pink) as a tribute to his Lordship's attendance. Sixty-four thousand spectators saw the start, although many would have missed McColl's first-minute goal. 'It was the best shot of the day,' commented the *Athletic News*. He got his third just before half-time (Jack Bell scored the other). McColl thought this the best Scotland team he had ever played in: 'Every man right for his position,' he said.

The 'Rosebery' team was Rennie, N. Smith and Drummond; Gibson, Raisbeck and Robertson; Campbell, Walker, McColl, Bell and A. Smith. Some believe this to have been the greatest-ever Scotland team. Lord Rosebery commented: 'I've not seen my colours so worthily worn since Lada won the Derby in 1894.'

The great mystery, however, is not that McColl went on to play professionally both with Newcastle United and Rangers (he was after all a superb forward), but that afterwards he was reinstated as an amateur, a very rare occurrence indeed, and allowed to finish his career with Queen's Park. What persuasion he had used to influence the ultra-conservative Queen's Park committee to take this unheard-of step is still not known. By this time, Robert Smyth McColl, or 'Toffee Bob' as he was known in the dressing-room, had become, with his brother Tom, proprietor of a thriving sweetie-shop business in Albert Drive, begun by their father who had made and sold his own toffees from the kitchen of his tenement flat. The brothers set up as a commercial company in 1901 and under the already-famous name of R.S. McColl they developed a company which in a little over a decade had thirty shops in Glasgow and a factory in North Woodside Road to supply them. Sergeant-Major

McColl returned from the First World War, having served in the RASC, to become chairman of the company, with Tom as managing director. Following a slump during the General Strike and the Depression which followed, the brothers sold their controlling interest to Cadbury's in 1933 but continued to run the company until their retirement in 1946. They remained on the Board until 1951, by which time R.S. McColl had extended nationally and diversified into newspapers and cigarettes as well as confectionery. In 1970 it was taken over by an American corporation and in 1985 was bought out by the Martin Retail Group, a subsidiary of Guinness PLC, who in turn sold it to the Panfida Group, a consortium of Australian investors in 1987. What a long way for a mere footballer to come in a hundred years. There is a famous photograph of the 1900 Scotland side, the first Rosebery team, taken in 1925, long after their retirement, and R.S. McColl stands at the back, assured and rich, looking like just Henry Ford among a group of his middle management. Toffee Bob was born to succeed. And not just at football.

The Rosebery International saw the return of the Scotland team to something of its old flashing form. The cumbersome selection process (often thirty-eight on the committee) had given way to a seven-man panel and this appeared to have served better. The 1900 team was a just celebration of the state of the game in Scotland as the century turned. In their own way, the 'Rosebery Rovers' were the equal of the 'Wembley Wizards' nearly thirty years later. Nothing else was talked about in Scotland for weeks. The Boer War was too removed and far away and the Scottish people, whatever the jingoistic press said, were not all that far away from sympathy with the Boers. Anything anti-English was pro-Scottish to the man in Sauchiehall Street. The Boxer Rebellion had just broken out on the same day as the Parkhead game, but the only boxer the average Glaswegian knew then was James J. Jeffries. What was much more interesting was that, in football, the Rosebery match marked the justification of Anglo-Scots in the Scottish team. The star at Celtic Park wasn't R.S. McColl or Jack Bell, for all their goals, but Alex Raisbeck, ex-Partick Thistle centre-half and captain of Liverpool, not to mention father of fourteen. He was magnificent in defence that day. He was evidence enough that the team needed the Anglo infusion if it were to play at the highest level.

Other Anglos had been returned to international duty since 1896, including Ned Doig, but one that was an enigma to many on both sides of the border was the mainstay of the Aston Villa side, albeit a thorn in the SFA's, Jimmy Cowan. Jimmy was always his own man and he could not have been a greater contrast to his sometime international colleague, the burly but circumspect Nick Smith of the Rangers.

James COWAN (1868–1918)
Centre-back for Vale of Leven, Aston Villa and
Queen's Park Rangers

16

Jimmy Cowan was unfortunate in that the best of his playing days were in that period when the SFA rather stuffily refused to pick 'Anglos', that is Scots playing for English clubs, for the national team. Consequently, excellent players like Cowan never got the cap credit they were due. However, he was a big name in England in his time and an idol at Villa Park. Tough, uncompromising and an expert tackler, he played the game the hard way. 'We're playin' fitba', no' larkin',' he would shout to his team-mates. Yet he might have been accused of doing just that when he feigned a sore back at training one year in order to get leave to go home to Scotland for the Powderhall Sprint in Edinburgh on New Year's Day. He had entered secretly and he and his Villa team-mates had a good bet on him, relying on his getting a good handicap. He did, and he won easily, returning quickly to Villa Park to celebrate. He was an all-out player on the pitch and an all-out liver-of-life off it. This was shown when he captained Scotland against England in 1898 rather the worse for a pre-match encounter with old friends. He said he wasn't drunk. It was just that he'd taken a drop of whisky for his toothache. Scotland lost and Jimmy's brief international career was over. Nevertheless, he continued to play and to enjoy himself. It was said that to talk while he was singing 'Loch Lomond' at the after-match social was a dangerous thing to do. After his playing days were over he became Queen's Park Rangers' first manager. It is not known if he also retired from singing.

Nicol SMITH (1873–1905)

Right full-back for Rangers

17

'Honest, fearless, upright, strong, yet fair,' Nicol Smith was the long-standing partner to Jock Drummond in the Rangers team and occasionally for Scotland. Rangers was his only club and he played twelve seasons for them with distinction before being struck down with enteric fever and dying in January 1905 at just thirty-one. Nick had come from Darvel as a youngster and took no time to establish himself as a regular in a very good Rangers team. He was fast, had a tremendous tackle and a famous shoulder-charge when that tactic was a prominent part of football. He first came to prominence when he produced a tremendous display for the Scottish League against the Football League in 1896. From then on, his calibre was recognised by honours despite the fact that Scotland was rich in backs at that time. Perhaps he was past his peak at his death but he was still playing up to that time and still had seasons in him. His final illness indicated that living conditions in Glasgow and the west of Scotland at that time, even for successful football players, were such that the strong, fit young man could be fatally struck down so unexpectedly. It was not only Glasgow Rangers mourned the passing of this formerly sturdy Scottish full-back when he and his young wife both died from the same illness, thought to have been caused by infected household drinking water.

This chapter ends with Rangers, particularly with a trio of their greatest players – half-back Jackie Robertson, outside-left Alec Smith, and big Bob Hamilton, their schoolmaster centre-forward – the last internationalists to be capped in the nineteenth century.

John Tait ROBERTSON (1877–1935)

Wing half-back for Morton, Everton, Southampton, Rangers and Chelsea

18

Professionalism was slow to come to Scotland after its recognition in England in 1885, but that didn't prevent Scottish clubs going into the market, albeit furtively, for the services of the better players like Jackie Robertson, one of the finest left-halfs of the time. Celtic, like Preston North End, made no secret of their paying their players in cash and kind for 'broken time' and other economic dislocations brought on players. Celtic made no bones about their status as 'paid amateur' – an acceptable Scottish compromise. However, it was to be 1893 before the SFA caught up with the times, and until then, the attempts by clubs to entice the quality player resembled a fashionable melodrama rather than sport. Agents thrived, but theirs was a risky profession to say the least, as supporters were robustly anxious to protect and preserve the best of their local football talent. Meetings between the parties concerned had to be secret and swift before the word was out. Not much has changed here either. Agents are still in the game, and to an even greater extent, although none is tarred and feathered today. When Celtic tried to sign Robertson in 1899, a better offer was made by Rangers, so he moved to Ibrox to make up the famous half-back line of Gibson, Neal (whom Celtic also sought to sign) and Robertson. He is said to have introduced the pass back to the goalkeeper, a tactic unheard of at that time.

Alexander SMITH (1876–1954)
Outside-left for Rangers   19

Alec Smith was the very acme of consistency. He played twelve consecutive internationals for Scotland and his twenty-one years with Rangers, dating from his trial match on 30 April 1894 against Notts County, the FA Cup winners of that day, proved not only his durability but his loyalty as well. He was the greatest left-winger of his day, probably second only to Alan Morton as Scotland's best ever. An untiring provider of chances and the ever-reliable source of scoring opportunities from his crosses, he played with every good inside-left in the game for Scotland but his regular partner in the Rangers team was Finlay Speedie. In a popular poll taken among football supporters by the *Weekly Record* to find the most popular player in Scotland, he tied for first place with goalkeeper Brownlie of Third Lanark and Celtic's Jimmy Quinn. Alec had been recommended to Rangers by Nicol Smith, their international full-back, who came from the same hometown of Darvel, in Ayrshire. It must have been gratifying for both men to find themselves only six years later in the same Scottish team for the Rosebery International of 1900. Smith had been employed as a lace-maker before taking up his football employment. The tricky patterns he made on the left wing for Rangers and Scotland were probably as effective as anything he might have created in Darvel lace.

Robert Cumming HAMILTON (1877–1948)
Inside- and centre-forward for Elgin City, Queen's Park,
Rangers, Fulham, Hearts and Dundee

20

Bob Hamilton, the tall, elegant schoolmaster, was, without doubt, the finest footballer produced by the Highland League. He was the son of an Elgin businessman and played his first football for that city. In 1897, he went to Glasgow University to take his degree and signed for Rangers. In the nine years he was at Ibrox, he became something of a legend for his strong shooting. He scored regularly for Scotland too, especially at Brammall Lane in 1903, when he got the winner against England. As the local report put it at the time: 'Like a mountain torrent in flood, Bob Hamilton swept through the defence and, with a shot Bladdley never saw, brought victory.' Like the later George Brown, he continued as a schoolteacher while playing for Rangers. A cartilage injury precipitated his transfer to Dundee, but he still played for Scotland. He returned to Elgin to manage the family business and ended his playing days taking them into the later stages of the Scottish Cup. He became Lord Provost of Elgin, and Hamilton Drive in the city is named after him. His first cap and portrait are proudly displayed in the Borough Briggs boardroom of Elgin City FC and he is still a matter of Highland pride to this day.

The century was over with the story of just twenty of our Scottish football greats. There were still many to come as there is much of football's story yet to be told. It's a long way from Parker's Piece, Cambridge, in 1848 to the Bosman ruling in Luxembourg in 1995, but in the fifty-two years so far we've seen much. This includes the acceptance of Anglos and professionalism, Arbroath's beating of Bon Accord 36–0 in 1885 (still a record score for an official match) and the gradual decline of Queen's Park in the face of the rise and rise of the Old Firm, Rangers and Celtic. It was all in the game in Scotland. Finally, 'The Simplest Game', for all the arguments it provokes, the interest it creates, the passion it arouses, the discussion it causes, had virtually reduced itself to one very simple rule: 'Only the ball must be kicked.'

Chapter Four

The Celtic Ascendancy

The period between the death of Queen Victoria in January 1901 and the assassination of the Archduke Ferdinand in Sarajevo in June 1914 marked the last Great Idyll, a decade of peace and plenty (for some), general security and stability that the world was never to know again. If one accepts as comparative sideshows the Crimean, Afghan and Boer Wars, Britain hadn't been involved in a major European conflagration since Waterloo, as military action would all too soon show. The last campaign to engross the British people as a whole had been the sea-battles of Horatio Nelson, hence the plethora of Nelson Streets and Trafalgar Squares all over the English-speaking world. This was a considerable territory of the earth in 1901, as could been seen by the amount of blood-red on the map, but it was also a time of assurance, confidence and total trust in the continuation of the British Empire. There was just the slightest surprise that old Queen Vic should have allowed herself to die at all. With her going the old Victorian values of cast-iron certainties and biblically justified expansions wavered somewhat but still held firm and this continuing confidence was shown in Scottish football, particularly by Queen's Park.

They had come into being when there was still hope for a British League as William McGregor had hoped, hence the title, the Football League, not the English Football League. Queen's Park, and later Rangers, played many of their first fixtures in English football and both did well in the FA Cup, but now with first-rate stadia at Parkhead and emerging at Govan, the Queen's Park committee recognised that their ground, the second Hampden Park, was not quite up to the same standard. With all the flair of the new Edwardians, coupled with the efficiency of previous Victorians, which most of them still were, and with only five thousand pounds in the bank (hardly the cost of the new stands), they set about building not the best football ground in Glasgow, or even in Scotland, but in Britain. They promised old Hampden to Third Lanark, to whom it would become the new Cathkin Park, and work was begun. Rangers, meantime, carried on where they had left off in the previous century, winning the first League title of the new era as well as the 1901 Glasgow Exhibition Cup. This special tournament had been played on the pitch especially created for the event at Gilmorehill, adjoining the University – but then tragedy struck – the Ibrox Disaster of 1902.

Rangers had spent more than twenty thousand pounds on a ground improvement scheme in order to bring Ibrox into line with Celtic Park and the second Hampden. They had engaged the father of Victorian football grounds, architect Archibald Leitch (1866–1939), a Glasgow-born engineer and draughtsman, who had designed the original stadium at Parkhead for Celtic and the second Hampden for Queen's Park. He was later to build his magnificent grandstands for Everton, Blackburn Rovers, Tottenham Hotspur, Arsenal, Fulham and Leeds United, as well as for Hearts and Hamilton Academical at home – but for Rangers, he gave them their first great main stand which still survives in their ultra-modern stadium of today. The custom at the turn of the century was to have a main stand with terraces open on the other three sides but Ibrox was provided with new wooden stands on the East and West terracings, both reached by staircases. It is not known if these additions were part of Leitch's remit but, in any event, it all looked very splendid and the SFA had no hesitation in naming the ground for the 1902 international against England. The selectors also chose the first-ever all-professional team to play for Scotland. In the absence of Liverpool's Alex Raisbeck, the regular Scottish captain, Albert Buick, then of Hearts, was chosen to lead the Scottish team which contained star names from the home League. Among them were team-mates Bobby Walker and goalkeeper Harry Rennie, as well as the charismatic Bobby Templeton, then playing for Arsenal. It was a confident Scottish team with such players in it.

Alexander Galloway RAISBECK (1878–1949)
Centre half-back for Hibernian, Stoke City, Liverpool, Partick Thistle and Hamilton Academical 21

Alex Raisbeck was born in Stirling but brought up in Larkhall, that veritable cradle of football in Lanarkshire. From the local Larkhall Thistle and Royal Albert junior teams, he signed first for Hibernian in 1896 before joining Stoke City two years later. He was bought by Liverpool for a modest fee but he was one of the best investments that club ever made. Raisbeck spent seven years on Merseyside, most of them as captain of the team. It was from Liverpool that he made his mark as a Scotland player following a splendid debut in the 1900 Rosebery International against England at Celtic Park. In 1909, he returned to Scotland to lead Partick Thistle until the outbreak of the Great War in 1914. He ended his playing career with Hamilton Academical, becoming a director, and also their manager, in 1917. He occupied the manager's seat next in Bristol (1921), Halifax Town (1930) and Chester (1938) before returning finally to Liverpool as their chief scout, a post he held until his death. Alex Raisbeck was one of the great centre-halfs, capable of playing the old game as pivot in the centre of the pack, and the new game as a third back at the rear, being very fast and excellent with his head. Only big Charlie Thomson of Hearts and Sunderland could compete with Raisbeck in the command of the field. But no one could compete with big Alex as a sire. He had fourteen children. Yet there is no record of another Raisbeck in first-class football. Perhaps Alex's huge talent was enough for all of them.

Henry George RENNIE (1873–1954)
Goalkeeper for Morton, Hearts, Hibernian, Rangers and Kilmarnock

22

Arguably the finest goalkeeper of the first decade of the twentieth century, Greenock-born Harry Rennie learned his football trade in his home town before joining the local Morton but not as a goalkeeper. He was a half-back at first and not until 1897 did he move between the goalposts. It was as a 'keeper' that Hearts paid fifty pounds for him soon afterwards and it was with them that he won his first two caps for Scotland. His further eleven until 1908 were all won with Hibernian, where he moved next. He had a long and worthwhile club career including a spell with Rangers before finishing at Kilmarnock and it was this total experience he put to good use when his playing days were over. He and Ned Doig could still remember the days when the goalkeeper was just another member of the team, wearing the same strip as everyone else in the team and wearing a cap as many outfield players still did. Rennie, however, set out to make the goalkeeping position a unique one, studying the narrowing of angles from the goalmouth and the gestures of players as they prepared to shoot. Positioning was therefore paramount and this scientific approach begun by Harry Rennie so long ago is part of every ambitious goalkeeper's training today. Jimmy Cowan, also of Morton and of Scotland, was only one of his many goalkeeper pupils.

Robert WALKER (1879–1930)
Inside-forward for Hearts

23

Bobby Walker was not known for his pace. In fact, some commentators thought him slow. What he did have was fast feet and an even faster brain. His captain in the famous 1900 Scottish team, Jackie Robertson, said of him: 'You would think Bobby Walker had eight feet. You go to tackle him where his feet were, but they're away by the time you get there.' He had an even faster football brain and not for nothing was he once described as 'the father of altruistic football'. He made the ball do the work and his positional sense brought the best out in his team-mates. So well did he pace himself in a game that his stamina was never suspect and so well did he pace his career that he played in twenty-nine internationals in almost as many years in first-class football. He played his first trial for Hearts in 1896 and his last appearance was as a partner to the great Welsh winger, Billy Meredith (who himself played till he was almost fifty) in the 1915 Belgian War Relief Match. It can be seen now that Walker's style was not slow but subtle and he anticipated a long line of thinking inside-forwards that have been the backbone of so many Scottish teams and the delight of Scottish crowds. A gas engineer to trade before he moved to Hearts, he knew no other club and had no wish to. He was also an excellent golfer and Edinburgh gave him ample chance to play that game as well. In addition, he owned a shop and was a partner in a cinema. Bobby Walker had few complaints.

Albert Thoroughgood BUICK (1875–1948)
Centre-back for Arbroath, Hearts and Portsmouth

24

Albert Buick was one of the many unsung football heroes in the early decades of the game. Nicknamed 'Spider' because of his exceptionally long arms, he was a most unlikely footballer because of a cumbersome appearance but that only belied the athletic skills he showed during a game. Unusually slight for a defender, with a slight stoop and shuffling feet, he was the antithesis of the footballer at the turn of the century, but on the park he was a dynamo and the centrepiece of the Portsmouth team for years. Almost single-handedly he turned that club's fortunes around and he has remained a favourite figure in their club history. He played most of his football in England and so was inclined to be ignored by the Scottish selectors. In any case, Alex Raisbeck was the man in possession of the centre-back position at the time, but

Albert was proud of his Arbroath birth. He became a Hearts player by answering their advertisement for players. When asked what was the secret of his success on the football field, Albert replied tersely: 'Man, I just play the game.' This was always his first aim and behind that simple statement lay a sophisticated football mind allied to a tough mental attitude. This allowed him to overcome his physical shortcomings and 'play the game' totally, all over the field and to the very highest standards. He captained his country on his first appearance against Ireland at Belfast in 1902 and scored. He also scored against Wales soon afterwards but was never picked again. Portsmouth was a long way from Glasgow in 1903.

Robert Bryson TEMPLETON (1879–1919)
Outside-right for Hibernian, Aston Villa, Newcastle, Arsenal, Celtic, Kilmarnock and Fulham

25

Bobby Templeton was Scottish football's first showman. Always a smart dresser, he did much to lift the image of the professional player from that of a scruffy proletarian dragged straight from the tenement or the pub to match what he really was, a successful executive selling his skills to the highest bidder, honing his public image to take advantage of mass recognition and admiration. Templeton was not the public schoolboy playing at it or the professional man enjoying a hobby. He was the full-time professional who gave of his best in return for the best he could get. He belonged to that select band of footballers of his day who were paid throughout the three-month close season. These months of May, June and July in any year were always tricky for the professional footballer before the advent of summer tours and international competitions. Even when these became commonplace, the vast majority of footballers were unaffected and had to return to ordinary work in the summer. However, for extraordinary players, close season wages were paid. Such players were household names and papers like the *Scottish Referee*, *Scottish Umpire* and *Scottish Sport* were eager to fill their pages with their doings. Templeton knew the value of publicity right from the beginning. When he was with Kilmarnock in the final phase of his career, he entered a lion's cage at Bostock and Wombwell's Menagerie in the New City Road after a game at Parkhead, and for a wager of ten pounds put his head in its mouth, giving its tail a tweak for extra measure. The owners of the menagerie gave him a special gold medal to mark the feat. Not that he needed such gimmicks. His dazzling ability on the right wing shone as brightly as the glister of a circus manager's golden trophy, for Bobby Templeton could play, his international recognition testifies to that. He won eleven caps between 1902 and 1913 but his high reputation was much greater than his toll of caps. He was the Stanley Matthews of his day and he drew the crowds wherever he played. Good to look at and exciting to watch, he was nicknamed 'The Blue Streak' because of his exceptional speed along the touchline on either wing, and he left most full-backs floundering. He was described as a 'sand dancer' and when in play he 'danced like a sunbeam, gliding here and there in mazy waltzes or darting for goal as the notion seized him'.

Born in Coylton, Ayrshire, he began his career with Kilmarnock Roslin Rugby XI in 1897, transferring to Hibernian a year later. He moved on to Aston Villa soon afterwards, despite Hibernian's attempts to retain him, and in 1903 he joined Newcastle. From there he moved to Woolwich Arsenal in the following season, in the manner of the many wandering Scottish stars of the period, who flitted from club to club as the whim, and the financial inducement, dictated. Celtic brought him back from Arsenal in 1906 as a left-winger, but he was too much of a 'star' for their particular needs at the time, even though the supporters obviously loved him. However, 'The Blue Streak' did not always please his superiors – especially the dour but all-powerful Willie Maley at Celtic Park. Once, when on tour in Denmark, his dizzy dribbling on the wing delighted the Copenhagen spectators, so much so that they chanted his name in unison – 'Tempel-ton! Tempel-ton!' – and spurred Templeton on to even wilder extravagances. This 'silly, selfish display' so infuriated Maley that that martinet-manager had Bobby on the carpet immediately and then put him in goal for the next two games. When the Celtic party returned home to Glasgow he was immediately put on the transfer list. The massive Celtic support protested strongly at his going, but the management was adamant and Templeton was allowed to go. No player could be seen to be greater than the club, a point of contention Celtic were to have with so many of their star players down the years. So he travelled south again, but this time only as far as Kilmarnock. He had, in a sense, come home. He stayed in the Burns Country until 1913 when he was transferred to Fulham for fifty pounds. He retired two seasons later and returned to Kilmarnock where he went into partnership with his old Celtic mate, 'Sunny' Jim Young, at the Royal Hotel in George Street. He had got used to hotels in his playing days. Unlike most players, his accommodation was subsidised and the debonair Bobby made the most of it. Before the Great War of 1914–18 he would have been earning, in real terms, much the same as any professional man. In other words, he was a success and his lifestyle reflected it. His fame of course rested entirely on his ability to perform on a Saturday afternoon. People flocked in their thousands to see their new heroes and the dashing Bobby Templeton, of the flashing feet and centre-parted hair, was one of these. He enjoyed it too. He had the looks and status of a matinee idol and all that went with that kind of fame. However, as Douglas Lamming quotes in his excellent *A Scottish Internationalists' Who's Who* (Hutton Press, 1987), some commentators of the time thought Templeton 'wayward and irresponsible. He never fully realised the tremendous possibilities in his superb ball control and tactical genius.' Nevertheless, he remains one of the great personalities of the Scottish game. He had everything – speed, control, two good feet and a whole range of tricks. What else would anybody want? Except more, perhaps.

Sadly, Bobby Templeton did not have long to enjoy his hotel. One Sunday morning in November 1919, he was lacing up his boots when he keeled over and died of a heart seizure. Perhaps an appropriate end for a footballer, to die with his boots on, but forty-one seemed rather young, even for a man who had lived as fully as he had. After his death, his brother Andrew, a bit hard-pressed for cash, sold a case of his famous brother's medals. The collection found its way to Australia, but in 1956 the owners returned the medals to the Templeton family. It was a generous and thoughtful gesture and it rightly honoured one of Scotland's most colourful football sons.

One wonders how much Bobby Templeton remembered of the Ibrox Disaster. It was said that people at the top of the overcrowded West terracing had leaned forward to watch one of his mazy runs up the right wing on the terrible day. They pressed on the spectators in front of them, who also pushed forward against those in front of them and so on all the way down to the front so that people spilled on to the track and even on to the pitch. Templeton found himself dribbling round them at one point as they ran in front of him. 'I'll never forget it till my dying day,' he said.

On the day of the match (5 April 1902) it had been raining heavily, and it continued to rain as the game began in front of 68,000 spectators who paid a shilling each to get in and sixpence for boys. People were still flocking in after the game had started and those already in gave way by climbing the narrow stairs that led to the top of the new East and West terraces. More and more climbed higher, trying to get a view of the pitch in the heavy rain, till there were just too many men in too small a space. The steel uprights supporting the wooden planking began to buckle, the platform began to sway and in the rush to get clear people became jammed at the top, having no escape except by the staircases leading down to the pitch. Most of the crowd were watching the game and few realised the panic that had now set in at the top of the west terracing. Suddenly, about ten minutes into the game, there was a mighty crack and a hole appeared, dragging down four hundred spectators among the tangle of twisted girders and broken planking. Twenty-six of them died. For a time, the game went on, but as spectators flooded onto the pitch in terror from the lower tiers of the terracing, people realised what was happening and the game was stopped. It was said that people at the top of the overcrowded west terracing had all leaned forward at one point. The extra pressure had told on the iron stanchions in the possibly weakened undersoil after a long day of rain, and they buckled and gave way, taking with them the seven rows of planking seats which they supported. The unsuspecting spectators fell into the gaping hole which opened up under them, others collapsed onto the tiers of spectators in front of them, who in turn fell forward against those in front of *them* and so on until the men and boys at the front spilled out onto the track around the playing pitch.

Among the dead was a professor of hypnotism, eight professional men, seven white-collar workers, a milkman and the rest were mainly skilled workers and men from the shipyards. There was one solitary housewife. The prices were beyond the very poor and poorly paid Catholics, who were the bulk of Celtic supporters – but then the fateful game was at Ibrox. There had been a crowd incident at Ibrox before. From the beginning they had had a large following and too often they were too much for the stadium at that time, but at least no one had been killed. At least not until 1902. At the official inquest, the architect blamed the builders for using inferior wood and iron, the builders blamed the architect for a poor design, and both parties blamed the weather, but in the end they were all just excuses and all joined to grieve what was a tragic accident. There was to be another tragedy on the Ibrox terracings and even more people were to die but that was over half a century in the future.

The game of 1902 was eventually played out against a background of rescue workers and spectators carrying out the dead and injured on improvised stretchers made from the broken wood that littered the terracing. In all, 587 spectators were sufficiently injured to receive compensation later, but the one-all draw was declared void. It was replayed at Birmingham during the close season and the resulting draw was sufficient to give Scotland the championship, but somehow it didn't seem to matter. All proceeds of the replay were given to the Ibrox Disaster Fund.

Charles Bellany THOMSON (1878–1936)

Centre-half for Hearts and Sunderland

26

Charlie Thomson was big, brawny and brave and that's all one might say of him, but having originally been a centre-forward in his early days with Hearts, he was also an attacking centre-half-back blessed with a remarkable stamina. After the game against Ireland in 1911, one journalist wrote: 'Thomson was a great bustler and like John Walker was not too particular in his tackling, but he covered a great deal of ground and showed no signs of tiring.' This was a tribute to his training as much as to his natural physique. He developed into an inspirational captain of Hearts and of Scotland and was a reliable taker of penalties, with only one miss, that against Ireland in 1908. His value to any side was stressed when he was transferred to Sunderland in April of that same year. He was assessed as being worth exactly twice the transfer limit of that time, so Sunderland threw in another player to make up the balance, so keen were they to have Thomson. He then went on to become the cornerstone of the great Wear-side teams before becoming a prosperous licensee.

Like big Charlie Thomson above, Harry Rennie, Bobby Walker and Albert Buick were all Hearts players at one time. Only Bobby Walker, of that group, saw out his whole football time with them but that didn't prevent Heart of Midlothian FC being quite a football force in the first years of the first decade. Indeed, it looked at one time as if they, with a little help from Hibs, might drive a wedge between the two Glasgow giants. Hibernian were champions in 1903 and Hearts were Cup finalists. They took Rangers to three games before the Ibrox men squeezed a victory. Third Lanark won the League the following year, but the Edinburgh pair were there or thereabouts in all Scottish competitions. In the international against England at Sheffield, Ned Doig held back the English forward line on his own until Bobby Walker could hit the winner, but one development above all else dominated this age, and this was the emergence of Celtic as the first really great club side.

The first sign of this new level came when Rangers generously put forward the 1901 Exhibition Cup as a trophy to be played for by the leading English and Scottish teams in aid of the Ibrox Disaster Fund. Celtic won what was formally renamed the British League Cup, as they were to win all the national competitions set up as special events in the years to come. However, no one could guess at this time that something was about to happen as season 1904–5 got under way.

Something of a football phenomenon emerged from the East End and it had little to do with tenement soup kitchens or Catholic charities. By 1904, Celtic Football and Athletic Club had come of age and if they weren't given the key of the door in their twenty-first year, they were certainly given the key to football success at the top level. To appreciate this, one must understand that twentieth-century Celtic was not the ready-made side that had been bought into being, as it were, twenty-one years before. This new Celtic team was the result of shrewd junior signings by manager Willie Maley, and deft coaching by director James Kelly and some of the seniors at the club. Maley was able to boast later that the team cost less than two hundred pounds in minimal signing fees. There was a change of policy in that the stars, like Jack Bell and Bobby Templeton, would come to Parkhead, dazzle for a time, and then, like meteors, zoom on. Meantime, the younger players, having benefited from the experience, would become stars themselves in time. In this way, Celtic built up a remarkable stable of players that was to see them through the next decade. The group was all the more remarkable because it was comparatively small – no more than twenty players were used on first-team duty throughout the seven years of ascendancy. These were Adams and Sinclair (goal), Watson, McLeod, Weir and Orr (full-backs), McNair, Young, Loney and Hay (half-backs) and a forward line which still reads like a prayer, not only to Celtic supporters, but to all Scots who appreciated the best in Scottish football. The line was Bennett, McMenemy, Quinn, Somers and Hamilton. Various others, like Wilson, Garry, McCourt, Campbell and Munro, were available, and, as mentioned, star imports came and went, but for the most part the men named were the players who carried the club through a momentous chapter in their story.

It began in earnest when they beat Rangers in a League decider at Hampden after they had finished level in the 1905 championship. In 1907 they completed the double, the first Scottish club to do so, beating the holders, Hearts, in the final. An interesting sidelight to Celtic's small playing staff at this time: when both their goalkeepers were injured, Rangers loaned them their reserve keeper, Tom Sinclair. Sinclair went on to win a Glasgow Cup medal with Celtic after a run of nine games without letting in a goal, then returned to Rangers reserves in time to help them win the Second Eleven Cup. He was then officially transferred to Newcastle, where he was in the team that won the English League Championship. They do say you need luck to be a keeper. Luck didn't desert Celtic either, for they repeated the double of League and Cup in 1908. They might have made it an astonishing triple in 1909 but for a drawn Cup final with Rangers, which led to the infamous 'extra time' misunderstanding between the teams and the consequent crowd trouble.

The clubs had thought there would be extra time in the event of a draw, and Celtic stayed on the field, encouraging the crowd to think that the game would go on. When it was pointed out to Celtic that Cup rules demanded a replay on another day, they also left the field at which the huge crowd, now thoroughly confused, rioted, burning the pay-boxes and setting alight a bonfire in the middle of the field. A regiment of police was called out to restore order and, as a consequence, the Cup was withdrawn from both clubs. It was a disgraceful incident and the two clubs must shoulder a lot of the blame, particularly Celtic, who had suggested to Rangers that extra time might be played rather than another game. It was this which caused the initial confusion and fuelled the disappointment which inflamed both sets of supporters. The SFA rules were clear, but the clubs thought they were too big for the rules, and a riot resulted. Rangers and Celtic took a joint stand in the matter but relations between them were never cordial thereafter and Celtic, in particular, lost the chance of a unique triple. In addition, they had to pay towards the damage done to the new Hampden, which had been opened only six years before. It was already the showpiece of Scottish football, and that it should also have been made the forum for an outbreak of hooliganism was unfortunate to say the least.

The point was made in the Glasgow press that many of the spectators, in trying to escape the confusion, were run down by police horses and attacked by batons. In naturally resisting this onslaught, they were held to be hooligans as well, and matters were only compounded. As always on huge crowd occasions, it is a small nucleus which seizes on the opportunity for mayhem or profit and their action draws a response from the authorities in which the innocent often suffer more than the villains. After this there were calls for soldiers with fixed bayonets at football matches, but as time passed tempers cooled and anyway there was another whole new fresh season to look forward to.

During 1909–10, it looked as if Celtic had been shaken by the Cup final events and the first cracks began to appear in the hitherto impregnable unit. The players were all getting older at the same time, which was a natural hazard, but what they lacked in pace they now made up in guile and still won the League championship and the Glasgow Cup in this, their swan-song season. All in all, it was a remarkable achievement in consistency and stability and even the actual statistics, nearly a hundred years later, still make incredible reading – they won three Scottish Cups, five Glasgow Cups and three Charity Cups while winning six Championships in a row. In acknowledgement of this feat, the Scottish League presented the club with a shield naming all the players who took part in the great run. Everyone was sure such a thing would never happen again in football. Little did they know it would be surpassed by the very same club fifty years later and surpassed yet again by Rangers in our own day. All this was in the future, however. In 1910, the day belonged to Captain Scott of the Antarctic, Dr Crippen and Glasgow Celtic.

In Edinburgh, Hibernian, founded and run by Irish Catholics for Irish Catholics, was unashamedly sectarian but it could never hope to emulate the immediate success of the Glasgow Irish – mainly because it had lost half its team to the new Celtic, a cause of much ill-feeling between the two clubs for many years afterwards. Even if the Edinburgh side had kept its players (most of whom came from Glasgow anyway), it is unlikely that it would have played 192 games, won 136, drawn 23, lost 33, scored 444 goals, lost 153 goals and amassed 305 points in six seasons as this Celtic squad did. It seems invidious to select individual players for particular honour, but a special place must be given to the cool captain of the rearguard, Alec McNair, to the brains at inside-right, Jimmy McMenemy, and, perhaps above all, to that human dynamo at centre-forward, Jimmy Quinn.

James QUINN (1878–1945)
Centre-forward for Celtic   **27**

Jimmy Quinn of Croy ranks with R.S. McColl, Hughie Gallacher and his fellow Celt, Jimmy McGrory, as one of the great Scottish centres. No one could have wished for a better debut, against Rangers in the Cup final of 1904, for he scored a hat-trick to win the game. He was known as the iron man of football, yet for all that he retired earlier than he might have done, due to persistent knee injury. This proneness to injury cost him caps in his career but he still managed to accrue eleven and in one game he hit four goals against Ireland. His last game for Scotland was as an outside-left, where his unabashed, direct style and chunky miner's shoulders gave England's famous full-back, Bob Crompton, an uncomfortable afternoon. He was not the first defender to feel the impact of Quinn's physical presence. Quinn spent fifteen years with Celtic (1900–15) and in that time his was a royal reign. His fine frame was used frequently in advertising, particularly for Boag's Rheumatic Rum, which was retailed at Bridgeton Cross for a shilling a bottle on the strength of his endorsement. He was a great crowd favourite, and once, in 1905, when he was ordered off, the Celtic fans invaded the pitch. Jimmy Quinn was never far from controversy. He gave as good as he got and he got a lot, but his manager at Celtic, Willie Maley, said of this shy, simple man with the quiet ways: 'He was dogged and damaged in almost every game he played. Yet it's astonishing how many men are still living whom Jimmy Quinn is supposed to have killed.'

James McMENEMY (1880–1965)
Inside-forward for Celtic, Stenhousemuir and Partick Thistle 28

Rutherglen-born, Jimmy McMenemy earned himself the cognomen 'Napoleon' due to his skills in football strategy and his ability to dictate play by the accuracy of his defence-splitting passes. He saw the football pitch as his chessboard, and by scheming, plotting and subtle positioning, he made his moves deliberately and without the need to over-exert himself unduly. In this, he was like Bobby Walker, to whom he lost so many international opportunities, although as late as 1919 he partnered Alan Morton in the Scotland side. Jimmy, like a later Celt, Bobby Evans, was never on a losing Scottish side. He earned twelve caps, but would have had more had he not been a contemporary of Bobby Walker's. They were both the same kind of player who appeared to walk through the game while others ran themselves ragged around them. Like Templeton, he was a natural, with small regard for arduous training – he had no need of it, being a natural. He was one of that lucky band of players who grew up to play for the club he supported when he was a boy and was at Celtic Park from 1902 until 1920. After his best days were supposed to be over, he was given a free transfer to join Stenhousemuir and then Partick Thistle, whom he led to victory in the 1922 Scottish Cup final against Rangers. He was forty years old at the time and returned to Celtic as trainer-coach. He was the father of two footballers – John of Motherwell and Harry of Newcastle – but once again, like so many of the football greats, the strain did not improve on the sire. McMenemy might never have played football at all because of his early job in a glass factory which damaged his feet. Celtic found him a job making chairs and his feet were saved for football. He was often the voice of sanity on the field and his cry, 'Keep the heid!' was often heard in the heat of the fray for both Celtic and Scotland.

Alexander McNAIR (1883–1951)
Right full-back for Stenhousemuir and Celtic

29

Unlike his Celtic colleague, McMenemy, who went from Celtic to Stenhousemuir at the end of his career, Alec McNair went from Stenhousemuir to Celtic in 1904, at the start of his, and he stayed at the club for twenty valuable years. He was a cool, intelligent player whom nothing disturbed on the field, and no matter the tensions of the game, he always appeared unruffled, hence his nickname, 'The Icicle'. In addition, he had quite a remarkable versatility as a footballer. He could have played in any position on the field – even goal – and distinguished himself, he was that kind of all-round player. He filled in wherever was needed on the day. He lived all his life at Larbert, worked a 5 a.m. to 5 p.m. shift all week and yet had one of the longest careers in football. Hugh Hilley, his final full-back partner at Celtic Park, started school in the same year (1903) that Alec signed with the club. Sadly, his wife died early in their marriage but Alec manfully brought up his young family on his own, while working down the pit and playing football on a Saturday. He must have had a hundred things in his mind at any time, yet he personified calm and ease on the pitch. Perhaps playing in a match was a welcome escape from the weans. He was first capped at wing-half, but soon made the full-back position his own and was recognised by his country on fifteen occasions and by the Scottish League on fourteen. His last appearance for Scotland was as captain in the high-scoring (5–4) defeat by England at Hillsborough in 1920. Altogether, he made almost six hundred club appearances for Celtic in a remarkable career. This equalled Alec Smith's playing record for Rangers (later surpassed by another Ranger and another right-back, Dougie Gray). McNair was the quiet type, highly respected by his fellow players and appreciated by management. Not for him the flamboyance of Templeton or the derring-do of Quinn. He got on with his job, which was to prevent the other team from scoring while at the same time assisting his own side to do so. He saw the simple game for what it was – simple – and in doing the simple thing well he played his part to the full. He was the ideal team man and it was this which gave him his status in the game. On his retiral, he managed Dundee for a time before resigning to become a Referees Inspector for the SFA. He finally set up as a stockbroker in Falkirk, not far from his Larbert home. He gave his telegraphic address as 'Celtic'.

William Struth, the Clyde trainer, left to join Rangers and found a dynasty. A new era would now begin for them as new players were brought in, like Alec Bennett from Celtic and Tommy Cairns, who would become their captain. The League was won again and twice retained but Rangers did not have all the best players. Other names loomed large in Scottish football at this time and none more so than that of Jimmy Brownlie.

James BROWNLIE (1885–1975)
Goalkeeper for Third Lanark and Dundee United   30

'Confident and daring, but not wildly so' was how Jimmy Brownlie was described as a goalkeeper. Bert Bell, the Third Lanark archivist, says that Brownlie's arrival at Cathkin Park in 1906 from Blantyre Victoria was one of the best things that ever happened to the historic old club. Despite a firm offer from Celtic (for whom he had played a trial), he was to remain with the 'Hi-Hi's' for seventeen years. On his mid-week debut against Partick Thistle he saved two penalties taken by Neil Gibson. It was an augury of things to come. Jimmy was a bricklayer with hands to match, extra large and extra strong. When he held the ball in these huge hands it seemed to disappear. The press referred to him as 'The Man with the Iron Clutch'. He once scored a goal against Motherwell and, uniquely, their goalkeeper, Clem Hampton, also scored in the same match. Brownlie conceded only eleven goals in sixteen appearances for Scotland and was especially memorable against England in 1909, against Ireland in 1910 and Wales in 1913. He also played in the Victory Internationals of 1918–19. Yet even in the six years of his international career, he rarely earned more than a skilled workman of the day and was entirely satisfied. His lifestyle was as plain as the man himself, even on the day he had to play for Scotland at Hampden. 'I worked as usual on Saturday morning,' he said. 'Then at dinner-time I headed for the Horseshoe Bar in Glasgow to have my normal half-pint and toasted cheese, the speciality of the house. I then took the tramcar to Mount Florida to meet up with the rest of the lads . . .' Compare that with today's pampered preparations for players not a quarter his size or status in the game. His only real bonus was to be paid to take his family 'doon the watter' every summer and to join the other star players on the annual overseas tours. On the 1921 tour to the United States and Canada, he was astonished by the attendant on the sleeping car, the first black man he had ever met in his life. Brownlie was constantly surprised by his own fame and success and was often awe-struck by the football company he kept on occasion. This modest big man didn't realise he was among his peers. When he was voted with Quinn and Alec Smith as Scotland's favourite footballer one year, all he could say was that he 'thought it was a great honour on myself'. When he retired from playing he became secretary-manager of Dundee United. On one occasion, the third replay of a cup tie against Hearts at Tynecastle, Paterson, the goalkeeper of Dundee Hibernian (as United were then called) was suddenly found to be unfit just before kick-off, and manager Jimmy Brownlie, aged forty-five and weighing more than fifteen stones, took his place seven years after hanging up his gloves. He had to pick the ball out of his own net no less than six times. Afterwards, no one laughed louder than Jimmy. He continued to attend games at Cathkin right up till his death in 1974. Far from football's honouring him, it was he who had honoured football.

Willie Maley, now almost a legend at Celtic Park, and the last link with its very beginnings in 1887, was now beginning to build another great side and his new signings included a wisp of a young man from Ireland, Patrick Gallagher, known as Patsy. Round the ageless McNair and the timeless McMenemy, he fashioned a new side which regained the Championship from Rangers in 1914 and wrested the Cup from Hibernian after a goalless draw at Hampden. Hampden Park, now restored as the venue for all great occasions in Scottish football, was again the finest ground in Scotland, even in Britain, which at that time meant the football world. The Queen's Park investment hosted a crowd of nearly 130,000 to see Scotland play England in April. The gates had to be closed against thousands waiting twenty minutes before kick-off. Brownlie was in goal for Scotland and McNair and McMenemy found places in the side as did Charlie Thomson, who played at right-half. He scored a wonderful long-range goal early and this inspired the Scottish team to one of its best displays before a home crowd, especially the inside play of Celtic's McMenemy and Croal of Falkirk, who baffled and bemused the English defence to such an extent that Scotland ought to have scored six. As it was, McMenemy, having his best-ever game for Scotland, scored one and laid on another for Ranger Billy Reid and the game finished 3–1. The huge home support was elated by the display and Scottish football was on a high. Celtic had not only completed a rich chapter in their own history but in British football as a whole. Now another chapter was about to begin. The idyll was over and in the new game that was about to start the goals were slightly different and the result was to change the world for all time. Kick-off was scheduled for a sunny Saturday afternoon in August 1914.

Chapter Five

Injury Time

During the August Bank Holiday of 1914, most of Britain was at the nearest beach, the Kaiser was enjoying his annual yachting holiday along the coast of Norway, and his Army Chief of Staff, General von Motke, was taking the cure at an undisclosed spa. The French president was on a state visit to Russia, the Russian ambassador to Vienna was on leave and the Serbian prime minister was out of Belgrade preparing his election speeches. Somehow, in this vacational atmosphere, and during the football close season, most of these same people were involved, by a bewildering process of national pride, egotism, blundering incompetence and fatuous short-sightedness, in drawing most of Europe into a war that would cost most countries a whole generation of its young men. Millions were to be killed because a Balkan student shot a relative of the Kaiser at Sarajevo and Britain was held to a piece of paper signed as long ago as 1839 in which the country guaranteed the safety of the French and Belgian coasts against the rise of another Napoleon. The truth was the military wanted to play soldiers, the young male population wanted a paid holiday in France, and, worst of all, Europe was bored with peace. The straw boaters were thrown into the air as war was declared on Germany by Herbert Asquith in the House of Commons and the National Anthem was sung outside the railings of Buckingham Palace. Posters appeared everywhere, with a finger pointed straight at you from behind a pink face with a big moustache: 'Your country needs you!'

Young men all over the country rushed to the recruiting stations to join up 'before the fun was over'. The nation was in a state of utter euphoria. 'It will all be over by Christmas,' drawled a typical army nincompoop, Field Marshal Sir John French, but he neglected to say which Christmas. My Uncle Phil, the one who nearly signed for Middlesbrough in 1939, told me a story he had heard from his own father about football in the First World War. It seems that on the actual Christmas that year:

> There was an unofficial truce on the Western Front. English soldiers of the Scottish regiment were seen to be fraternising with the enemy. After Christmas carols had been sung from the opposing trenches, presents were exchanged, and a friendly game of football was begun. Officers intervened, and ordered the men to return to their positions. Several refused, and were shot.

When I mentioned to Uncle Phil that I had never heard about this terrible incident, or read about it anywhere, he just shrugged.

'It wasn't in the newspapers,' I said.

He looked at me keenly. 'It's no' the sort o' thing they'd put in the papers, is it?'

From a newspaper report:

> The East Surrey Regiment was attacking German positions. The Captain of one company ordered his men to dribble footballs in front of them as they crossed No Man's Land, one for each platoon. The men kept up a dribbling competition over the mile-and-a-quarter of land they had to traverse. The platoon commanders kicked off and the match against Death commenced . . .
>
> The gallant Captain himself fell early in the charge, and the men began to drop rapidly under the hail of machine-gun bullets, but still the footballs were booted onwards with hoarse cries of defiance, until they disappeared in the dense smother behind the German line . . .
>
> When the bombs and bayonets had done their work, and the enemy had cleared out, the Surrey men who had survived, returned to the German lines to look for their footballs. They recovered two.

Against such a backdrop, League football seemed trivial but fixtures continued even if only because people had imagined the war would be over in no time, and when it wasn't the battle on the football pitch was a relief from the horrors that were happening across the English Channel. International matches were suspended because so many of the four countries' teams were on active service but a Scotland Select played an England Select at Goodison Park in aid of the Mayor of Liverpool's War Fund. An unrecognisable Scottish side lost 4–3. What was noticable was that players from the smaller clubs were quicker to enlist than the stars from the bigger sides. Queen's Park players virtually enlisted as a man. So did Hearts. Rangers and

Celtic certainly didn't. Although one Celtic player, Willie Angus, a reserve, won the VC for rescuing an officer from the trenches, losing an eye in the process; and later in the war, Peter Johnstone, their regular centre-half was killed in action. Key players like Gallagher, Dodds, Loney and McAtee were all in reserved occupations in the shipyards, factories and mines. Which is no doubt why they went on winning, sharing the football spoils with Rangers in those five wartime seasons, Celtic taking four League titles to Rangers' one. There was some pointed comment about this at the time, especially as the huge gaps on the terracing indicated the number of men who were still in France – and would stay there. Cigarette-card photos of players, in full colour, continued to be issued, but this times with added legends – 'OHMS' or 'Killed in Action' or 'Died of Wounds'. Conscription came in 1917, all clubs were equally affected, and players often reported for matches in uniform. But once stripped for the game, they were back again to what they were, football players, and the fans cheered them on much as before. Willie Maley introduced teenager Tommy McInally to the Celtic team and another character player made his mark.

Scotland seems to specialise in this kind of player. Eccentric and individual, often unthinking and selfish but with an undeniable skill that almost amounts to genius, they are let down by an engaging fecklessness that undoes the brilliant work they do on the park. McInally was such a player for Celtic near the end of the Great War. He may have had all the gifts but he lacked consistency, which is often the refuge for the safe and second-rate. Tommy McInally was anything but second-rate. Since his time, there have been others in our own time whose talent was greater than their concentration. Players like Andy Ritchie of Morton and Chic Charnley of Hibernian, who were never capped. They may not have been of the very top class but they had colour and spectators loved them for it.

The Armistice was announced at the eleventh hour of the eleventh day of the eleventh month of the nineteenth year of the twentieth century and football hurried to get back to normal as quickly as possible. After the strained and straitened conditions of wartime, the players themselves were keen to take the opportunity of improving their conditions. They held a meeting in Glasgow to consider the changeover to peacetime football, especially as it might affect the ceiling fixed on wages and the limitations on transfers. All the power lay with the clubs, and it was to stay that way. The maximum wage remained at a pound per week with another pound being added after 31 December 1918 to a limit of three pounds at the discretion of the clubs. Even given that the average rate of pay for a working man at that time was half of that, it was a poor return for a player who was bringing in thousands at the gate every week. Of course it is supposed to be the team that draws the spectators, but in fact it is the personality player who really does, as the records show. Football is a team game, and an individual player can't play on his own, but every great team has its share of great players at some time. Kilmarnock may not have had a big name since Bobby Templeton but that didn't stop them beating Albion Rovers in the Scottish Cup final of 1920 and signal the gradual return to normality, despite the fact that any Scottish Cup final without Rangers or Celtic was exceedingly abnormal. The players of all the clubs in Scotland still felt disgruntled about their pay and contract conditions and it was a very aggrieved group of professionals who reported for training at the start of the first postwar season scheduled to begin in August 1919. However, 'lest we forget', the SFA instituted the Army and Navy Fund for the dependents of professional players killed or wounded in action, and all over the country, in every village, town and city, the building of war memorials began. In Edinburgh, the Town Council and Club combined to erect a clock tower at Haymarket Cross in remembrance of the Hearts team of 1914 who enlisted together after their tour of Denmark in that summer. Not all of them came back.

And at the final whistle, we shall remember them . . .

On the other side of the memorial they added, less than forty years later and with almost the same wording, a memorial to the Hearts players who lost their lives in the Second World War. It was almost as if there had been some kind of ghastly replay. And with the same appalling result.

The resumption of the official Home Championship in 1920 was important in the Scottish football story for only one thing – the introduction of one player to the international arena, Alan Morton. From his debut against Wales at Cardiff till his swan-song against France in Paris in 1932, he was Scotland's outside-left, unless injured or unavailable. Alec Troup of Dundee was his stand-in, and he made only a handful of appearances. It was a tenacious hold that Morton had on the outside-left spot, missing only one game against England, at Old Trafford in 1926, which Scotland won through a goal by Alex Jackson. It was known as the game in which Alan Morton *didn't* play.

Alan Lauder MORTON (1893–1971)
Outside-left for Queen's Park and Rangers

31

When the Scottish Football Association held its Jubilee Dinner in 1933, the only player invited to its select gathering was Alan Morton. This says much for the status of players generally at the time but it also points to the unique place held in the game of his day by this precise little man who stood high at five foot four inches and hardly weighed nine stone. He was Scotland's gentleman player *par excellence* and on and off the field he carried himself with a correctness that firmly indicated a man who knew his place and that it was an extremely comfortable slot. More than a legend, he is a titan of the Scottish game, one of its few genuine icons. Yet he was a slight figure of a man, more intent it seemed on his day-to-day job as a mining engineer. So many of Scotland's greats have come up from a mine to win fame on the football park but generally they have come, grimy and sweating, from the coal face. Here was a mineworker who came instead from the office and the drawing board, spick and span in his three-piece suit, with watch chain and stiff collar, to exchange it in the dressing-room for a light blue or dark blue jersey which transformed him immediately into a 'wee blue devil' ready to run the stoutest full-back ragged and delight the fans.

He never married. Little is known of his private life. What demon was in him that could create this metamorphosis from douce little gentleman to football imp? Was it that football was his only love, his only distraction from the daily business of earning a living in a respectable profession? He earned more than enough from football to give up his day job, but he never did. He managed to maintain a balance between sober executive and public entertainer throughout a long career and never once did anyone think to question it. His private life was his own but his public persona was happily given to Scotland throughout twenty years of impeccable professional conduct. Yet one can only wonder how this Wembley Wizard got on with Alex James and Alex Jackson, not to mention Hughie Gallacher, when they came to London for that wet Wembley in 1928, when together they made football history. How could he avoid the japes and jinks got up to by that trio? The answer is probably that he remained true to his own code wherever he went, a quiet little man who kept himself to himself, except when he played a game of football. Who, then, was the enigma, this little Jekyll and Hyde, whom every one knew as Alan Morton?

His father was a coal master who started off in Jordanhill, where Alan was born. The family then moved to Airdrie where Alan began training as a mining engineer. At the same time, while a schoolboy at Airdrie Academy, he trained his left foot to be as accurate as his natural right and practised the lob that was to bring him fame by aiming the ball at the hole in his father's garden shed. Everything he did, he did thoroughly and neatly and even on the field he was, in Bob McPhail's words, 'always going in a straight line – for goal. He could take the ball into the penalty area faster than anybody I ever saw . . .'

And McPhail should know. He partnered Morton in the Rangers and Scotland teams. So did Tommy Cairns, who compared the little winger to Stanley Mathews, only he thought Morton was better: 'The greatest winger of all time,' he said simply. Mr Morton could do it all – dribble, pass, run, cross and shoot and he was also a good team man. In short, he was a football paragon, and Scotland doesn't boast too many of those.

Alan Morton began his football career in 1913 with Queen's Park (which he joined merely to keep his brother Bob company) yet won the first two of his thirty-one caps as an amateur before joining Rangers in 1920. He was new manager Bill Struth's first signing. In his thirteen years with Rangers he played in 495 games and scored 115 goals and while doing so created a legend. The 'wee blue devil' was the soubriquet given him by English sportswriter, Ivan Sharpe, after watching him torture yet another hapless English full-back. He had watched him bob and weave, shimmy and dummy, dance and prance to such an extent that he pronounced him 'un-get-at-able'. Yet there was a coldness, a *hauteur* in the manner of his play that belied the 'imp' or 'devil' labels. The crowds gasped and admired but they did not warm to him as they did to Templeton or Quinn. One could not *love* Alan Morton but he demanded respect, admiration, awe and he got all three in his long career. Off the field, he shed his devil image immediately and became 'the wee Society man', which was his other nickname, after the neatly dressed collectors of insurance premiums from the better kind of Glasgow tenement. In fact, his attention to sartorial detail became mandatory for the other Rangers players and it must be said that some did not suit the bowler and city suit as much as did Mr Morton. However, no one dared laugh at this particular emperor's new clothes.

The same fastidiousness applied to his football gear: socks always neatly pulled up, shirt tucked in and buttoned up and only three studs in each boot, the better to let him pivot on either foot. He exemplified a disciplined approach to everything but it was this very sense of discipline that made him the player he was. He described his own approach to becoming a player as follows:

The three essentials are balance, ball control and quickness off the mark. They can only come from intensive practice, practice mark you, that was never a labour, but a love. It gave me confident use of both feet . . . proficiency came slowly but in a way that became natural the longer I kept at it. At first, it was all deliberate, but then it became automatic.

This was obviously a man who thought about his game. As a boy, he supported Airdrie, his local team, and though given a trial by them against Motherwell, it was at centre-forward, a position he did not enjoy and the trial came to nothing. Alan was very disappointed. Then came the Queen's Park opportunity and he found himself entirely satisfied. The strict amateur traditions of the Hampden club suited his temperament even though he had to provide his own shirt and wash it as well. After seven seasons of this kind of austerity, his engineering apprenticeship completed, he made the move that had been impending for some time and turned professional.

In June 1920, after protracted negotiations between club and player, Rangers signed him for a substantial fee and a weekly wage that made him the highest-paid footballer of his day. It was also agreed that he could keep his day job as a now-qualified mining engineer. Everything was tidily arranged as befitted the man and a new, great phase was to begin for him – and for Rangers. One irony, not lost on Morton, was that in the hat-trick of League Championships for Rangers from 1923 to 1925, the closest challenger was Airdrie. Indeed, the Ibrox team went through their greatest-ever period, eleven fine years from 1923 till 1934, while Alan Morton was on the left wing – even though they had players of the calibre of Tommy Cairns, his partner Andy Cunningham, Davie Meiklejohn, Tully Craig and many others on the playing staff. Morton was certainly in good company. One can never think of Alan Morton in bad company, but his playing colleagues were exceptional. In 1931, there were thirteen full Scottish internationalists on the Ibrox playing staff (a record only to be beaten by Celtic's fourteen capped players during Steintime at Parkhead, thirty-four years later). Altogether, Morton made almost six hundred League appearances in his career. Only Bobby Ferrier, an Englishman playing on the left wing for Motherwell, played in more matches for his club.

After his final game in 1932, Alan Morton was immediately invited by Rangers to become a director, the first of their players to be so elevated. He remained on the Board till his retirement in 1971. His final days were spent in a wheelchair. He was still a bachelor but he was still the original 'wee blue devil' and when he died at the end of that year all of Scotland could only remember that between the two World Wars, Morton's was the first name put on the team sheet when the Scottish selectors met to name their side. If the greatest-ever Scottish team were to be similarly chosen today, who is to say that the name Alan Lauder Morton would not still be the first put down?

There is a photograph of Ibrox Park in 1920, an aerial view of a match in progress (possibly one in which Alan Morton was playing), and one cannot help contrast the density of the vast crowd packed onto the terraces with the almost desert-like emptiness of the surrounding grounds. No buses or cars, only one white van parked by the perimeter. Not even a pedestrian. It looks as if the whole population of Govan was at the match, which it probably was. No doubt, beyond the picture, trams clattered and shoppers shopped, and life outside football went on as usual, but for the great majority of Glaswegians, Saturday afternoon in 1920 meant only one thing – the match. They were made for each other. They talked about it all week, in the pubs at night or at the tea-break in the yard or factory. It was the one common subject for working-class conversation, other than money. Football had taken a hold on the male population, those who had survived the war, and it was never to let go until television brought it into their homes. Even the walk to the ground had its ritual, always going by the same route, picking up people at the same points, the same old banter in the queue for the turnstiles, getting your money ready, wondering if you could afford a programme. It was all part of Saturday, no matter the club, no matter the game. And depending on the result, you walked back by the same route either singing or sullen. Then, with the resilience of all working people, by Monday you had started to look forward to the next Saturday – and so on, from August till May, season after season. Football supporters never talk of years. Those empty months of June and July are limbo days to be got through as quickly as possible until you can get to Ibrox again, or Celtic Park – or even Firhill. There are teams other than Rangers and Celtic, you know. Teams like Partick Thistle, who drew big crowds to Firhill because they had players like Jimmy McMullan.

James McMULLAN (1895–1964)
*Wing-half for Third Lanark, Partick Thistle, Maidstone United
and Manchester City*

32

Jimmy McMullan started his career with Third Lanark but it was with Partick Thistle that he made his name as a cultivated and 'thinking' left-half. A dispute with the club (who had turned down a large bid from Newcastle for him) led to his leaving Scottish football to play with non-League Maidstone United. This cost him in caps but not in reputation. He returned to Firhill only to move on again to Manchester City when another large offer came for his services. McMullan was a master tactician but had a chequered career as a manager with Aston Villa, Notts County and Sheffield Wednesday until the Second World War when he left football to work in a Sheffield factory. However, without any doubt his greatest hour was just after 2 o'clock on 31 March 1928 when he led out the Scottish team to be introduced to the then Duke of York and future King George VI in the presence of the King and Queen of Afghanistan. It had rained, as he had hoped, and his tiny forwards revelled in the mud to the consternation of the more cumbersome English defence. Nearly 90,000 spectators saw the Scots win 5–1 to become the Wembley Wizards. As long as they are remembered so will Jimmy McMullan. Even if he did end up in a factory, what tales he could tell at the tea-break.

In 1922, promotion and relegation were introduced into Scottish League football. Wartime football had meant the exclusion of clubs like Aberdeen, Dundee and Raith Rovers for geographical reasons. When they returned to the playing field, as it were, the League decided to expand the First Division and disband the Second. This led Dunfermline and other Fife clubs to found the Central League on their own, which was successful enough to persuade the League to think again. The two divisions were restored but with the possibility of clubs going up or down depending on results. No side was exempt, not even Rangers or Celtic, nor even the venerable Queen's Park, and so it was done, and football might be said to have started properly again. The Old Firm was still in business but this time it was Rangers as the senior partner, a position they were to hold for the next thirty years or so, with interruptions from Celtic from time to time and occasional strong challenges from Airdrie and Motherwell, but in the ragtime '20s the football theme song would appear to have been 'Follow, follow, we will follow Rangers . . .'

The Scottish Cup was a more democratic piece of silverware.

Partick Thistle, Morton, St Mirren and Airdrie were all winners, and Kilmarnock won it twice in the decade – but Celtic also claimed it three times and Rangers once, in 1928, beating Celtic 4–0 in the final. This broke their Cup hoodoo, but real success at Ibrox stemmed from the appointment of Bill Struth as manager, after the accidental drowning of Willie Wilton. The first thing Struth did was to sign up Alan Morton but he had good players on the books at the time – like Andy Cunningham.

Andrew CUNNINGHAM (1891–1973)
Inside-forward for Kilmarnock and Newcastle United   33

Described as 'brainy, breezy and bowler-hatted', Andy Cunningham was the golden boy of his era. He was unlucky in losing his best football years to the First World War, which is why he made his international debut at twenty-nine. He had played for the Scottish League in 1912 when with Kilmarnock, where he had been spotted by Rangers for his excellent close control at inside-right. He joined Rangers soon after and captained them in their eight-in-a-row Championship run during the 1920s, becoming a household name in the process. He was essentially a forward but he played centre-half for Scotland against Wales in 1923 when Willie Cringan was injured early in the first half. He had the height and positional sense, as well as an all-round ability to play anywhere on the park. What he lost at the start of his career he more than made up for at the end, signing for Newcastle in 1929, only eighteen months off his fortieth birthday, the oldest-ever Football League debutant. He stayed on to manage Newcastle and one of the first things he did was to transfer his former team-mate, Hughie Gallacher, to Chelsea. There had never been much love lost between the two. He left Newcastle in 1935 to become the firm but astute manager of Dundee until 1940. He then became a sports journalist for the *Scottish Daily Express*.

The main aspect of the Struth regime was the discipline imparted to the players which made them not only the best pool of players in Scotland, but made them *feel* the best. They were encouraged to live well, dress well, take taxis instead of buses and generally maintain an image of Rangers as the superior club. Progress for a young player was slow. He had to make his way through a hierarchical system of team levels until he broke into the first team, and even then he had to earn his football boots before being admitted to the inner circle around the captain of the day. It was ponderous to some extent but it worked in keeping Rangers ahead of the pack between the two wars. Of course, they had the talent. Players of all persuasions were keen to play for Rangers, but it did help if you were a Protestant. Whatever the truth of this, the players certainly came forward to place themselves under the Struth aegis. Jimmy Gordon, whom some reckoned the finest all-rounder ever seen in Scotland, was coming to the end of a noble career but he had a ready successor in Willie McCandlish. Tommy Cairns was still there in the attack but Morton's arrival signalled the start of Rangers' supremacy. This chapter belonged to Struth and the Rangers he created. The outside world may have been going through a bad time, but inside the palace of Ibrox all was as desired – and expected.

Fortunately, all the industrial unrest and political turmoil seemed to happen in the close season and football was hardly affected. There would have been a Russian-style revolution had the strike happened in the winter and the footballers had decided to stay in the pavilion. As it was, the ordinary people were almost glad to get back to the real problem of who would win on Saturday rather than who would win between workforce and owners. It was soon almost forgotten as Bobby Jones became the first amateur since 1897 to win the Open, the future King George VI played in the men's doubles at Wimbledon (he and his partner lost in straight sets), and Hobbs and Sutcliffe won the Ashes for England at Leeds. The country was agog over the impending meeting of Jack Dempsey and Gene Tunney for the World Heavyweight crown. (Tunney won on a TKO.) Sport, not religion, was the real opiate of the people, although the zeal shown by Rangers supporters in Scotland, who 'followed, followed' their team to victory in almost everything they played in, amounted to fanaticism of a religious order – the Orange Order, at that. The Struth regime was functioning smoothly and Rangers' supremacy was unquestioned. They won the League Championship, losing only a handful of games although they tripped up to Falkirk in the Cup. In the following four seasons, Rangers won the title every year, losing only one game in 1928–29. It was an example of determined and consistent application by the management and playing staff and it more than paid off in the second half of the decade. They played to their strength as much as to their strengths and left little to chance. It was quite the opposite to their Glasgow rivals on the other side of the city. Celtic could take one's breath away on occasions, but that was the trouble, it was only occasionally. Rangers, breathing more slowly, lasted the pace better, and finished stronger every time. It had to be remembered that Bill Struth had been a runner in his time, and a good one. He also knew how to ring the changes in the playing staff. Even the senior players had to look over their shoulders now and then. Youngsters climbed steadily through the ranks, but it didn't mean that Struth had first pick on everybody who could play. Rangers signed Andy Cunningham at the height of his career, but they missed Andy Wilson. He didn't play for Rangers, although he appeared to play for almost everybody else.

Andrew Nesbit WILSON (1896–1973)
Centre-forward for Middlesbrough, Hearts, Dunfermline, Chelsea, Queen's Park Rangers and Nîmes

34

Andy Wilson was still in the army at the end of the First World War and made his first international appearance by accident. He was wounded in action in France and nursing a shattered right arm in Stobhill Hospital when he was allowed out in an ambulance with the rest of the walking wounded to see the Victory International against England at Hampden. Two of the Scottish players, Alec McNair and Jimmy McMullan, were delayed by a train breakdown. McMullan arrived just in time to change but McNair never made it from Falkirk. The Scottish team was hurriedly rearranged and Wilson was drafted in at centre-forward. He scored two goals and made the position his own for the next twelve games. He shares with R.S. McColl the honour of having captained a Scotland team from the centre-forward position. Counting his two wartime appearances, he had a scoring rate of seventeen goals in fourteen internationals – a feat which has still to be bettered at that level. Andy Wilson reversed the usual trend in that he was a west of Scotland man who continued his professional career in the east of Scotland, first with Hearts and then with Dunfermline in the rebel Central League, although he was a registered Middlesbrough player at the time. He was with Dunfermline when he received his first cap in 1920 and a year later he was the Football League's leading goalscorer with Middlesbrough. He was also the sensation of the Scottish tour of the United States and soon after his return, in 1923, he was transferred to Chelsea. He returned to France to end his career with Nîmes. This time, he came home without injury. He was then employed by Chelsea to coach their younger players, among whom were Hughie Gallacher and Alex Jackson. It was obviously time not wasted. After the Second World War, Wilson played bowls for England. Presumably, by this time, his arm had got better.

*

In a year that began with the first successful transmission of pictures by television by a Scotsman named John Logie Baird, the miners, for so long the backbone of the football force in Scotland, came out on strike against the coal-owners who wanted to cut the miners' wages and increase their working hours. There was even talk of a return to Saturday afternoon working. The miners were incensed and appealed to the TUC for help. The resulting General Strike of 1926 was an attempt by the Trades Union Congress to call out every worker in Britain in support of the miners, and the action cut the country in two. The middle and upper classes looked on it all as rather fun and they came out in their college scarves to drive trains, buses and trams in defiance of the pickets and to deliver the mail defended by armoured cars. Despite the conservative attitude of the Rangers Football Club and the fascist tactics of Billy Fullerton and his thugs from Bridgeton, the working classes were totally with the miners. But as the strike went on, the lack of wages began to bite. One by one, the other unions slowly drifted back to work, leaving the embattled miners to carry on alone under their leader, Arthur Cook. Eventually, after holding out for most of the year, even Cook was forced to concede the day to the owners and the miners went back to a Black Christmas and worse conditions than they had come out against. This was the first time in history that the working classes had tried to take unified industrial action against the Establishment but it failed because university undergraduates, stockbrokers, retired Army officers, barristers and civil servants had thrown off their white collars for a few weeks to play at working while a whole underclass who had to work, and work hard, were left a few shillings short of a weekly wage that hardly covered their needs as it was. It was a shameful exhibition of class exploitation and it did not reflect well on Great Britain and its upper-middle classes. But then, few of *them* had any interest in football. Yet the irony is, theirs was the very class that had given us Association Football.

On the international scene (in the football sense, that is), Scotland wasn't quite so consistent as Rangers were in club action, but the country's select was not without its successes. The '20s were good for Scotland. Up till 1924, the year of the change in the offside law, they rarely had a settled side, yet won three Home Championships in a row. The new law meant a change in defensive tactics, and the centre-half position was the one that caused most problems throughout the '20s. No fewer than nineteen players were tried in thirty-four internationals. It must be borne in mind that the centre-half then was the pivotal player in the team, who could play forward and in defence from the centre of the field. The totally defensive 'stopper' was ten years away yet. McMullan played centre on occasions but he was really a wing-half. Gilhooley (Hull City), McBain (Manchester United), Cringan (Celtic), Morris (Raith Rovers), Townsley (Falkirk), Gibson (Partick Thistle) and Gillespie (Queen's Park) were just some of the fine players involved. Goalkeepers didn't offer the same problem. Up till 1927, only four were used – Willie Harper of Hibs, Willie Robb of Rangers, Alan McClory of Motherwell and Jack Harkness of Hearts – and between them they kept Scotland with a clean sheet for 747 minutes, the longest spell of defensive containment in Scotland's international history.

However, another international match was imminent and would rely little on centre-halfs and goalkeepers. The attack would come into its own on this occasion and in a manner that would make them immortal and add another chapter to football's lore. They were to become known to the entire football world of the time as the Wembley Wizards.

Chapter Six

Tunes of Glory

Scotland's record throughout the '20s was exemplary – played 34, won 24, drawn 5 and lost 5. And in the defensive phase already mentioned, they had scored 20 goals without reply. These figures say much for the state of the Scottish game, at least as it applied to the individual players available. Those who didn't feature in the Home Championships were given representative experience in tours of Canada and show matches against Norway in Norway as well as games in Germany and the Netherlands. Visits were arranged to Paris as well, but the main problem on such trips, according to trainer Mattha Gemmell of Clyde, was that there was nowhere he could buy his thick black tobacco. Clubs, too, had the travel bug in the post-war euphoria. Celtic had toured to Czechoslovakia in 1922 and Raith Rovers sailed to the Canary Islands in 1923 and got shipwrecked off the coast of Spain. In response to the offer of generous financial guarantees, Rangers went to New York and made a lot of friends and a lot of money, as guarantees on such tours were usual. Football had settled quickly in Scotland, and by now a Third Division was in place, which introduced new names like Queen of the South to the League and brought back famous ones from the past like Vale of Leven and Arthurlie. However, one regret was that, following the introduction of promotion and relegation between the Divisions, Queen's Park lost their First Division status for the first time. It was as if a very grand old lady had to vacate her mansion for a lodging-house. This was a fact of football life, and hard though it might seem, it had to be borne by one and all in the game. The former Dundee Hibs were readmitted to the League as Dundee United, and the League secretary, Willie McAndrew, got a nice rise in wages to five hundred per annum, tax free. This was more than twice what the retaining wage was in the First Division. 'Twas ever thus. The man in the office always got more than the man on the shop floor. With the better footballers, however, there was more than one way of skinning a cat, and rarely was a well-known player 'skint'.

This was often a problem as they were frequently given handsome signing-on fees in a lump sum. Stories were told of players who spent all of their wages over the weekend in the company of the kind of friends that easy money always attracts. Michael McKeown of Celtic was one such instance. His drinking ruined what might have been a very good career as a left-back for Celtic and Scotland. He is said to have struck John O'Hara, the Celtic secretary, in an argument about money. Although appointed captain of the new Celtic, he had an ongoing feud with James Kelly and several of his other colleagues and once went absent to Ireland, missing a vital cup tie against Queen's Park. He resigned from the club in anger in May 1890. However, he was too good a player to let go, so he was persuaded to come back. But not for long. Despite his good play on the field, there was more trouble in the dressing-room and he was allowed to go to Blackburn Rovers. Unfortunately, his drinking worsened and he was sacked by them soon afterwards. He joined the Army but was dismissed after 288 days as being 'incorrigible and worthless'. He returned to his native Ayrshire, where he became known as 'The Wanderer', living off hand-outs and free drinks. He was only thirty years old. Eventually, he was found dead in a lime-kiln at Camlachie, within sight of Celtic Park. The club buried him to save him from a pauper's grave.

Willie Groves, of Hibs and Celtic, 'Darlin' Willie' to everyone, was an even greater player than McKeown, his some-time colleague. He was one of the first superstars in football, but was forced to live out the final years of his life in abject poverty. He was considered on a par with Bobby Walker, and ranked with him as one of the finest footballers ever produced by Edinburgh. Unlike Walker, he was a dainty, almost delicate, kind of player, with a lady-like touch on the ball, but with a powerful shot nonetheless. 'An amazing dribbler with a puzzling swerve' was how he was described in his day. When moved to half-back, he showed masterly distribution, so they said. Yet it all came to an end so suddenly. Celtic had bought him from Hibernian and set him up in a pub in Taylor Street, Glasgow, but they couldn't stop him following Dan Doyle to Everton and then changing his mind and selling his services, first to West Bromwich Albion (with whom he won an FA Cup medal in 1893), and then to Aston Villa, whom he helped to win the Football League in 1894. Then, at the height of his manhood, he collapsed with tuberculosis and was forbidden to play again. Even so, he returned to Scotland and played a few games for Celtic – but he was finished. Celtic opened a subscription for him, but Willie died at thirty-seven, a labourer for Edinburgh Corporation, and with not a penny to show for a brilliant career.

A footballer's lot is not always a happy one, especially as it ends so early in a man's life. The risk is in letting what comes from your feet go to your head, and the temporary temptations are many. Most club pros, however, were sensible lads, well conscious of their brief flit in the sun, and they prepared for their retiral by frugal and prudent care of themselves and their wages. Or their wives did. The majority of players were from working-class homes and had learned early the need to count the pounds by pennies. If one needed to look for examples of players who used the game as well as it used them, one need look no further than the respective Old Firm captains, Willie McStay and Davie Meiklejohn. The latter was already an outstanding player, and although he never became a Wembley Wizard on that Saturday afternoon of 21 March 1928, he has his place in the pantheon of players.

David Ditchburn MEIKLEJOHN (1900–59)
Wing-half or centre-half for Rangers

35

A captain of men, a captain of Rangers and a captain of Scotland, Davie Meiklejohn, or 'Meek' as he was known to his team-mates, was a natural leader of a side, even when with Maryhill Juniors on the north side of Glasgow, and a great player who was capable of turning a game single-handedly. He succeeded the great Jimmy Gordon as Rangers captain and won every honour there was to win in the game of his time. He was awarded fifteen caps in all and scored a hat-trick of goals but his value was as a defender who also had the skills to be a playmaker. He made 635 appearances for Rangers and scored fifty-four goals, the most important of which was the penalty he took in the 1928 Scottish Cup final which broke the Cup hoodoo for Rangers, who had not won the trophy for twenty-five years. Typically, as a Govan-born Glaswegian, Davie Meiklejohn was a one-club man, and with Jimmy Simpson and George Brown he formed one of Rangers' finest half-back lines. Meek represented the vast bulk of players in the Scottish game – unshowy, effective and thoroughly professional at all times. He never sought superstardom but worked away quietly in the engine-room of the team. Rather than the great captain he was, perhaps Meek was really more of a chief engineer. For which post, by the way, he was professionally qualified.

As the time approached for the now-established fixture against the 'Auld Enemy' at Wembley towards the end of the 1927–28 season, controversy raged about the team selection. There were so many names vying for contention. Apart from McStay and Meiklejohn, men like Bob McPhail of Airdrie, now with Rangers, and, even more pressing, Jimmy McGrory of Celtic, whose goal-scoring facility was already being noticed, were being touted on all sides as probables. The possibles included talents like Jock Hutton, Aberdeen's redoubtable full-back, Tommy Muirhead of Rangers, a stylish wing-half, and Tully Craig, his fellow half-back at Ibrox, not to mention the veteran Ranger, Andy Cunningham, as well as George Stevenson of Motherwell, a clever inside-left. John Thomson, Celtic's brilliant young goalkeeper, also had his supporters. All these players had the right credentials for the right to wear a Scottish jersey and yet none was chosen on that particular occasion, although Craig was named as travelling reserve.

The team eventually chosen by the SFA selectors was J.D. Harkness (Queen's Park); Nelson (Cardiff City) and Law (Chelsea); Gibson (Aston Villa), Bradshaw (Bury) and McMullan (Manchester City), captain; Jackson (Huddersfield Town), Dunn (Hibernian), Gallacher (Newcastle), James (Preston North End) and Morton (Rangers).

This was the side that has entered the pantheon of great teams of all time and, for years afterwards, every Scottish schoolboy was able to recite these names like a litany, an incantion in memory of high excellence on the football field – but at the time the same names elicited only howls of outrage, anger, surprise, consternation and disbelief on all sides. The outcry was vehement and the older diehards wanted to know why it wasn't an All-Tartan side of home Scots, like the great teams of before, men who had resisted the lure of English gold and stayed true to their roots. Why have eight Anglos in the line-up? Have we not got as good, or better, at home? And so the debate went on. The controversy about McGrory was particularly heated. He was the player in form, whereas Gallacher was just completing yet another period of suspension and would be out of match practice, and so on. This was the atmosphere that greeted the players as they met at the Regent Palace Hotel in Piccadilly, London, on the night before the match.

They all made their various individual ways there as was the custom, only the three home Scots, Harkness, Dunn and Morton, with reserve Craig, travelling down by train from Glasgow with the official party. The London-based players travelled by tram, and Jackson, of course, rolled up in a taxi. It was all very casual for the players. They were all professionals, and knew the job they had been picked to do. For the officials it was another junket and no expense was spared and they gave little thought to the comfort or morale of the players.

Officials then still regarded themselves as gentlemen and the players as little more than hired hands. One of them condescended to approach the captain, and suggest that he might talk to the players about the game on the morrow and make sure that none skipped out for the night into London's West End. As it happened, prankster Jackson, with the connivance of James and Gallacher, changed rooms without telling the trainer, who spent most of the night pacing the hotel. One wonders how the decorous Morton fitted in with all the horse-play. They were a mixed lot, but they were to mix well when it mattered. Jimmy McMullan's team talk that night was economical: 'All I have to say is, go to your beds, put your head on the pillow – and pray for rain.'

Their prayers were answered. The rain came and the pitch was heavy. This wasn't ideal for the taller, more physical English players but it was perfect for the little Scots (Jackson, at five foot seven inches was the tallest of the forwards). They would be able to use their ball skills to better advantage if the English defence was slow to turn. This was why the experienced McMullan had wanted rain. He was the only one in the Scots side with significant international experience. Law and Bradshaw were winning their first caps, and James only his second, and the others didn't have all that many between them. That had been another of the many objections to the line-up. Never mind. Whatever had been said, it was all in the past now. From 3 p.m., the game was the thing. After the preliminaries were over and the royal party had taken their seats, the English started aggressively and in the very first minute a fierce English shot hit the post. Harkness, in goal, had been so nervous he was holding on to the other one to steady himself, but the gods were with the Scots, for the ball rebounded to McMullan where he stood just outside the penalty area. He turned quickly and passed to Dunn, who immediately placed a long ball in the path of Morton on the left, who scampered down the wing before chipping a cross over which met the flying Jackson's head as he sped in from the opposite wing, and before the English goalkeeper knew anything about it, the ball was in the net. Scotland had scored in three minutes.

From then on, they never let up. Everything seemed to go right for them on that wet, overhanging afternoon. The forwards played as if inspired, and at the back Tiny Bradshaw never gave the famous Dixie Dean a chance to show his prowess. Not that he had many opportunities. As one English journalist wrote: 'The little lads in navy-blue shirts took the ball as if on a string, from one end of the field to the other without an opponent touching it.' It was a wonderful justification of the traditional Scottish passing game and the three impish inside men, Dunn, Gallacher and James, revelled in it, turning and twisting, darting and feinting to the astonished delight of the few Scottish supporters who had travelled down. Every Scot played well but Jackson was the star of the piece, his running and exuberance tormenting the whole English left flank. His three goals were just reward. As Morton was doing much the same thing on the other wing, England were glad to go in at half-time only two down, James having scored the second. When play resumed, it was the Scots who hit the post this time with a volley from James, but then Jackson got his second goal despite some fine work by Hufton, the English goalkeeper. Then Gallacher set up his pal James for the next goal, Morton gave Jackson his third, and the despised team were five up. Not unnaturally, they tired towards the end and England got a goal from a free kick in the last minute but it didn't matter. The Wembley crowd had been given a display of Scottish attacking play they would never forget and it provided all of Scotland with a sweet memory that lingers on even yet.

What is unfortunate is that, for one reason or another, the team never played together again and for Tiny Bradshaw it was his one and only appearance for Scotland. The side has gone into legend as the Wembley Wizards and takes its place along with the Rosebery Rovers of 1900 as a Scottish team, where, on the day, no player could be bettered in the position played and both fine victories were won with class and an impudent panache. The one surprise on the day was that Hughie Gallacher didn't score, play well as he did. He was, after all, a natural striker but he played here as a team man, as they all were on that great afternoon – Harkness, James, Jackson and Gallacher *et al*.

Hugh Kilpatrick GALLACHER (1903–57)

Centre-forward for Queen of the South, Airdrie, Newcastle United, **36**
Chelsea, Derby County, Notts County, Grimsby and Gateshead

Hughie Gallacher was literally and metaphorically a shooting star who zoomed to fame from virtually his first serious kick of the ball with his first club, the local Bellshill Tannochside Athletic, in 1919 and maintained this fame until signing for his last club, Gateshead, in 1939. Each signing was a launching pad to further heights, beginning with Queen of the South in 1921, then Airdrie, Newcastle in 1925 and culminating in Chelsea in 1930. His fall therefore was all the greater when he slid down to Derby County in 1934, Notts County and from there to Grimsby Town in 1938 and finally to Gateshead and retiral into obscurity. In his heyday he was full of goals for his eight clubs (369) and for his country (twenty-two). He scored five against Ireland in 1929 – an international record that still stands for the old Home Championships. He was as much an automatic choice for centre-forward in internationals as was Alan Morton on the left wing, but the best thing that could be said about little Hughie Gallacher was that he kept Jimmy McGrory, the Celtic scoring machine, out of the Scotland team for most of the latter's long career.

Gallacher was in his time one of the most famous names in football, but there was another side to this shooting star. This side, which most people tried to keep dark, was, however, the part of the star from which he made his own black hole. He had always been temperamental, but he was allowed that because of his outstanding ability. Then it was realised that what he really had was a dreadful temper in conjunction with a growing mental problem. He was only five foot two inches, and had a similarly short fuse. In addition, his vast football talents were not compensated by any balance in his character or personality and this was to lead ultimately to professional decline and private tragedy. It was almost as if he had a wish to self-destruct, a hazard for more than one Scottish football name, as we shall see. Gallacher also had considerable boxing skills, honed in the tough mining community from which he and so many other famous footballers emerged. Bellshill was a rich seam for more than coal. He might indeed have been a contender at light-welterweight, but he elected for the football pitch instead of the ring, although he wasn't above displaying his pugilistic skills on the park and in the dressing-room. He was disliked by many of his fellow professionals but he was loved by the crowds. He had all the charm in the world when he was sober but his was a disturbed personality, and the origins of this disturbance lay far back in his own roots.

His parents were respectable Ulster working-class, firm in the Orange Order and stoutly anti-Catholic. Yet the first thing their son did as soon as he received his first five pounds in football in 1919 was marry Annie McIlvaney, a Catholic. The match was doomed from the start, damned on both sides. Their first child died in infancy and they parted after little more than a year. Gallacher sued for divorce, which was not granted until 1934. The massive legal bills that accrued bankrupted him and when he signed for Notts County the two hundred pounds signing-on fee was paid straight into Carey Street. In 1935, he married Hannah Anderson, the daughter of a Gateshead publican, but not before he was arrested for fighting in public with her brother. Like so many Scots before him, such as James Boswell and, after him, Peter Marinello and Charlie Nicholas, London was bad for Hughie Gallacher. He took to fame and the bottle in much the same way, greedily and indiscriminately, and gave in happily to the high living in low places and to all the other temptations that surrounded a celebrity in London between the wars. The mercurial feet began to stumble and then to plod painfully as he gradually descended the football ladder he had sprinted up in such an electrifying fashion only a decade before. It was obvious that the little Bellshill hard man was his own worst enemy and perhaps in the end he knew it. The pity is that his undeniable football worth has been diminished today by the memory of an unhappy, bedevilled sporting genius who had been trained for football but not for life.

Nevertheless, he remains a genuine Scottish football immortal. One has to remember that in his own time he may have been one of the most talked-about sportsmen in Britain. He was news and he made it whether he liked it or not. In Belfast he was shot at – but whether for scoring five goals against the Irish that afternoon or for marrying a Catholic, we can never be sure. He had married at seventeen and the child of that marriage had died before a year was out. At the very outset of his career, he was struck down by pneumonia at Dumfries after scoring nineteen goals in nine games for Queen of the South. While he was on the danger list in hospital he was also on the wanted list of nearly every big football club in England but instead he elected to go home to Airdrie, for whom he was to score a hundred goals. In 1923, the Diamonds finished runners-up to Rangers, thanks to Gallacher and another young teenager, Bob McPhail, and in 1924, they won the Scottish Cup. At twenty-one, he won his first cap against Northern Ireland. He was on his way in earnest. He had everything needed in a footballer except height and he made up for that by well-timed jumps that often saw him towering over much taller defenders. In his best days, he had a limitless, terrier-like energy that could cause havoc around the penalty area. He had strong, boxer-legs and a powerful shot with the shortest of back-swings. This allowed him to act quickly in crowded situations. He could think fast on his feet, an attribute the footballer shares with anyone brought up on street corners. He moved like a streak over short distances and his ball control saw that he could beat anyone who stood in his way. He said his best goal was scored against Wales in 1925 when he beat five men in a row and hooked it over the diving Welsh keeper. 'As I turned to walk back, I saw the Welsh players applauding me,' he recalled. Newcastle thought they had a bargain when they paid a record fee for him that same year. He scored two on his debut and was an immediate Geordie hero, and from there to being an idol was only a matter of more goals, and from that to being a legend was only a matter of time. It was not that long ago when Newcastle children could be heard singing at their street games:

> D'ye ken Hughie Gallacher, the wee Scotch lad?
> The finest centre-forward N'castle ever had.

That may have been so but when Chelsea came for him in 1930 the Newcastle Board, prompted by manager Andy Cunningham, signed him away without even telling him. In this way Gallacher was turned, against his will, towards London and the beginning of the end. He teamed up with fellow Wizard, Alex Jackson, but despite their twin talents, Chelsea never won anything with them except a feud over money. Gallacher now had an increasing drink problem, as well as a growing police record, and finally was discharged as bankrupt in 1934. He played his last game for Gateshead on the day before war broke out – 2 September 1939. Fortunately, his marriage with Hannah was good and they had a son, Matthew. The family remained in the north-east and for a time Gallacher was a sports columnist, but his match comments were so barbed that he was banned from St James' Park.

He played occasionally with his boyhood pal, Alex James, in charity matches, but even though the old skills could be glimpsed occasionally, he cut a wretched, skeletal figure on the pitch. Then, in 1950, Hannah died and for 'Wee Hughie of the Magic Feet' it was the end of the line. A family row with the growing Matthew resulted in the boy being taken into care. Deprived of the two things he loved most, football and his family, and faced with the shame of legal proceedings at Gateshead for the maltreatment of his son, he stumbled out of his empty house one day and threw himself under the York–Edinburgh express on the morning of 11 June 1957. His decapitated body was found at Dead Man's Crossing at Low Fell. Who knows if the famous feet were left unscathed, but what is certain is that the volatile and volcanic Hughie Gallacher, the man with the magic in his feet but the demons in his head, was no more. Ironically, his son, Matty, tried out later for Newcastle United but he never made the grade. It was almost to be expected. Hughie Gallacher was a one-off.

Alexander Skinner JACKSON (1905–46)
Outside-right for Dumbarton, Aberdeen, Huddersfield Town, Chelsea, Ashton, Margate and Nice

37

Alex Jackson came from Renton, near Dumbarton, a place with a historical football pedigree and in 1922, at the age of sixteen, he signed professionally for Dumbarton. However, soon afterwards, he and his brother, Wattie, emigrated to America to join their oldest brother, John, in a works team, Bethlehem Steel, in Pennsylvania. Both brothers returned in the summer of 1924 at the invitation of Pat Travers, the wily old Aberdeen manager (later to be manager of Clyde). He paid a mere hundred pounds for both of them and Herbert Chapman (later to be manager of Arsenal) paid more than fifty times that amount to entice Alex south to Huddersfield. In 1930, even that amount was doubled to take him to Chelsea, but he grew lazy about his career after that and devoted his energies to his pub in St Martin's Lane and his partnership in the Queen's Hotel, Leicester Square. Why should he worry about a mere game of football when the life it gave him was so good? He was handsome, healthy and hearty, with a zest for living that matched his dash on the wing. Known as 'The Flying Scotsman', he had scored a hat-trick with the Wembley Wizards, had helped Huddersfield to cup success and was the idol of Chelsea – that is, until his famous dispute with them over the iniquities of the maximum wage in 1932. He described himself as a freelance professional footballer available on hire to the highest bidder, but the clubs at that time were hostile to such ideas and remained inflexible. So Jackson quit League football to play for Ashton National in Manchester, then Margate and finally Nice, in the south of France, until he drifted out of football altogether. He wasn't yet thirty. It was a terrible waste of a great talent. In 1946, in North Africa, the truck which Major Jackson was driving skidded on a desert road and overturned. The laughing cavalier of soccer was no more. For reasons that had little to do with the game and more to do with his personality, he had left first-class football too soon. He also met his death too early, but his football immortality was assured as the most complete and physically imposing winger of his era.

Alexander Wilson JAMES (1901–53)
Inside-left for Raith Rovers, Preston North End and Arsenal

38

If Hughie Gallacher was the James Cagney of football, then Alex James was the George Raft. The former was the greater star, but the latter made better use of lesser gifts. Gallacher and James were opposites. They had been boyhood friends in Bellshill, both had idolised Patsy Gallagher of Celtic, though neither was a Celtic supporter, and both favoured the snappy dresser image that went with their similarly stocky frames. Yet there their mutuality ended. Gallacher may have soared away beyond his pal in the game, but when he fell, there was James, an almost comical figure in baggy shorts, just getting properly started. Hearts had turned him down for being too small but he was big enough for Raith Rovers, who placed him on a diet of cod-liver oil to build him up. He hated it but became part of the very famous Raith Rovers forward line of 1925: Bell, Miller, Jenning, James and Archibald. Each was a good player in his own right but all agreed that James was the mainspring. Described as 'having wonderful footcraft', he also had a gramophone tongue that never stopped talking from kick-off to final whistle. He moved to Preston North End in a general exodus of Scots into England at that time and soon the Deepdale team was known as 'Alex James and ten others'. James began to reappraise his own value. He said himself, 'Dear old Jock Ewart, my playing pal at Preston used to tell me, it's you the crowds come to see. Get all you can out of this racket. You're worth it. Cash in while you can.' And Alexander Wilson James certainly did that. He went to Arsenal because Herbert Chapman, their omnipotent manager, had secured a well-paid, part-time sinecure for him as a 'sports demonstrator' at Selfridges. Here, James learned about the value of publicity and gimmicks. The famous baggy shorts were just such a stunt. They were the idea of Tom Webster, the cartoonist at the *Daily Mail*. The idea caught on and James became a well-known figure in London's West End but, unlike his pal Gallacher, James knew when to go home. On the field, he had turned Arsenal's fortunes around virtually on his own and when he – and they – won the FA Cup in 1930, he had started on a run that was to continue through two more Cup finals and four Championships until his retiral in 1937. In all, he made 261 appearances for Arsenal and scored twenty-six goals, but his contribution was more than a matter of statistics. Dubbed the 'Clown Prince of Soccer', he was the dynamo around which the team revolved, the playmaker *par excellence*. The spectators on the North End terracing at Highbury worshipped him.

For them, he could do no wrong, and the more mischief he got up to off the field, the more they loved him. He would have earned more caps if his first loyalty had not been to Arsenal but James knew best which side of his bread had jam on it. He dabbled in various commercial ideas but when they all failed he became a personality sports journalist for the *News of the World*. In 1945, he returned to Arsenal to coach the Arsenal 'A' team at Hendon. He also coached in Poland but in 1953 he came home to London to die of cancer. The *Times* honoured him with an obituary. He was the very embodiment of the archetypal Scottish footballer, with all the skills and tricks of his trade, and he won for himself a place in the imagination of a whole generation of Londoners. He made a point of never going home to Bellshill, but he was shrewd enough never to lose his accent. It was just another part of the public picture he had so assiduously built up. He may have talked too much on the park, but he had an astonishing all-round vision of the game for one so near the ground.

John Diamond HARKNESS (1907–85)
Goalkeeper for Queen's Park and Hearts   **39**

Jack Harkness won the first of his dozen caps in 1927, when an amateur with Queen's Park, and the rest until 1934 when with Hearts. He was an immortal 'Wizard', of course, yet his memory of the great occasion is of the rail journey down from Glasgow with Tim Dunn, Alan Morton and Tully Craig of Rangers, a Scottish reserve. (This made nonsense of the famous cartoon in the *Bulletin* of 30 March 1928 which showed the three Scots regretting that they didn't have four for a rubber of bridge. It's doubtful anyway if Tim Dunn, the joker of the pack, would have known how to play bridge.) Harkness and Morton, the extrovert and introvert, would have been ideal partners, one thinks – Jack of Diamonds and the King of Clubs. They were good friends in any case. Jack Harkness was a friendly kind of person. He had what many wanted in a goalkeeper – dependability and coolness in the penalty area, with that extra flair all the great custodians have. He was Scotland's goalkeeper at a time when a cap for your country meant something, and it meant a lot to him. He was made an MBE in 1971 and after many years as a commercial traveller for a brewery firm he became a very successful sports journalist.

In 1986, a modest funeral in Coatbridge, Lanarkshire, attended by a mere twenty people, honoured the passing of the last Wembley

Wizard. Tommy Bradshaw, known to all as 'Tiny' due to his six foot four inches stature, had returned to his native parts after a career in football that had seen him move from Bury to become the Liverpool centre-half and captain. He was an attacking centre-midfield player and this disconcerted his own team as much as opponents, and no doubt lost him greater international recognition, but his fellow players recognised him as the quality footballer he was. Matt Busby was an admirer. Now he was dead, and the Wembley Wizards were no more, but as long as they are remembered in football, so will Tiny Bradshaw.

The 1928 summer tour of the continent by a Scotland party did not include a single 'Wizard', which seemed incongruous, but the SFA often used these trips to blood young, up-and-coming players, or seniors who had not had adequate recognition. There were other players who preferred to rest and stay at home with their families rather than go on these tours which were more often than not sprees for management. The first official game after the memorable Wembley occasion was in October of the same year against Wales at Ibrox. Scotland won 4–2 thanks to three goals by Hughie Gallacher and one from Tim Dunn but three Rangers played in this team – Dougie Gray for Nelson, Tommy Muirhead for Gibson and Bob McPhail for James. It was McPhail's second cap. He was one of Scotland's most popular players but he was to play only intermittently up until the Second World War, as he had to cede the place to either Alex James or George Stevenson. Still, one can't pick one's generation. Which was a pity, for he was a powerful player with a sharp instinct for goals, as his record shows.

Robert Low McPHAIL (1905–2000)
Inside-left for Airdrie, Rangers and St Mirren   **40**

Unassuming Bob McPhail may have been responsible for the Hampden Roar. If it doesn't belong to Cheyne's last-minute corner kick score in the 1929 game or McGrory's header in 1933, then it certainly belongs to the two goals scored by Big Bobby in the second half of the famous 1937 game before a record crowd to beat the 'Auld Enemy' at Hampden. When told afterwards by a friend that he had almost been crushed by the enormous crowds on the terracing, the modest Bob replied: 'You should've been where I was, I had plenty of room.' And so he had, as his two goals that day showed. But then, he was always able to find room for himself, even in his Airdrie days, scoring as many as his then club-mate, Hughie Gallacher, much to the latter's bluntly stated annoyance. However, McPhail remained as imperturbable as ever and after Gallacher left for Newcastle in 1925, he, in turn, left for Rangers in 1927 where he won every honour going until he retired in 1941, after a few games for St Mirren. He then became trainer of the Rangers reserves for some years, and it was surely a boon for any young player to have someone of his stature in attendance. His club scoring record (305) was second only to Jimmy McGrory's and his Rangers tally was only very recently (in 1996) surpassed by Ally McCoist. McPhail epitomised the big, uncomplaining, all-round, work-horse-type player whose high skills, both in defence and attack, are often obscured by his very industry. He was a perfect foil for Alan Morton both for Rangers and Scotland and he continues, in his nineties, to attend games at Ibrox Stadium where he is deservedly treated as an idol in the arena he had once adorned so modestly but so well.

In 1929 at Hampden, Scotland, with ten men (Jackson was injured) beat England again, but this time by a last-minute goal by Aberdeen's Alex Cheyne, scored direct from a corner kick. Scotland's last game of the decade, like the first, was against Wales (this time at Cardiff) and again Scotland won 4–2, Gallacher scoring twice, with others from James and Gibson At home, Kilmarnock beat Rangers to win the Cup but Rangers won the League with Celtic as runners-up. So what was new? The '20s had roared through their ragtime days, and the Charleston had given way to the quick-step just as the silent film, in the final year of the decade, capitulated to Al Jolson's immortal ad lib: 'You ain't heard nothing yet.' He might have been speaking of the rise and rise of Scottish football as the hungry '30s beckoned.

Chapter Seven

Lifting the Depression

More than two million men were unemployed at the beginning of the new decade yet two thousand guests attended the cathedral wedding of Lady Margaret and Mr James Drummond Hay of Seggieden, Perth. There were still two worlds, and the new heroes were the working-class wives who were making a penny do the work of a shilling in the course of a pinching week. Those heads of households in work were lucky to bring in four pounds a week and even that had to be made to stretch. Ramsay MacDonald dithered in Downing Street while Oswald Mosley was trying on his first black shirt around London's East End. It wasn't a happy world but even if bread had risen to sixpence a loaf, the football circus was still available at less than two shillings every Saturday and people flocked to it in their thousands. The Mills Brothers' hit song was 'Hold that Tiger' but there was no holding the lure of football, and its night sister, the cinema, in the grey days of that time. *All Quiet on the Western Front* was the movie hit of the day but things were not so quiet on the football front.

The year 1930 had started with Don Bradman making a record-breaking 452 not-out in Sydney, which was only thirty-four more than all the goals scored up till then by Scotland since internationals began officially in 1872. Nor did it look as if they would add much more to that total as the year got under way due to the Football League suddenly deciding to place a ban on the release of players for inter-national fixtures other than those selected for England. This imposed 'All-Tartan' teams on Scotland and the result was to deprive the inter-national side of such as McMullan, Jackson, Gallacher and James, a heavy loss to any team, and so the assured and sweeping successes of the '20s came to an end. The English embargo was in some way a blessing in that it allowed home-based players to be given an outing. Home-spun didn't necessarily mean lesser, as men like Danny Blair of Clyde and Joe Nibloe of Kilmarnock got their chance, but no one was more deserving of this opportunity than Jimmy McGrory of Celtic who had been stand-in to Hughie Gallacher for so long.

Centre-forward is the prima ballerina of the football ensemble. Today he is the equivalent of the centre-half of the earlier days, around whom the team pivoted. The modern centre, or striker, is the front-man, the flashpoint of the attack, who leads the line and strikes home the vital goal. It is the glamour position, the one that gets all the attention and most of the praise when things are going well and when they go badly the other forwards are blamed for not supplying the centre-forward with the proper opportunity. The public loves him. From the very beginning of organised football, centre-forwards have taken the eye. John Goodall of the Preston Invincibles, who was English-born but Kilmarnock-raised, was a famous centre-forward, as were G.O. Smith of the gentlemanly Corinthians, Steve Bloomer of Derby County and Middlesbrough who scored twenty-eight goals in twenty-four internationals, and William 'Dixie' Dean of Everton who scored sixty goals in a season. Not forgetting Jimmy Smith of Ayr United who got sixty-six, R.S. McColl of Queen's Park and Newcastle, and Jimmy Quinn of Celtic, who made his mark in whatever game he played. These were all famous centre-forwards, but none quite equalled the goal-scoring feats of another Celtic centre-forward who scored more goals in first-class football than any other player before, or at least since John Petrie scored thirteen for Arbroath against Bon Accord in 1885. McGrory scored eight goals against Dunfermline in 14 January 1928 and this still stands as a Scottish record for goals in a League match. He had been signed by Willie Maley in the 1922 season, but was loaned out to Clydebank for match experience. When he eventually came into the Celtic team he stayed there and soon established himself as a crowd favourite on a par with Jimmy Quinn and Patsy Gallacher. He was particularly effective with his head and scored many of his goals by diving fearlessly at a cross from either wing. Not unnaturally, other clubs envied Celtic their prodigious goal-scorer, none more than Arsenal, who made determined efforts to land him. So much so, that Celtic agreed to let him go, but the player refused to be transferred and went off on a pilgrimage to Lourdes with his manager, who had been ill. Whatever their prayers were, they seem to have done the trick and Jimmy McGrory, simple, honest man that he was, stayed at Parkhead till the end of his playing career and after, even though at the height of his fame he was paid a pound a week less than the other members of the teams. No one knows why, least of all Jimmy McGrory himself, and he would have been the last man to ask. His is the kind of football story it is a pleasure to tell.

James Edward McGRORY (1904–82)
Centre-forward for Celtic

41

Jimmy McGrory, or the 'Golden Crust' as Celtic supporters called him, is the greatest scorer of goals ever known in Scottish football history. With 'shoulders like a young Clydesdale and a neck like an Aberdeen Angus', he scored over 550 goals in his football career and that total is unlikely to be beaten in Scotland, as is his feat of eight goals in a first-class game scored against Dunfermline in 1928. The reason for his goal-scoring proclivity was his strength in either foot and an uncanny precision with his head. He was fortunate in a sense to coincide in a change in the off-side law which allowed a greater opportunity to the attacking player, but nevertheless, he showed an extraordinary courage in coming forward and by a relentless chasing of every opportunity he converted many possible chances into goals. His international career was limited because of Hughie Gallacher's contemporaneous occupancy of the Scotland centre-forward berth, and also, some said, because of a bias by the SFA against Celtic (and therefore Catholic) players which prevailed at that time. He was an undeniable Scottish legend and his paltry seven caps (like Alex James's) are a poor reflection of his prowess and standing in his own age. McGrory's is an imperishable name in the record books. Not only for his scoring feats but for his courage. His nose was broken frequently. So was his jaw on one occasion. He also lost two front teeth. Like Jimmy Quinn before him, he was fearless in the fray.

> Oft indeed he felt most grateful
> To escape from the attack
> With his head upon his shoulders
> And his jersey on his back.

During his 15-year playing career from 1922 to 1937, his athleticism and extraordinary scoring ability ought to have won him a greater international recognition but he retired to become a Celtic great, albeit an indifferent manager of that historic club, and he faded into an accepted nadir as Celtic's public relations officer until his death. Nevertheless, Jimmy McGrory exemplifies all that is meant by loyalty and total commitment to a game and to a club and he ought to be remembered for that as well as for all his wonderful and thrilling goals. One particular effort is worth mentioning. At a training session, McGrory, wearing his usual managerial bowler hat and puffing on his pipe as usual, stood watching a group of players dealing with high crosses from the wing. Suddenly, the players were startled to see the manager rush among them, hat in one hand, pipe in the other. As the ball came over he met it cleanly on his forehead and it bulleted into the back of the net. Calmly he replaced his hat and his pipe, saying, 'That's whit I mean, lads,' and returned to his place on the touchline.

His playing influence was never more clearly exemplified than in the 1931 Cup final against Motherwell, who were a good team at that time. They were leading 2–0 with ten minutes to go when McGrory impossibly scored from a sitting position. This so rattled the hitherto imperturbable Motherwell defence, that their centre-half, Alan Craig, harried as ever by the tireless McGrory, headed the ball into his own net in the last minute to even the score. Celtic easily won the replay, and almost as inevitably as Rangers won the League Championship. However, buoyed by a triumphal tour of America, the young Celtic team gave the first hints of threatening Rangers' armour-clad grip on that particular prize. They were keen to top the League, as another title win by Rangers would allow them to equal Celtic's famous six-in-a-row sequence from more than twenty years before. (As it happened, Motherwell, not Celtic, won the Championship and so the record remained at Parkhead.) However, prior to this, on Saturday, 5 September 1931, the Old Firm met at Ibrox in what both clubs considered to be a vital, if not a deciding, League fixture.

Eighty thousand spectators attended what was from the start a tense and engrossing encounter. There was no scoring in the first half but five minutes after the interval, Celtic were pressing hard when a long ball out of Rangers' defence caught the Celtic rearguard out of position and found the young Rangers centre-forward, Sammy English, on-side and in the clear. He rushed speedily into the Celtic penalty area with only the goalkeeper, Johnny Thomson, to beat. Thomson hesitated for a second and then threw himself full-length at the centre-forward's feet. There was the thud of a collision and both players fell prostrate. The ball went harmlessly past. English got to his feet almost at once but young Thomson lay ominously still. His brother Jim, sitting in the stand, remembered: 'I knew at once it was serious from the way his hand fell slowly . . .' One ambulance man watching said quietly to a colleague: 'That's the end of him.' At first, there were cheers and jeers from the respective supporters, and the Rangers supporters particularly were baying loudly from behind the goal, thinking Thomson was feigning injury. It was only when the Rangers captain, Davie Meiklejohn, went to them with both hands upraised, that they eventually fell silent. An eerie quiet descended over the ground. One of the Rangers players made a crude remark and was immediately rebuked by Alan Morton. By this time, Thomson's head was bandaged and he was lifted on to a stretcher. As it was carried past the main stand a woman's scream rang out. It was Thomson's girlfriend, Margaret Finlay. She was just nineteen. Although not officially engaged to Johnny, as the family called him, she was accepted as his sweetheart. She was taken by John Thomson to the dressing room and went on to the hospital where she held Johnny's hand until the end.

John THOMSON (1909–31)
Goalkeeper for Celtic

42

By his early twenties, John Thomson was Celtic's first-choice goalkeeper and had already played four times for Scotland. Great things were expected of him in the years ahead, but at the age of twenty-two he was dead, killed while playing football. The tragedy was not only his, or his family's, or Celtic's, it was Scotland's too and now, nearly seventy years later, the events of that September afternoon at Ibrox Stadium are still not forgotten. John and Jean Thomson arrived from their home at 23 Balgreggie Park, Cardenden, in response to a telegraph sent to Cardenden Post Office. The distraught parents reached the Victoria Infirmary only minutes before their son succumbed to the compression of his skull at 9.25 p.m. without regaining consciousness. A few days later, working men took time off work to walk more than sixty miles from Glasgow to Fife to see him interred in a wall-side grave which has since become a shrine. Thirty thousand people lined the route to the little graveyard in Bowhill. A railway wagon, packed with floral tributes, waited at a siding, not knowing what to do with them all. The shock had numbed everyone, but Scottish football had found its first martyr.

It had seemed so little time since he had signed for Celtic as a seventeen-year old on the lid of a roadside fuse box in Galton after a persuasive tram ride with the Celtic scout, Steve Callaghan, during the miners' strike of November 1926, and yet already he was Scotland's goalkeeper. He had come from Wellesley Juniors in 1925 after learning his goalkeeping trade with Bowhill Rovers. After a spell on loan to Ayr United, he made his debut for Celtic against Dundee in February 1927 and was an ever-present in goal thereafter. During his outstanding, if brief, career, he suffered a double fracture of the collarbone, a broken jaw, concussion and the loss of two front teeth. He seemed to make a habit of getting hurt, but it never deterred him for a moment from throwing himself into the heat of the action around his goalmouth.

His position was made all the more vulnerable through Celtic's reluctance at that time to utilise their centre-half and captain (Jimmy McStay) as a third back, as was the growing fashion of the time. Celtic still held to the traditional game. This meant that, while they were always an attacking threat, they often left a yawning gap in their own penalty area. Only Thomson's superlative goalkeeping saved the day time and time again but it was an unfortunate and, some might say, fatal tactic, in the way football was being played at that time. This is in no way to blame the club, or his team-mates, for the fatality which followed, but Thomson's job might have been made easier had it relied on some defensive cover rather than on his own daring instincts. A press picture of the time shows young John, his big goalie's cap set against the sun, jumping high to fist away a high ball. The jump is so high, the punch so defiant. It is an action so typical of his physical zest, yet within minutes of that picture showing him leaping like Nijinsky, another picture shows him, a bandage round his head instead of a cap, being helped onto a stretcher. The ball he had cleared so confidently was returned out of the Rangers defence and into the path of the onrushing Sam English . . .

It was hardly a matter of minutes but it was the difference between life and death. The late Hugh Taylor, an eminent Scottish sports journalist, wrote of Thomson:

> The thin boy had a veteran's coolness, uncanny anticipation, a sure clutch, and an acrobat's agility . . . to thousands of Celtic supporters who weren't even born when he died he is still the best goalkeeper who ever played. It is true his tragic death made him a hero for whom ballads were written, a footballer who will never be forgotten. But we must realise that when he played he was hailed as a genius, even though he was so young. He magnetised the fans; he was an idol. John Thomson would have been a great goalkeeper in any age because of his hands and his eye . . . His true greatness lay in the way he could find extra power to change course and find fresh drive in mid-air. Today he would probably have been named Batman . . .

Celtic full-back Hugh Hilley, who was still at the club then, and a good friend, insists that if John hadn't hesitated for a split second about coming out, he wouldn't have needed to dive for the ball. It was an act of daring, born out of sheer instinct and the result was tragically accidental. John Arlott, the English sports commentator, wrote of him in *Soccer – The Great Ones*: 'A great player, who came to the game as a boy and left it still a boy; he had no predecessor, no successor. He was unique.'

He had brightened grim days by his grace and thrilled plain people by his courage. His modesty and good looks endeared him to countless thousands who had never met him, this slim custodian armed only with a pair of gloves and a cap against marauding forwards in heavy boots, and all fighting for a leather ball that grew heavier in the mud and rain. He was required to be a hero on a regular basis. Now he was gone as a result of a knee-cap blow to the temple. At the official inquiry, Willie Maley was asked if it could have been an accident. 'I hope so,' he replied. What did the man mean? It could only have been an accident, as newspaper pictures and newsreels of the time showed. Sam English, inexplicably, was not called upon to give evidence.

Out of a split-second action on the football field, a legend was born; and it still lives today, more than sixty-six years on. Today, on each anniversary of John Thomson's death (5 September), Celtic supporters from all over the world gather round his grave in the little cemetery in Bowhill, Fife, to lay scarves and caps and flowers on the marble plinth together with scraps of paper and cards all giving the same message – they are remembering him still. On the tombstone it reads:

They never die who live in the hearts they leave behind.

The scenes at the funeral were incredible. The long road from Parkhead to Bowhill, covering as it does the broad Lowland waistband of Scotland, was a veritable rosary of salute. Knots of people stood at every crossing watching all those ordinary men with bare heads, some still in working clothes, walk from Glasgow to Fife. The Celtic team, led by Captain McStay, took turns to carry the coffin to the graveside. Only a few days before, he had run out onto the field beside them, full of the same youth. It was so hard to accept. It still is. The graveside service was conducted by an ordinary miner, John Howie, who, like the Thomsons, belonged to the Church of Christ, where there are no ministers. The congregation took turns to speak. When it was time for Mr Howie's turn, cap in hand, he spoke simply and plainly, more telling perhaps than any pious rhetoric, and then, in the late afternoon sun, they dispersed through the little village in silence . . .

When David MacLellan's play about Celtic, with music by Dave Anderson, was presented by the Wild Cat Theatre Company at the Pavillion Theatre in 1988, the funeral was re-enacted. When the 'coffin' was carried across the stage by the actors, the whole audience rose spontaneously and stood for several minutes in exactly the same kind of silence.

As can be imagined, the Celtic players seemed to lose heart for the title race and even the Rangers team was affected. Motherwell took advantage and, as mentioned, won the Championship of 1931–32. This was something their high quality of play had long deserved and was as much a tribute to their manager as a triumph for the team. John 'Sailor' Hunter had managed Motherwell for more than twenty years and had persisted in a style of close play which had won the team many admirers but few honours, but Hunter persevered with his young juniors until he had eventually moulded them into a sweet-moving, attractive side which nonetheless achieved a record-breaking 119 goals in their winning League campaign. This was achieved largely by three men in their forward line: centre-forward Willie McFadyen (who scored fifty-two of them), inside-left George Stevenson and outside-left Bobby Ferrier. The left-wing pairing of Stevenson and Ferrier was a delight of the age and has remained a legend with Motherwell fans ever since. Not since Celtic's McMahon and Campbell at the turn of the century had a left-wing pairing caught the imagination of the Scottish spectator, who loves to see his football played with finesse and precision. Ferrier, in particular, was deadly, as his 256 goals in 626 games clearly showed. He might have figured as a Scottish great, but although born in England of Scottish parents, he was denied international recognition just as he was deprived of English caps because of his wholly Scottish playing career. The same applied to other supposed 'Englishmen' like Jocky Simpson of Falkirk and Charlie Buchan of Arsenal, who, although born in England, were completely Scottish by blood. It must have boiled at being deprived, if not of their birthright, then at least of their blood right which proclaimed them Scots entirely. Today they would have played for Scotland but not then. They remain 'honorary Scotsmen', as it were. The same title might be bestowed on the great Patsy Gallacher of Celtic, and his modern successor with the club, Charlie Tully, who both came to football prominence in Scotland and in their respective careers added much to the gaiety of games in our dour Caledonian clime. Had they been Scots, you can be sure that both these players would have added a few decibels to the Hampden Roar.

This football phenomenon was born in 1933 when a depleted Scotland side met England on April Fool's Day. There were two amateurs in the side, Gillespie and Crawford of Queen's Park, a throwback to very early international days. Bob Gillespie was captain, in fact, and Jimmy McGrory was at centre-forward. 'McGrorious' was the epithet coined when, in the ear-splitting din of the capacity crowd, McGrory took a subtle pass from Bob McPhail and blasted the winner past Hibbs in the English goal. The roar that went up then became known as the Hampden Roar and it's been with Scotland sides at Hampden ever since, along with the swirling wind and the injury jinx. There have been many times when the Roar was worth an extra player to Scotland. Unfortunately, it couldn't travel and the team went through a lean spell in 1933–34, failing to win a single match. The same bad luck seemed to attend the players around that time. Harry McMenemy, son of the famous Jimmy 'Napoleon' McMenemy of Celtic, was named for the Scotland side to meet Wales in October 1933 but was injured. His place was taken by his brother John. It was John's only cap and Harry was never named again. Speaking of strange caps, Joe Kennaway of Celtic, brought from Canada to replace John Thomson, played for Canada against USA in 1928, and for USA against Canada in 1930. He was also capped for Scotland in 1933 against Austria, thus winning three caps with three different countries. The middle of the decade was no less strange. The effects of the Wall Street stock-market crash were still being felt and the consequent Depression affected everyone. It was said that Gary Cooper walked all over Hollywood trying to change a hundred-dollar bill but King Kong still got made and Shirley Temple was everybody's favourite. In football, however, things were much slower to change, and Rangers, operating from their marble halls at Ibrox, seemed a gilt-edged certainty to rule unchallenged, as much as Gordon Richards seemed to ride unchallenged on the race-track. Rangers had a Rolls-Royce conveyer belt of quality players passing through their portals and a royal succession of captains. Among these were Dougie Gray, Sandy Archibald, Jimmy Fleming and George Brown. There seemed no end to the quality of the thin, blue line.

It would be a mistake, however, to think that Rangers and Celtic had the right to every good player that came on the Scottish scene. Every team in the country had its own star and a nucleus of at least two or three good players. Partick Thistle had Peter McKennon and Alec MacSpadyen, the Motherwell trio has already been mentioned, Aberdeen had Willie Mills at inside-forward and Matt Armstrong at centre, Falkirk boasted Kenny Dawson, and Raith Rovers had a whole forward line of talents – Glen, Gilmour, Haywood, Whitelaw and Joyner which echoes their legendary line-up from the '20s (Bell, James, Bauld, Gilmour and Archibald). Every season, players seemed to come up as inevitably as rain at the Glasgow Fair Holidays. Of all the teams outside the Old Firm, perhaps Hearts had the strongest squad at any one time, and foremost among a strong Edinburgh presence were Glaswegians like Alec Massie and Andy 'Tiger' Anderson, both regular Scottish internationalists.

By this time, Adolf Hitler had come to power in Germany as leader of the National Socialists and already Winston Churchill was warning the House of Commons that another war was on its way but the members paid no attention, or if they did, they only scoffed. Even less interested were the ordinary people who buried their heads in the sands at Ayr or Portobello and followed the terpsichorean adventures of Fred Astaire and Ginger Rogers on the big, black-and-white screen or the more pedestrian adventures of their local team on a Saturday afternoon – and for colour, there was the occasional international, especially the annual Bannockburn or Flodden with England. 'Anglos' were back in favour and few were favoured as much as Dally Duncan.

Douglas DUNCAN (b. 1909)
Outside-left for Hull City, Derby County and Luton Town

43

Douglas Duncan was called 'Dally' because he did just that – dallied. Never in a hurry, he would loiter on the left wing then suddenly dart up to the corner flag and cross or move into the penalty area to shoot fiercely. He scored a lot of goals with his head – twice against England, and both from Charlie Napier corners. In each case, Dally had pipped Hughie Gallacher for the goal and Hughie had a few names for Duncan that day, none of which was Dally. Dally Duncan is one of the few Aberdonian schoolboy internationalists that Aberdeen missed. Hull City invited him down for a trial and after he had helped them to the semi-final of the FA Cup he was transferred to Derby County in 1930 – 'to help me get into the Scottish team, as they had a lot of internationals in their side at the time'. He scored on his debut against Wales in 1932 but Scotland lost that game 5–2 and Dally thought his career with Scotland was over, but he kept his place until the outbreak of war in 1939 and the end of all official internationals. At thirty-six, he helped the Rams win the FA Cup in 1946 then, as manager of Luton Town, took his club to Wembley in the Cup final of 1960. As recently as 1996, Dally Duncan took Third Division Chesterfield to the semi-final of the FA Cup, an event that took everyone in football by surprise and nearly straightened the town's famous crooked cathedral spire. Dally was still 'doing the business', as footballers say.

On 4 October 1933, when Herr Hitler walked out of the League of Nations in Geneva and tennis was still celebrating Fred Perry's win in the US Open, a Scottish football player won his one and only official cap in a mid-week match against Wales in Cardiff. Dally Duncan and Andy Anderson were his team-mates that day and Jack Harkness was playing his last game for Scotland, but the Scots went down 3–2 to a very good

Welsh team. A debut Scot on the day immediately lost his place to Alec Massie. It would seem that he had failed, yet this particular Scot went on to make a niche for himself among the game's immortals and to be known not only by his fellow Scots, but by people all over the world who follow the fortunes of the round ball wherever it is kicked. His name was Matt Busby. To many he is Mr Football, and by the end of his life he had a status in the sport second to none, but what is less known is that he assiduously built up to this height from very humble beginnings. In fact, the only way the future Sir Matt could go was up.

Sir Matthew W. BUSBY, CBE (1909–93)
Wing-half-back for Manchester City, Liverpool and Hibernian 44

Matt Busby's is a much-remembered name in Bellshill, Lanarkshire, where he was brought up, and he is a hero in Liverpool where, in 1936, he formed a half-back line with fellow-Scots Bradshaw and McDougal; he was a respected figure in Edinburgh when he played for Hibernian during the war, but he is a god in Manchester, where he recreated not one but three great teams, in 1948, 1958 and 1968. However, if one is to consider his life in football terms, then it must be like the game itself – in two halves with an interval – because Matt Busby had two lives, one as a player and one as a manager, and each is complementary to the other. It is hard to think of the revered Sir Matt as a young miner who played football for the Orbiston Cannibals. There was little else to do in the '20s between the end of a shift and bedtime. He signed for Manchester City when he was seventeen because it was better than working, and football he regarded as fun and enjoyment rather than work. Real work was underground. This was something that had also occurred to Sir Harry Lauder earlier and to Bill Shankly and Jock Stein later. The City manager of that time, Peter Hodge, had to move quickly to get young Busby because he was about to emigrate to America with his widowed mother. He was signed as an inside-forward but City moulded him into the classy half-back that he became. From the very beginning, Matt Busby had style. He had it in the way he played, even then, also in the way he danced (even if my mother preferred my father as a partner) and in the way he dressed. Like the rest of the Bellshill Brigade, Gallacher, James *et al*, he was a bit of a dandy dresser, from snap-brim bowler to spats, and he was known to have an eye for a pretty girl. Well, why not? You don't see many at the pit face. He got to like cufflinks and well-cut suits because pit clothes were grimy and dirty, and too often hid the man. He liked to put on a bet, because he saw that life itself was one big gamble. He would have put his shirt on a sure thing, but Sir Matt made sure it was a football shirt, and a red one at that. Matt Busby, the Bellshill boy, knew his place but Matt Busby, the footballer, had class, and over the years he passed on this poise to the man he became.

This sense of quality showed in the way he played – the calm trap of the ball, the studied pass, the playing ease throughout the game that is the hallmark of the world-class player. He was unfortunate that his best playing days were during the unofficial wartime years and it was as a temporary Hibernian player that he was recognised for the influential half-back and superb captain that he really was. He had offered his services to Celtic at this period, because he had supported them as a boy, but they, with the myopic stupidity and smugness that typified the Celtic Board of that time, turned him down. So he took his boots to Easter Road and made his influence felt with Harry Swan's youngsters, who were to grow into one of the great teams of the post-war era. He was in at the birth of the Famous Five – Smith, Johnstone, Reilly, Turnbull and Ormond – that was to be the basis of the future Hibernian Championship sides of 1948, 1951 and 1952. They were among the first to profit from the special Busby tutelage that was to be his hallmark even though he was then at the end of his playing career. He might not have known it, but his best days were to come. He was in the interval of his life and his football career, but the second half was about to begin.

When the war ended so did his playing days and even though he was invited to stay on at Liverpool, he was happy to accept an offer to manage a run-down Manchester United, who had lost their ground in an air-raid and were in a bad way. He became a manager simply because he wanted to stay in the game and Manchester United at the time would have been glad of anyone. Always a devout Catholic, his faith carried him through the death of his first great Championship team at Munich, when the same plane crash nearly cost him his own life, and it helped him build a new team to claim the European Cup in 1968. Now, in 1945–46, it helped him rebuild a club from the ground up. Ideally, he ought to have been manager of Celtic. He had always wanted to play for them, after all. In the same way, he might have managed Liverpool, a club that had the same peasant fire, but Fate decreed then that he should mastermind Manchester United into its world standing. Almost single-handedly, he made it into the dominating team of the post-war age, in the same way that Herbert Chapman made Arsenal, and Bill Struth made Rangers the pinnacle pre-war clubs. Sir Matt Busby, in his eighty-four years, sometimes gregarious, sometimes the loner, cigarette constantly in hand, had striven to provide the best for his family, his club, his country and his adopted Manchester. He gave all of them exactly that – his best – and he passed on knowing that his gift was secure in good hands. Players loved him, and when they are as disparate as Duncan Edwards, Bobby Charlton, George Best, Denis Law and Pat Crerand, you know that Busby must have had something. For the want of a better word one might well describe it as genius. His 1970 biography by David Muller was the aptly named *Father of Football*. His achievements are greater than the facts that anyone can see in the record book. He came to a prime club and gave it a passion. From good beginnings, he made it great, for he himself was touched with greatness. He gave it himself and from that blood-flow sprang a life that still pulsates in the game today. They call this life-force Manchester United and it, like Matt Busby, belongs to the world.

On 10 June 1934, Italy won the second World Cup at the Stadio Torino in Rome before a packed crowd and a delighted Benito Mussolini, *Il Duce*. Italy had equalised Czechoslovakia's goal to take the match into extra time. Scavio then scored the winner to give Italy the Cup and cap what had been an all-out Fascist jamboree rather than a football competition. Uruguay, winners of the initial World Cup in 1930, had been prevented from coming because of a footballers' strike, and Austria, the favourites, had been beaten by Italy in the semi-final. The other beaten semi-finalists were Germany. The British football nations, not being members of FIFA, did not compete. The FA preferred to stand aloof from what they considered to be merely a continental novelty, and the other Associations, Scotland, Ireland and Wales sheepishly followed suit.

In the meantime, the invincible Rangers, managed by Struth and marshalled by Brown, had won the League and Cup yet again and England beat Scotland 3–0 at Wembley. So what else was new? And in keeping with the darkening days of this chapter, 1934 ended with Gillingham's centre-forward, Raleigh, dying from concussion sustained in a match against Brighton and Hove Albion. Then one remembered poor John Thomson.

Chapter Eight

Distant Drums

The 1935 football close season was marked by a Civil Defence exercise where thousands of young women donned skull-like gas-masks in parks all over the country for the benefit of anxious civil servants who were beginning to feel as uncomfortable as the young ladies no doubt were, about the ominous noises across the Channel, especially as the Nuremberg Rally approached. Ramsay MacDonald retired 'for health reasons' and a piper played 'Will Ye No' Come Back Again'. He might've been the only one who meant it. It was ironic that the hit song of the moment was 'Red Sails in the Sunset' as Britain's first Labour Prime Minister tiptoed out of the back door of power and the Tory Mr Baldwin walked briskly in at the front, winged collar, top hat and all. With slightly more urgency, Sir Malcolm Campbell beat the world land speed record in his racing car, *Bluebird*, reaching more than 300 mph on the sands at Utah. The British people, meanwhile, had sought different sands as, with their usual apathy towards world events during the summer, they surged lemming-like to the coast for the August Bank Holiday. It was something to do while they waited for the football season to start. There is no record of anyone taking a gas-mask with them.

In the new fascist states of Germany and Italy, sport, especially football, was seen as a vital means of propagating the national image and every effort was made to upgrade and promote sporting skill as a means of promoting their new ideologies. Winning mattered now more than ever and the game was rapidly becoming a matter of high politics abroad.

Rangers toured Germany and Austria, being careful to be beaten now and then, Motherwell went to the Argentine and Queen of the South to North Africa, but none of these tours was in the same frolicking atmosphere of just a few years before. The Foreign Office now took a keen interest in teams up for temporary export. National prestige was at stake. Xenophobia raised its ugly head in every kind of international encounter, and although Scotland had risen to its full national height in every encounter with England, there was no ideology involved other than a risible supra-patriotism, and anyway, it was only once a year – but now things were getting more serious, especially in Europe. This affected all British sides involved in touring but it was less important for Scotland.

In any case, Scottish players might have been better represented by the Football League, as nearly all good Scots were lured over the border at some time or other in their careers. It was a very cushioned few with the bigger clubs who could resist the continuing lure of English gold. In England, Lord Roche had decreed that anyone earning more than two hundred and fifty pounds per annum could not be classified as a manual worker, and therefore could not draw the dole when unemployed or get sick benefit when off work with illness or injury. Since many players spent a lot of time 'off work' with some kind of injury, this was a problem. No doubt some kind of personal arrangements were made privately, but then they always had been, where skilled players and their clubs were concerned. Somehow, the less skilled player didn't seem to be injured as often. The iron-clad full-backs were still indestructible and the thick-necked centre-forwards seemingly impervious to any hurt.

Scotland, however, could still boast its football aristocrats. Like children of grace, they appeared in every generation, coming as if from nowhere to bloom like a rose on the cabbage-patch. It is not known why some players can play a rough game with some finesse. For football was still a rough game in the mid-1930s. It had not yet become a dirty game, full of tactical, sly fouls and strategic play designed to stop the other side playing rather than playing oneself. The stakes were not quite so high and the ordinary exuberance of the players meant that football was still a physical encounter between two teams of strong men. Yet somehow the cultured player thrived. He had that extra acumen that kept him out of the worst trouble and the flash of unexpectedness and originality that caught his opposition on the wrong foot. This was because the good player is a thinking player and always has a yard in hand at any time in the game. He has the ability to remain calm even in the tensest of situations and it's this repose that gives him the extra few seconds in which to act.

Tommy Walker of Hearts was exactly this kind of player.

Tommy WALKER OBE (1915–1993)
Inside-right for Heart of Midlothian and Chelsea

45

Tommy Walker had originally wanted to become a minister. Instead, he became a footballer. There is no record of his ever having regretted it. From schoolboy caps with Livingston, he ascended the conventional football ladder with Hearts, Chelsea and Scotland to earn for himself a place as one of the most popular players ever to play for his country before the Second World War. There is no doubt that, but for that war, he would have won himself many more honours. He was an exemplary young man, on and off the field, with an ice-cool temperament for the big occasion, as witness his penalty kick at Wembley in 1936. Twice the ball was blown off the spot by the wind, and twice the nineteen-year-old Walker replaced it only to ram it home cleanly at the third attempt. Scotland had found a new hero. In his fifteen years with Hearts he never won a medal, yet enjoyed an enormous reputation as a player, especially as Sergeant Walker, T., in the famous Army team of All-Stars. He attracted a large fee from Chelsea in 1946 but his stay in London was brief. The war years had been his best years. He came back to Hearts as manager and his final years were as an administrator with Dunfermline and Raith Rovers. He was awarded the OBE in 1960 for his services to football. Tommy Walker was, in fact, a throwback to the Scottish Corinthian, the old-style gentleman-player but with a weekly wage.

Herbert Chapman, like Willie Maley (and Alex Ferguson in our own day), was a moderate player who became an exemplary manager. Chapman had begun at Leeds City when they were expelled from the Football League for 'irregularities'. The Leeds players were publicly auctioned like so much cattle, which says much for the status of the player then, and Chapman moved with a nucleus of the Leeds players to nearby Huddersfield, which was in a similarly parlous state financially. In three seasons, he took them to Division One and runners-up in the top grade by 1925. This was the year of the offside change whereby a player could be offside only if one outfield player was between him and goal when the ball was played. This resulted in a quick upsurge of goal-scoring and teams quickly sought measures to counter this offensive advantage. Herbert Chapman is credited with bringing in the totally defensive centre-back as a tactic towards this end. Speed became the need as the offside trap, perfected by such as McCracken of Newcastle, had so often thwarted previous attackers. Given fast wingers such as Chapman had at Arsenal, like Bastin and

Hulme, as well as accurate passers of the ball from inside, like James and Jack (and Buchan before him), as well as Ted Drake at centre-forward (who had scored seven against Aston Villa in December), he had exactly the players on hand to put the new concept into practice. Essential to the scheme, however, was the right kind of centre-half, who had to be commanding and cool at the centre of the defence, allowing the wing-halves to tie up with the inside forwards. Chapman had Bernard Joy and in him the prototype of the stopper centre-half was gradually fashioned. Soon every club in the country was following Chapman's methods and trying to find their own version of the stopper. Rangers had theirs in big Jimmy Simpson.

James McMillan SIMPSON (1908–72)
Centre-half for Dundee United and Rangers   **46**

Had it not been for a serious ankle injury, big Jimmy Simpson, this footballing Fifer (from Ladybank) would probably have broken the record for the continuous captaincy of Scotland. He had to pull out of the team against Czechoslovakia in 1937 because of injury. Had he played, he would have beaten Charlie Thomson's run of thirteen appearances as captain. Simpson never played for Scotland again, retiring, like so many others, with the onset of war. Jimmy Simpson was one of the pioneers of the centre-half as 'third back', or stopper between the two full-backs. Originally, like Kelly of the Celtic and Charlie Thomson of Hearts, the centre-half-back was the pivot of the team operating at the centre of the field, but with the new offside laws being brought into operation there was a greater need to defend and the centre player dropped back. Gillespie of Queen's Park was thought to be the first to do so in Scotland and by the '30s it was the accepted practice. Except, noticeably, by Celtic. Simpson, by his commanding height and good ball sense, was just right for this kind of role, despite his obvious football artistry, and when brought from Dundee United he played it effectively both for Rangers and Scotland. Like Davie Meiklejohn, he was a professional engineer – and like many other famous footballers, he could draw a good pint in his bar. His son, Ronnie, a Scotland goalkeeper, was part of Celtic's all-conquering Lisbon Lions in 1967. Despite his father's persistent attempts, young Ronnie never followed him to Ibrox. Perhaps he wisely realised how big his father's shadow was.

*

Celtic made an attempt to get in on the 'third back' fashion by signing Willie Lyon, an Englishman, from Queen's Park. Lyon was one of the very few amateurs to have been signed by Celtic, but he fitted the bill exactly as the new commanding centre-half in the manner of Simpson and Joy, although Alec McNair had played something of the same type of game in an earlier era. Bob Gillespie, too, as has been mentioned, had played as a third back in the great Queen's Park team of 1923–24, when he was flanked by J. McDonald and W.S. King and had T.K. Campbell and W. Wiseman at full-back. That side had J.B. McAlpine at inside-left, he of 'the educated feet' who would have won many caps for Scotland had he not, like Willie Lyon, been English-born. Lyon filled the place at Celtic left by Jimmy McStay who had gone to Hamilton Accies after a minor dispute about money. Charlie Napier left because he didn't get a benefit after six years and the O'Donnell brothers, Frank and Hugh, because Frank didn't get on with the Celtic supporters. Lyon came then at the right time to take charge of the cubs now claiming their places in the first team, like Malcolm MacDonald, George Paterson, John Divers, Johnny Crum and Willie Buchan. However, an even greater influence was the appointment of the great 'Napoleon', Jimmy McMenemy, as coach to the younger players. From this time on, Celtic looked as if they could seriously challenge Rangers again for the League Championship. From fourth place in 1933, to third place in 1934, to second place in 1935 – the gap was closing all the time – and in 1936, they closed it by winning the League by five points ahead of Rangers, and with Jimmy McGrory, a veteran now, getting fifty of their goal tally. He needed only three more to beat the Scottish record for goals in a season held by McFadyen of Motherwell but injury kept him out of the final games and the chance was lost. He was unlucky again. Meantime, in England, Ted Harston of Mansfield Town set a record for Division Three of the Football League by scoring fifty-five goals in forty-one games and not long afterwards, on 13 April 1936, in the same Division, Joe Payne scored ten for Luton Town against Bristol Rovers. One can only speculate on how many McGrory might have scored had he gone to Arsenal instead of Lourdes ten years earlier.

Rangers resumed their normal programme by regaining the Championship in 1937. 'Struth' (meaning 'God's Truth') was a common epithet, but to many Rangers supporters, God did reside at Ibrox in the person of manager, William Struth, who, by this time, by dint of eagle eye and firm hand, had moulded an Ibrox dynasty in his own image, so that he had a younger stable eager to make their mark as seniors. Names that were to become famous were already being seen on the Ibrox programmes but their day was yet to come. Meantime, as the Spitfire took to the sky in trial flight and the *Queen Mary* took to the sea in her trial voyage, and the Civil War broke out in Spain, regulars in the Rangers team were still the bulk of the great team that had served them so well throughout the decade under captains Meiklejohn and Brown. Rangers were now the Establishment team and had that status and high prestige that belongs to long-lived success. Like Celtic earlier, they were now the team that everyone had to beat, Celtic being the only side capable of doing it with any kind of consistency. Although at this time, as commentator Archie McPherson put it, Celtic were a green-painted ship becalmed in a blue-painted ocean. Really there were two competitions going on in Scotland, one between Rangers and Celtic and the other between the rest. What impressed about Glasgow Rangers was that they seemed to get there by order, while Celtic did it by inspired improvisation. Whichever the way of it, the Old Firm was still in business, because they had players like . . .

James DAWSON (1909–77) 47
Goalkeeper for Rangers and Falkirk

James Dawson was called 'Jerry' after the Burnley and England goalkeeper, Jeremiah Dawson, who was famous at the time of our Jerry's boyhood in Falkirk. Jerry had a ghoulish beginning in the senior game, making his debut for Rangers at Ibrox as successor to the redoubtable Tom Hamilton in the game in which the opposing goalkeeper, John Thomson, was killed. However, despite his parents' natural anxiety about such a profession for their son, Jerry went on to become Scotland's best goalkeeper since Jack Harkness. In a sense, Thomson's untimely loss gave Dawson his Scotland chance and in 1934 he took it. He had wonderful agility and a keen positional sense which often made saves look easier than they were. Like Harkness, he was safe rather than spectacular, but he had his best hour in the 1937 Hampden game against England when he held out against the Englishmen in a series of wonderful saves in the first half, allowing Scotland to win in the second. He played on until 1943 at the very highest level and then went home to Falkirk to play out the last years of a fine career and become manager of East Fife. Jerry Dawson was noted for his ability to put spin on his goal kicks. What good this did to his team is not stated except perhaps to put the ball quicker into touch. Still, he was employed for his goalkeeping not his goalkicking.

James DELANEY (1914–89)

Outside-right and centre-forward for Celtic, Manchester United, Aberdeen, Falkirk, Derry City, Cork Celtic and Elgin City

48

Jimmy Delaney also went to Falkirk in the closing years of his career but he went on to serve three more clubs after that and only stopped playing when they took his boots from him. A natural athlete with an electrifying burst of speed and a lethal shot, Jimmy was the kind of player who had the crowd roaring in anticipation as soon as he received the ball. He was in the direct line of Alex Jackson in his fast approach and deadly finishing. In a long and trophy-filled career, from 1934 until 1957, he won the hearts of supporters throughout Britain by his attacking flair and the sheer excitement of his involvement in any game. He had been an unemployed miner when he was signed by Celtic, from the local Stoneyburn Juniors, and, like those other Lanarkshire escapees, he couldn't believe his luck. He trained hard and played hard and his long career is a tribute not only to his fitness but to his continued enthusiasm for the game at whatever level. He loved playing football and it showed. It showed in those dashes up the wing, in all the last-minute goals and in the joy he gave to so many thousands. He said himself that he thought the day would never come when he would give up football, but when it did it left him famous, with a trunkful of caps and medals – and arthritis. But being Jimmy Delaney, he thought it was well worth it.

Delaney never saw Celtic Park until he played in it. In fact, had the letter inviting him for a trial been written a week later, he might've been a Hibernian player, as he also received an invitation to play a trial for them, but the Celtic date was the first. He went along, intending to take up the Edinburgh offer if nothing came of the Glasgow one, but Celtic asked him to join them, and he did. He signed for a bonus of twenty pounds and four pounds a week if he made the first team. He did so within the year and it was these football wages which kept his whole family in Clelland, just as McGrory's kept his in the Garngad. In the mid-1930s, there were few men working in the Scottish industrial belt. The only people making money at that time were pawnbrokers, publicans, bookmakers, variety hall performers, boxers and footballers. It was almost the norm for the young son of a large family, who was clever with his feet, to keep the whole house going on what he brought home from the football club. The ball-winner was also the breadwinner. This was the reason why so many young players were always in dread of the autocratic managers who could dispense with their services at a whim. It was not so much a blow to the player's pride as a threat to the whole family's standard of living. A man on the dole, the head of a house, was bringing in less than a pound for himself, ten shillings for his wife and two shillings for each child. Small wonder a lot of west of Scotland Scots were small and thin with bow legs. They also had spirit and a sense of humour. It would have been hard to survive otherwise. This was why players like Delaney, McGrory, Gallacher, James, Busby and Shankly played all out all the time in all games. They were hungry, and they were taking no chances. In Delaney's case, his enthusiasm for the game was genuine, his long career is proof of that, but it was underpinned by a need to keep the money coming in from season to season and year to year. As his success grew, so, of course, did his earnings but he was never rich. In his entire career, he never earned more than a respectable tradesman, but that was enough for this extraordinary, ordinary man.

A broken arm sustained against Arbroath in August 1939 seriously affected his club and international career. The SFA was reluctant to risk him in the national team because of insurance problems and it wasn't until a huge crowd demonstrated outside the SFA offices in Carlton Place, chanting 'We want Delaney! We want Delaney!' that he was finally selected again and his international career resumed. He was as much an inspiration at this level as he was with Celtic and every other club he played with, at whatever level. As Malcolm MacDonald, his Celtic team-mate said, 'You don't play with Jimmy Delaney. You just play to him.' Yet, to the end, he remained the same modest, unassuming man from Clelland. There was nothing modest or unassuming about his play, however. Like so many players, he put on his playing persona with his jersey, and as soon as the green and white hoops girded that lithe frame, he was another personality altogether, as eager as a racehorse and as brave as a lion. Like Stanley Matthews, he had extraordinary speed over the short distance and had the same uncanny ball control. More than Matthews, he was loved by spectators and worshipped by Celtic fans. Whatever his club in his career, his loyalty was total. He had his only disagreement with the club when he was refused a two pounds rise and for asking for this trivial sum he was put on the transfer list. The support was enraged but Matt Busby travelled up by train to escort Delaney personally to Manchester. They met at Motherwell station and you can be sure that Matt would have offered to carry Jimmy's bag. He knew the value of the bargain he was getting and Delaney didn't let him down. Right to the end of a very long career, he gave his all in every match, and fully earned the high reputation he never lost. He played in Scotland, England, Northern Ireland and Eire and won cup medals in all four countries by the time he reluctantly left the game in 1956 after almost a quarter of a century of running at speed with a ball at his feet. It was said that they had to hide his football boots or he would be playing yet.

It was 17 April 1937 and the largest crowd in Europe gathered at Hampden Park to see Scotland beat England 3–1 to the accompaniment of the loudest sound ever heard in a football stadium: 149,547 voices (one of which was my own seven-year-old treble) raised to greet a Scotland side. The England team, already on the field, were taken aback by its huge intensity. 'If ever a match was won and lost by a roar, it was this one,' said young Stanley Matthews, the new England outside-right. The whole England forward line was recast. Horatio Carter played inside to Matthews, Freddie Steele was at centre, and Starling and Johnston made up the left wing. Most Scots would've liked to have seen Denis Compton of the Arsenal play, I think. Anyway, we were to see enough of him on all the billboards advertising Brylcreem. The English forwards must have been good all the same because Jimmy Simpson, the Scottish centre-half, said later: 'I had a sore day. The interchanging of those inside-forwards had me nearly out of my mind. I had to be more of a cat than a policeman.' As it happened, it was the more skilful England who scored first, through Steele, five minutes before half-time, but it was when the teams came out again for the second half that the giant crowd really roared the Scots on. It was taken up right from the kick-off and swelled to an unbearable level as Frank O'Donnell, the ex-Celt now with Preston North End, playing at centre-forward, equalised. From then on, the sheer noise of the Hampden Roar impelled the ball towards the England goal and it was no real surprise when Bob McPhail scored twice in the last ten minutes to give Scotland a memorable, if perhaps undeserved, victory. If it hadn't been for the heroics of Jerry Dawson in the Scottish goal, England might have won handsomely. It was the best display by a Scottish goalkeeper since John Thomson ten years before. The Rangers man became a folk hero from this game on, but the Scots had a twelfth man – the huge crowd, and *they* had their own weapon, the Hampden Roar. People living ten miles away from the ground could tell if Scotland had won by the sound of the roar. The Scots did well to savour the moment because they weren't to beat England at Hampden again in an official international until 1962.

My own recollections of the actual game are hazy, but I do remember the long walk to the game. At least it was long for seven-year-old legs. I think I was carried piggy-back part of the way. I do remember being passed over the heads of the men with the other young boys – raised hands passing us easily down to the track where we sat in front of the little perimeter wall only six feet or so away from the touchline at the Aikenhead Road end of the stadium. The English players, in the whiter than white shirts and black shorts, seemed Gulliver figures to the Glasgow Lilliputians huddled by the red cinder track, and I had the impression they were all suntanned. The Scottish players were paler, and more boy-sized from where I sat. For the record, the Scottish team that day was: Dawson (Rangers), Anderson (Hearts), Beattie (Preston North End), Massie (Aston Villa), Simpson (Rangers), Brown (Rangers), Delaney (Celtic), Walker (Hearts), O'Donnell (Preston North End), McPhail (Rangers) and Duncan (Derby County). My most vivid memory is of the pipe band passing at half-time. My father was a piper, of course. The crowd seemed to go mad and we little boys at the front couldn't hear ourselves speak, so we just shouted out anything in a kind of wild hysteria. If one hadn't joined in, I suppose it might've been frightening. It was like a wall of noise behind me. I felt I could've leaned against it. The game itself is just a blur of coloured images. All I do know, even now, was that I *loved* those Scottish players in their dark blue jerseys with that splendid red lion on their chests. At seven, I could hardly tell Andy Anderson from Andy Beattie, or George Brown from Dally Duncan, but I did know Jerry Dawson and Tommy Walker because I had seen their pictures so often in my cigarette card collection, and Jimmy Delaney of the Celtic was already my hero.

I remember being so disappointed that he didn't score. I gather now that he almost did. He always got a big roar all to himself whenever the ball came to him, he was such an adventurous player. At the end of the game, a policeman came and told us to stay where we were until the crowds cleared a bit. When I turned and looked up at the massed terracing behind me, I panicked a bit. I wondered how my Dad would find me. What if he forgot all about me in the excitement, or couldn't get down to the track through the crowd? I also remember wanting to pee. The policeman said I should just step over and do it against the wall. I did. I'm glad Dad never saw me. Or my Uncle Phil, who had come to the game with us. Dad had said that I was to stay where I was at the trackside and he would come to me at the end of the game. And he did, grinning all over his face, with all the other fathers and uncles, collecting their offspring as if they were parcels, and hauling them up the slope of the terracing to the exit gates on the other sides. It was as if we were going up a mountain, but it was a concrete mountain, stepped all the way and littered with empty beer bottles, cigarette packets, chewing gum wrappers and all the residue that belongs to an assembly of nearly 150,000 males who have been standing in one spot for more than two hours. Some were still leaning on the iron stanchions, still in the excitement of the game, going over it again, as they would countless times in the coming week no doubt. I remember seeing lots of caps and hats and umbrellas lying about but what I remember most was that Dad found half-a-crown.

'Must be my lucky day,' he exclaimed.

'Shouldn't you hand that intae a police station?' said my Uncle Phil, who was known as a bit of a joker in the family. 'Lost property, an' that,' he added.

'That'll be right,' muttered my Dad, pocketing the big, bright, silver coin and taking my hand. 'Come on, then.' And we continued the long climb up the concrete steps.

That's my big memory of that great day. It was my lucky day too, in a way. I only wish I could remember more of the match.

It was the very first all-ticket game. You can see a picture of mine on the front of this book. As you will see, it cost my Dad two shillings then, which for him was quite a lot of money. (Of course, if you count the half-crown he found, he still made a tanner.) There was no Boys' Gate then for international matches. Some 150,000 tickets were actually sold, although just slightly fewer than that went through the turnstiles at Hampden on the day. The stadium had been extended to take 200,000 (thought to have been the unofficial attendance in 1935 when those locked out climbed the walls) so there was room for everybody, although it didn't seem like it at the time. Gate receipts for the 1937 game were announced as £24,303, but the players still only received six pounds a man and any legitimate expenses, for which they had to sign. Nobody even thought to complain. It was still an honour to play for your country despite the fact that the Oxford Union debate not long before had concluded that it was silly to die for it. It probably still is. Not that we cared. My family didn't even know anyone who went to Glasgow University never mind Oxford or Cambridge. We walked all the way home again – home then being the tenement room and kitchen a mere bottle's throw from Celtic Park, where my mother had the soup ready and little brother Jim was waiting to hear all about it. No doubt I told him – several times over – and of coming home, this time on my father's shoulders, like a hero being taken from the field. I *was* a hero. After all, I had been to Hampden and I had seen Scotland play and, best of all, win. I put my ticket carefully away in my special drawer so that I might bring it out again proudly – sixty years later.

Football internationals were important events in 1937. You waited impatiently outside Carlton Place, the offices of the SFA at that time, to hear the team announced by a man who wore a wing collar just like Stanley Baldwin. Or you waited outside your local newsagents for the first of the three Glasgow evening papers to arrive with the names of the team in big, black capitals on the 'Stop Press' column. The excitement of reading them out was almost sick-making. Then the two weeks of waiting for the Big Day. The suspense was unbearable, but the day itself was unforgettable. There were so many unforgettable football days then. Joe Louis may have won the World Heavyweight title, Sydney Wooderson may have broken the world record for the mile, the abdicated Prince of Wales may have finally married Mrs Simpson, but that was all incidental to the football peaks that seem to loom up regularly like a range of Everests in those immediate pre-war years, even though people were raging against the growing menace of the Football Pools. Post Office workers wanted extra money for dealing with the massive sorting that the Pools entailed and there were cries that gambling on such a scale was a disgrace. Football ought to be banned, said the letters to the Editor. What a hope. It had never been so popular. Only twenty days after my 'Lucky Day' with Scotland, 146,433 spectators returned to Hampden to watch Celtic beat Aberdeen 2–1 in the Scottish Cup final, while 20,000 milled around following the game by the shouts of the crowd. It was a classic game and yet another record attendance. My dad must have been on pipe band duty elsewhere that day, or I might have been there too.

The crowds had also gathered around Buckingham Palace to celebrate the Coronation of King George VI, that reluctant and unexpected King, and his Scottish Queen, Elizabeth Bowes-Lyon. A year later, the royal couple agreed to come to Glasgow to open the Empire Exhibition at Bellahouston Park. To mark the event, a football tournament was proposed involving the top clubs from England and Scotland. Rangers, Celtic, Aberdeen and Hearts represented Scotland and Everton, Chelsea, Sunderland and Brentford were the English standard-bearers. All the matches were to be played at Ibrox, near to the Bellahouston Exhibition site. Celtic, in their haphazard way, had by this time discovered a magical forward line – Delaney, MacDonald, Crum, Divers and Murphy. Each was a striking individual player on his own, yet they combined and interchanged as if they had been playing together for years. They all played for Scotland but never as they played for Celtic. It took a war to break them up just as they were getting into their full stride. In the summer of 1938, however, they were all young and new and it showed in the exhilarating way they played football.

The Scottish teams did well but the favourites were always Celtic and Everton, the latter having disposed of Rangers in the first round, but Celtic were lucky to get through against Hearts in the semi-final. The final went to extra time between two well-matched teams, with Delaney and Tommy Lawton the respective danger men, but it was little Johnny Crum who stole the winner from a neat Divers flick with a powerful shot from the edge of the penalty area. Celtic had won for Scotland, and even Rangers could not deny that the Parkhead team always seemed to produce something for the special football events, and now the 1938 Exhibition Trophy was added to the 1901 Exhibition silverware – and there was more to come.

By this time, the war drums could no longer be ignored, except by those gallant few who supported East Fife. The tiny club from Buckhaven startled everyone in Scotland by getting to the final of the Scottish Cup, after requiring three games to overcome the Edinburgh St Bernard – or St Bernard's, as they were called. Even the final against Kilmarnock was drawn, but when they replayed the following Wednesday, East Fife scored twice in extra time to lift the trophy. They are the only Second Division side ever to have won the Scottish Cup and John Harvey, their goalkeeper, won his only medal after having been quickly transferred from Hearts a few days before the injury suffered by Herd, the Fifers' regular keeper. Harvey returned to Hearts to become their manager, but poor little Herd got none. The Kingdom of Fife was making itself felt that year in footballing Scotland. Raith Rovers, the club from just further along the coast at Kirkcaldy, won the Second Division title with 142 goals, the highest aggregate ever scored in a season. Notwithstanding, Celtic won the big League by three points over Hearts, with Rangers third and the world went on its usual way, rumours and tensions abounding.

Mr Chamberlain returned from seeing Herr Hitler in Munich, waving a bit of paper at Heston Aerodrome, declaring to all that it was a signed Peace Accord with Nazi Germany, and that it meant 'Peace in our time . . .' His watch must have been slow. Never mind, most people believed him. I think because they wanted to. People would believe anything but another war. They cheered the launching of the Queen Elizabeth at John Brown's, and Len Hutton's record cricket stand of 364 at the Oval. The newspapers carried grim pictures of Japan's invasion of China but that was too far away for anyone to bother about. People, especially New Yorkers, were more worried about the reported invasion by Martians which was organised by twenty-three-year-old actor-director, Orson Welles as a Hallowe'en spoof on radio, and terrified half the American population for a couple of days. It was odd that no one linked the theatrical prodigy to

H.G. Wells, who had written about much the same thing years before.

The New Year of 1939 opened with Rangers beating Celtic 2–1 at Ibrox, on their way to still another championship, before a record attendance for a club match of 118,561. Rangers were undisputed masters of the domestic football scene once more, accounted for perhaps by the fact that they had thirteen internationalists on their playing staff, although Jerry Dawson was the only regular in the Scottish team at this time. The team toured in North America that summer and one of the highlights was when full-back Jimmy Carabine played centre-forward against the American League – and scored a hat-trick. Proof that a good player can play in any position.

James CARABINE (1911–1987)
Right full-back for Third Lanark

49

The 'Quiet Man' they called him. He was nevertheless by no means placid, as was shown by his being ordered off on the afternoon of the day he was married, with his brand-new wife sitting in the stand. His mind may have been on other things. He typified his only club in many ways. He was unostentatious but effective, modest but proud of the tradition he played in. In all, he played four hundred games for Third Lanark between 1934 and 1946 and also 'guested' for Hearts during his war service. He was a member of the famous British Army side that included players of the calibre of Frank Swift, Stan Cullis, Tommy Walker, etc. Most of his fourteen appearances for Scotland were unfortunately unofficial and he had only three pre-war caps. However, it was as a 'Hi-Hi' man that he is best remembered and when his playing days were over he served them just as well as manager until he went into sports journalism in 1949. Jimmy Carabine had a great knowledge of the game and of players, and this served him effectively in his post-playing days. He had been a player of some pride and this informed his entire football life with the club he loved. Sad to say, Jimmy was killed in a road accident in Rutherglen High Street on 2 December 1987.

Our next football character was neither quiet nor self-effacing but he was to loom larger than most in the panorama of the sport. At this time, however, he was hacking his way up the provincial managerial ladder after a solid, workmanlike playing career in England. No one ever guessed what heights he would attain on that ladder. No one, that is, except the man himself – Bill Shankly. With him ends the first half of this Scottish football story.

William SHANKLY OBE (1913–81)
Half-back for Carlisle United, Preston North End and
Partick Thistle

50

Outside the village of Glenbuck, on the borders of Ayrshire and Lanarkshire, in an otherwise inconspicuous landscape, stands a stone cairn built in memory of a man of football. It was built by the subscriptions of thousands of ordinary football supporters, most of whom came from Liverpool, out of love for a man who came from Glenbuck. Glenbuck. When you've said that, you've said what is essential about the man. You have to pronounce Glenbuck as it is, directly, almost tersely and with no nonsense. He spoke that way all his life. In rapid, machine-gun phrases that somehow conveyed a whole depth of feeling in the man. A sensibility he would vehemently deny but it must have been there or he couldn't have won the adoration of Liverpool's Kop for two decades. Humour too. How often has his famous quip been misquoted – 'Football's not a matter of life or death. It's much more important.' What he actually said, according to the *Sunday Times* of 4 October 1987, was: 'Some people think football is a matter of life and death. I don't like that attitude. I can assure them it's much more important than that.' The middle sentence prepares one for the pay-off. His sense of humour was assisted by a considerable natural comedic technique. Every one of his aphorisms, delivered in that well-honed rasp of a voice, has a grin in it. There was also a deep sensibility in him. The man was a poet behind the stone mask.

He started his football with the Glenbuck Cherrypickers. You had to have a sense of humour to play for a team with a name like that. In 1932, he signed professional forms for Carlisle United, moving on the next season to Preston North End for a fee of five hundred pounds. A windfall for the Shanklys – or at least ten per cent of it. He had come up the hard way, like most of his contemporaries, and now the selectors beckoned. Playing for Scotland answered all his emotional, cultural and aesthetic needs. 'When you pull that Scottish jersey over your head,' he told Tommy Docherty in 1952, 'the lion will grow twice the size it is . . . Just run about, the jersey will take care of the rest.'

Football was in his blood. One uncle played for Rangers, another for Carlisle, his brothers were all professional players in various degrees, but none, even the successful manager Bob, was to achieve the Olympic status of the 'Shanks'. He knew he was going to make it. Right from the start. It was all part of the Great Plan. He just had to keep himself in condition for it. He was fanatical about fitness. He told his great Liverpool side: 'When I die, I want to be the fittest man in the graveyard.' When he did die, he had managed Carlisle, Workington, Grimsby Town and Huddersfield before he arrived at Anfield to create a legend out of the derelict remant of a Liverpool club always in the shadow of the mighty Everton. When the barber asked, 'Anything off the top?', he replied, 'Ay, Everton.'

His total obsession with the game is further illustrated by the fact that for their honeymoon he took his wife, Nessie, to see Tranmere Reserves. He could be pithy too: 'The trouble with referees is that they know the rules but don't know the game.' Again, when Liverpool could only tie with Leeds, thus conceding the Championship to them, he growled to Don Revie from the dressing-room door, 'The best team drew.' There was no such thing as a defeat for Bill Shankly, only a thwarted victory. In 1974, he was awarded the OBE and Liverpool won the the FA Cup. He was top of the Kop, but only he knew how jaded he was. He had done it all now, but in his own words, he was done. He astonished everyone by retiring suddenly. Nessie asked if he knew what he was doing. 'I do,' was all he said. It was not a happy retirement. He died on 29 September 1981, totally spent, but he had created the team that was to win everything it played for and laid the foundation of the great Liverpool sides of today. 'Liverpool was made for me and I was made for Liverpool . . . Anfield is my memorial,' he had said.

He was a prophet, an inspirer and a zealot, and the fire that he instilled in others eventually burnt him out. When he walked into the Celtic dressing-room after they had won the European Cup, the first British club to do so, he embraced Jock Stein, saying, 'John, you're immortal.' If anyone should have known that, Shankly should have. He had had his eye on Parnassus from the beginning. According to Hugh McIlvanney in *McIlvanney on Football* (Mainstream, 1994), Shankley's creed was simple: 'I am a people's man. Only the people matter.' All his life he trumpeted his working-class origins, and as a man of the people he moved and worked among them. Yet Bill Shankly had an aristocratic football pedigree. It was in his blood as much as coal dust had touched those iron lungs. Uncle Bob, on his mother's side, had played for Rangers and Portsmouth, and became a director of the latter club. His Uncle William played for Carlisle and was made a director there. Postman John Shankley (who spelt the name with an 'e') had five sons and they all did him proud on the football field. The oldest son, Alec, played for Ayr United but his career was cut short by the First World War. Jimmy, four years younger, played centre-forward for Carlisle, Sheffield United and Southend United, earning himself nice transfer cuts on the way. The middle brother, John, played for Portsmouth, Luton and Alloa but suffered from heart trouble and had to retire early. He later went back down the pits. The other brother was Bob, who played for Falkirk and later became their manager. He also managed Third Lanark, Hibernian and Stirling Albion whose ground was at Annfield in that city. At the other Anfield, in Liverpool, Bill Shankly's was a very different football operation.

He took the club from the English Second Division in 1959 to the European Cup in 1973. Under him they won the FA Cup twice and the Championship three times. He never managed the European Cup, but when they did win it in Rome in 1977, everyone knew that it was won by the team that Shankly made. Sadly, at this time, a rift had developed between him and the Bob Paisley regime at the club they had both served so long and so well and when Shankly died in 1981 they said it was a heart attack. Perhaps it was just broken. The *Times* wrote of him: 'Some rush into the limelight, some back into it. Shankly tramped into it and showed little surprise when he was treated like a god.'

Now they have built a statue to him behind the Kop. The man who spoke in stone sentences will be immortalised himself in stone by those who worshipped him – ordinary people like himself. His journey was carved in stone from the hillside cairn to the statue on the Kop. It was a hard road at times but he took hundreds of thousands along with him. He wasn't just Bill Shankly. He was much more important than that.

By the early summer of of 1939, iron railings were being cut down all over Glasgow, brick raid shelters were being built on every open space and Anderson shelters were being dug in every back garden. Things were looking ominous and plans were made to evacuate all schoolchildren out of the cities but the League fixtures for the new season were printed as usual, and, as usual, most heads were buried in summer sands. When football restarted after the break, the teams had only played five games when the season was interrupted on 3 September. Hitler had invaded Poland and Prime Minister Neville Chamberlain, in a BBC broadcast, told the nation 'that this country is therefore at war with Germany'.

And all for a bit of paper, a political treaty as meaningless as the 1839 jumble of words on a piece of parchment which had started the First World War.

Now, exactly a hundred years later, ostensibly for the sake of the port of Danzig but really just for a bit of paper, Europe was at war again. It was as if the first one had never ended. It seemed as if the lull between the two wars, which our parents had known as the Depression, had only been half-time and the second half was just about to begin. For the moment, however, nobody did anything and everyone waited to see what would happen.

Chapter Nine

Wartime Rations

It was to be a particularly hard winter but even in September 1939 everything was already 'frozen'. It was if a spell had been cast all over the British Isles. A black-out covered the country as all the lights went out and a hush seem to fall over everything. Normal living was subdued as everyone waited for something awful to happen, but it was only when a rabbit was killed as a lone German plane straffed the Firth of Forth that people realised there indeed was a war on; and the country got a new song to sing: 'Run, rabbit, run'.

It was a funny war, a phoney war and very soon it became a 'bore' war. To counter this reaction, this sense of anticlimax, it was decided that football should resume on a limited, regional basis and that players should be retained on a semi-professional basis at two pounds per week. It was no surprise when most of them opted instead to become physical training instructors in the Services. Better a sergeant instructor in the Army than a civilian footballer on half-pay. The more famous quickly became temporary officers, their shaky grammar obscured by their sporting charisma. Besides, most of them spent more time playing football for the nearest First Division side than serving King and Country with their respective units. It was indeed a topsy-turvy football world and the rewards as always, in the spiv civilisation of wartime, went to the more audacious and enterprising. Spectators were often roped in as players and often played better than the professionals – even if only for the first half. Sunday football was sanctioned for the first time and the handshake was introduced at the end of each match – possibly because the players themselves had never been introduced to each other.

The new football aristocrats were no longer the Arsenals, the Rangers, the Celtics and the Aston Villas, but the new, emerging Service teams containing the cream of the country's footballers. The Army team had Sergeant Tommy Walker, the RAF could boast Flight Lieutenant Ken Chisholm of Queen's Park and the Navy had Petty Officer Bobby Brown of Queen's Park and Rangers. In addition, because of the presence of so many Europeans in the country, their influence was also felt as they, too, were drafted into local sides. Mass recreation was now seen as a vital part of war work in relieving tension and, more particularly, boredom. The war had not yet 'hotted up', as it were, and people's first patriotic enthusiasm was rapidly wearing off. Three things took their minds off everything – the cinema, ballroom dancing and football matches. *Mass Observation* reported in 1940:

> In a society where things like sports and jazz are just as important as politics and religion, it might well be thought that first-class sportsmen were as important to the community as say watch-makers and curates who are in reserved occupations. Sports like football have an absolutely major effect on the morale of people, and one Saturday afternoon of League matches could probably do more to affect people's spirits than the recent fifty thousand pound Government poster campaign urging cheerfulness.

It might have been merely coincidence that so many well-known players were in reserved occupations at the outbreak of hostilities but, as in the first war, people remarked on how few Old Firm players were in uniform. Yet Willie Thornton of Rangers was to win a medal for bravery in action and Willie Lyon of Celtic won an Army commission. Football did restart quite soon after the artificial period of uncertainty but when it did it was divided into regional divisions and crowd limits were at the discretion of the local chief constable. Some clubs, like the smaller country teams, couldn't cope and dropped out; other city sides amalgamated until, in Scotland, the final arrangement realised a League in the west and another in the east which was good for the minimising of travel and the saving of petrol and fuel but it didn't do much good for the game. The war posters said 'Is Your Journey Really Necessary?' but travel restrictions meant that Aberdeen was virtually cut off and the Edinburgh teams were denied the big money fixtures with Rangers and Celtic. However, there was a war on and everybody just got on with it. Nevertheless, not even the common needs of a National Emergency could force the Scottish League officials and their counterparts in the Scottish Football Association to get on. That is perhaps an essential part of officialdom, to disagree on principle. At any rate, for the first time in history, Edinburgh resented being cut off from Glasgow. Meanwhile, the SFA's War Emergency Cup went ahead with limited club support and was won by Rangers without turning round. By the time Norway and Denmark had fallen to the German panzer divisions the make-up of Scotland's internal football divisions seemed, in comparison, a very trivial matter, but not to officialdom, still entrenched in its pre-war, imperial mentality. Holland and Belgium were over-run and as France was threatened people were singing 'The Last Time I Saw Paris'. Even the football writers were beginning to get impatient. One of the best known, *Waverley*, writing in the *Daily Record* said: 'Any attempt to run football as though nothing was happening in the world outside would be sheer lunacy ...'

One way or other, it looked as if the lunatics were ready to take over the asylum. Rangers, to their credit, tried to make any scheme work that would give the public credible football. Celtic, on the other hand, were apathetic to all changes and wouldn't even take advantage of the star players that the wartime Service posting situation made available to them. They allowed their Exhibition team to disintegrate, and people wondered if they were contemplating seeking asylum in neutral Dublin. Willie Maley was now a sick old man and his fifty-two-year-old relationship with the club was in crisis. Like everything at Celtic Park, it turned on a dispute about money and about the players' eating at the Bank Restaurant, owned by Maley. It was all very petty, and all very Celtic, and it did no one involved much credit. The upshot was that Maley himself was abruptly sacked, as so many of their best players had been, and he spent the next eighteen years in bitter retirement. Then to cap it all, Jimmy Delaney broke his arm and it seemed that the Celtic team fell apart. From being the best in Britain only three years earlier they were now a team of dispirited, inexperienced tyros unable to compete with the forward-marching, relentless Rangers. Playing standards had fallen to an all-time low under the new manager, Jimmy McStay. He had been a great player, but that does not always mean a great manager, as the players realised. He was too nice a man, for one thing. And he was director Kelly's man as well. It was felt at the time that the Celtic Board had really wanted Jimmy McGrory to succeed Maley, even though McGrory seemed firmly tied to Kilmarnock. Small wonder that McStay always felt he was a stand-in manager at best. The decision to do without guest players, the Board's decision, not McStay's, was disastrous. R.E. Kingsley (*Rex*) of the *Sunday Mail* put it neatly when he wrote, in February 1943:

> It used to be a big thrill to beat Celtic; now clubs consider it an indignity if they don't. It may be dire necessity which demands the fielding of so many youngsters who should in the ordinary way be in the reserve side, but it's a bit sad to watch all the same. These

Celtic youngsters are all very clever, but they are all at the same
stage and need a Matt Busby to father them.

Matt Busby had actually trained at Celtic Park and was known to
be 'Celtic-daft' but still the directors not would have him. Former
players like the O'Donnell brothers, Willie Buchan and Charlie Napier
all offered their services but were also refused. Celtic gave the
impression of being on a course of self-destruction, which succeeded
in discouraging their massive and previously loyal support. Celtic did
not appear to be taking wartime football seriously and this ended in
no one in the new League structure taking Celtic seriously.

The Southern League had now been in place for a few seasons, and
although still geographically restricted, it did include Hearts and
Hibernian. Since there was no Scottish Cup, the League introduced
their own League Cup where the teams were divided into four
geographical sections and the winners of each section provided the
semi-finals. It was a brilliant idea which satisfied the restrictions of the
times yet gave the public back the special thrills of the cup tie. A
Summer Cup was also introduced, which was won by Hibernian on
the first occasion, and also by St Mirren, Motherwell and Partick
Thistle in subsequent summers. Otherwise the name of Rangers was
writ large over everything in wartime, much as England's was written
all over the unofficial international scene in those unreal years
between 1939 and 1945. Both swept everything before them. Rangers
beat Celtic by a record 8–1 at Ibrox and England beat Scotland by a
record 8–0 at Maine Road, Manchester – but fortunately for the losers
neither of these results stands in the record books. Crozier of
Brentford had taken over from Dawson in the Scotland goal and
Delaney had returned after his broken arm, but despite the presence of
players of the calibre of Carabine, Busby, Walker, Gillick, Macauley
and Caskie, Scotland could only beat England three times in sixteen
games, and Jock Dodds scored in all three, including a hat-trick in
their 5–4 win over what was arguably the strongest team England has
ever put out in the international field. It is a tragedy for that team, too,
that it reached its peak in unofficial, wartime conditions. It was lucky,
though, for an inferior Scotland.

Although it must be said that it was difficult to know where one
was with the Scottish team in those days, and who was what and
where, with the ubiquitous guest situation complicating selections and
then players not being available because of war work or Service
demands, clubs were unable to build a settled side. Guest players came
and went but most clubs stumbled on, appealing for players from the

crowd on occasions. Many famous players got their first chance this way. It was difficult, too, for supporters. They weren't the prize-hunters of today, interested only in the result – at whatever cost. Supporters then lived up to their name, they supported. They didn't flock to bask in the successes, bought at all costs by the richest team. They rallied round their own. Local men supporting local boys through the worst of it. It was something they didn't choose to do. Theirs wasn't a meek acceptance. They complained loudly, week after week, but they did so with a loving loyalty. They knew that *they* were the club.

The war itself had by now become more serious. Bombs fell on cities and many of these same supporters, civilians, were being killed as regularly as servicemen on duty. Coventry, Clydebank, Bristol and the East End of London now became the new battle grounds and every convoy putting out from the Tail of the Bank ran a gauntlet with killer U-boats. Rationing tightened but what was ironic was that there was more football than ever. The season now lasted for most of the year and clubs, even the biggest of them, were beginning to feel the strain. Dundee Football Club almost went under, but Dens Park was saved by the prompt action of locals from becoming another greyhound stadium. In the same way, Britain itself was saved by the United States who came into the war after Pearl Harbor in 1941. Japan then bicycled into an undefended Singapore. These were the darkest hours of the war, but Britain and her Empire armies won the Battle of El Alamein in 1942 and the corner was turned. As Churchill put it: 'It was not the beginning of the end but it was the end of the beginning.'

Germany had made the Napoleonic error of invading Russia, but Stalingrad held out, and cracks had begun to appear in the Third Reich's previous invincibility. The U-boat was beaten by the discovery of the radar principle and the breaking of the Enigma code led to the destruction of most of the Rhineland by the RAF. The Allies took the initiative now and they had the Nazis on the run, but the Japanese looked as if they might hold out indefinitely until Hiroshima was engulfed in a mushroom cloud and the world hasn't been the same since. Victory came in 1945, as everyone expected. Hitler killed him-self in the ashes of his Berlin bunker and Winston Churchill gave the V-sign to the free world, but all the celebrations had a hollow ring even allowing for all the hysteria of VE night in Britain and VJ night in America. The world was exhausted and drained and just relieved that it was all over for the second time. The only difference was that

that same mushroom cloud hung over victor and victim alike. And it still does. For Hiroshima read Chernobyl.

Football celebrated the resumption of peace with the 1946 Victory Cup won in Scotland by Rangers, of course, and with a Victory International against England at Hampden, won unbelievably by Scotland in the very last minute with a header from Jimmy Delaney. The bunnets went up for a Scotland win at last, but everyone walked home more relieved than victorious. I should know, because I was one of the 139,468 spectators who were there. This time, I didn't see the game from track-side in short trousers but high above on the Somerville Road terracing as a skinny sixteen-year-old in long trousers who walked home to Parkhead not with my Dad but with my school-mates, sorry that the war was over before we got a chance to get in on it. Such is stupid youth. Only National Service loomed for us, but that was two years away. It was time to take a break now. It would take a little time for everything to get back to normal anyway.

The whistle blew for the interval.

Interval Talk

John Stein, CBE (1922–85)

So let us talk of the Big Man, the Boss, the Gaffer, Goliath with a limp. He was all of these, but what he was most famously was the manager of Celtic and of Scotland, and for this latter reason, despite the fact that he was never capped for his country, he has a place in the list of great Scottish football names. Whenever the topic of managers comes up, the same three names emerge every time: Busby, Shankly and Stein – the Blessed Trinity, the Unholy Triad of British football, at the mention of whose names, every Scottish head, at least, is raised a little higher. There is no question of their importance to the game in both England and Scotland, and this was recognised in their lifetimes, but what is seldom realised is the similarity of their backgrounds – all miners, all Lanarkshire, and all, it must be said, lesser players than managers. Busby was the best footballer of the three in his day, Shankly, the toughest tackler and Stein, the steady defender at the rear, but while the three might have made a decent half-back line for a better-than-average club had they ever played together, world-class they were not.

Yet what made them each of them world-class as managers? The answer is that they knew men and recognised that footballers were just men with a special talent, but that they were men first. This is why Busby was the only one who could handle George Best, Jock Stein could control Jimmy Johnstone and Shankly was able to rein in Steve Heighway. The three managers were rich in character and integrity themselves and they found it in their charges, even where it seemed most unlikely. They were also very strong personalities and this radiated from them like light, blinding some, illuminating others, but all the time giving out energy. When that energy is returned from a group of men such as a football team one has a formidable resource on one's hands and this explains much of the success this trio of Scots had at Manchester, Glasgow and Liverpool with their different clubs in different eras and with the various groups of combustible young men under their charge.

No three men could have been more different in their temperaments and individual approaches but what they had in common was a total commitment to and involvement with the job at hand, and for each that job was to weld a football team out of eleven disparate psyches lurking in eleven fit and highly trained bodies. It is not the easiest of jobs in football. To do it well, the manager must be part despot, part witch-doctor, and part father-figure. Busby, the seeming introvert, was obviously the last, with submerged quantities of the other components. Shankly, the seeming extrovert, had his own depths but Stein was neither introvert nor extrovert – he was a practical combination of each so that he appeared self-contained and balanced, and therefore trustworthy. This gave him a striking air of authority, a front he did not disdain to use on occasions. Busby had Frank Murphy to do his shouting for him, Shankly had Bob Paisley to deal with complaints. Stein had no one but himself. He found that sufficient. After all, it was his own self-sufficiency had carried him over a long and winding rough road to success and fame. He had learned the hard way but he had learned well.

John Stein was born in Burnbank in 1922 and, like everyone else he knew, he went down the pits as soon as he left school at fourteen. At sixteen he was playing junior with Blantyre Victoria. He played his football as he worked at the coal face – seeing it as hard graft in order to get results. He never forgot this lesson. Exempt from armed service during the war, he signed as a part-timer with Albion Rovers and stayed with them for seven years until they refused to transfer him to Kilmarnock in 1950 and he walked out. He had to walk as far as Llanelli, in Wales, to get his next job in football after answering an advert: 'Wanted – Players of Proven Ability. Transfer fees no detriment'. Jock got the job. Although it paid well, it was non-League football, and it was getting him nowhere. Besides, his wife was unhappy in Wales. He made up his mind to quit and was on his way to see the manager when he met that gentlemen on his way to see Jock. Celtic made an offer for him out of the blue, on the suggestion of Jimmy Gribben from Baillieston, the assistant trainer, and in 1951 Jock was back in Scotland and back in the big time – at twelve quid a week plus bonuses: two pounds for a win, a pound for a draw.

No one was happier than Mrs Stein. Officially, Jock was hired to coach the reserves but, as Fate would have it, both Celtic central defenders, Alec Boden and Jimmy Mallan, were injured and Stein found himself in the first team. He was to remain there for three years until a bad ankle injury in a game against Rangers ended his playing days and left him with a permanent limp. In 1955 he was appointed coach of the Celtic reserves. He had hoped to become manager after the retiral of Jimmy McGrory, but instead was offered the post of commercial manager. He opted for Dunfermline in 1960 and a year later they won the Scottish Cup. In 1964, he was asked to manage Hibernian and they won the Summer Cup – their first trophy for years. It was then that Celtic realised their error and he became their manager in 1965. The following decade made history not only for Celtic but for the entire Scottish game, and even for British football too, when Celtic became the first British club to win the European Cup in 1967. Under Stein's guidance, Celtic won ten Championships (nine of them in a row), eight Scottish Cups (finalists in the other three) and six League Cups (finalists in seven) between 1965 and 1978. It is an astonishing football record. He was elected to the Celtic Board in 1978 but resigned to join Leeds United after refusing Manchester United – twice – Wolves and Coventry City and even Rangers.

He did not stay long at Elland Road because he was offered the Scotland job soon afterwards and Leeds released him to take it up. He had been in charge of the Scotland team before for a short tenure after the departure of Ian McColl but he had left them to rejoin Celtic. The Scotland job was not a sought-after appointment at that time. The SFA had an unhappy record in its dealings with its managers. Andy Beattie was the first in 1954 but he walked out in 1958 and Matt Busby stepped in for a year as caretaker until Andy returned in 1960 only to walk out again. This was when Ian McColl took over. When Jock left for Celtic John Prentice had the job for a few months but was sacked and replaced by Malcolm MacDonald, who had done so well as manager of Kilmarnock, but his stay with the SFA was brief. Bobby Brown took over and saw out his four-year contract. Tommy Docherty then blew in like a whirlwind but, after a typical flurry, just as quickly blew himself out again.

Then came unexpected success with the best Scottish manager so far, Willie Ormond, but ill-health forced him to retire early and he was replaced by Ally MacLeod. Argentina put paid to the luckless Ally in 1978 and the way was made ready for Stein to take up the reins. Everything he had ever done in football up to that time had prepared him for this appointment.

He had learned what work was in the mines, he knew what real blackness was like. When you have been down a pit you can cope with anything on the surface. This helped him to make the best of things at Albion Rovers and Llanelli, to employ tactics instead of speed on the park when with Celtic, to take full note of every step he made at that club from reserve coach to a seat on the Board, and to savour the experience of success at all levels and to use it now for Scotland. He also had a new zest for life itself, having survived a horrific car accident when returning from holiday in 1975. Now all that was behind him and the way ahead seemed clear. There was perhaps a twinge of regret that he hadn't tried his managerial hand more in England or even on the continent but now he had both hands full to prepare Scotland for another World Cup. He had an unexpected ally in big George Young, who knew the ways of the SFA, and Bobby Evans, who was good with the players, and Danny McGrain, his captain at Parkhead. It looked as if Scotland might even do well. It all depended on how Scotland fared against Wales at Ninian Park, Cardiff, on Tuesday, 10 September 1985. If we lost then we didn't go to the 1986 Finals in Mexico. A draw would do. Could we do it?

With just over half an hour to go, Scotland was down 1–0 and Stein substituted Gordon Strachan with Davie Cooper. Strachan wasn't very pleased and might've spoken out as was his way, but a signal from Alex Ferguson, the Scottish assistant manager, made him bite his tongue. The substitution was a masterstroke. With ten minutes to go, the revitalised Scotland got a penalty. Cooper took it and scored. Scotland was through. Stein rose from the bench to push a photographer out of the way, but he held onto him for too long. On the way back to the tunnel, only five minutes later, he stumbled. He died on the dressing-room table from a heart attack. He was sixty-two years of age. The after-match celebrations stuck in every Scot's throat that night and the Scottish football world has been muted ever since. The huge vacuum he left has never been filled.

PS (Post Stein):
'How do you spell Stein?' asked someone.
A well-known Scottish player replied, 'G.O.D.'

Chapter Ten

Rangers Supreme

When the second half of the Scottish football story resumed after the war, the pre-war Divisions One and Two became the post-war Divisions 'A' and 'B', but the only real difference to the wartime situation was that Aberdeen was back in 'A' with a restored Kilmarnock and a resurrected Queen of the South, and Dundee was back in 'B' with Leith Athletic by 1947. After the atomic big bang it was boom-time in football. Attendances everywhere soared and few noticed that teams like King's Park and St Bernard's were no more. On the other hand, Tam Fergusson, the coalman, created a whole new team, Stirling Albion. Later, Hal Stewart was to import Scandinavians to Cappielow to create an ongoing Greenock Morton for the '60s. Tom Fagan supported Albion Rovers single-handedly from his scrap-yard and to offset the demise of Edinburgh City, Willie McCartney, the big man with the flower in his buttonhole, created a forward-looking Hibernian. These were the large characters that kept football going. At least they had a little more colour than the faceless little bureaucrats who appeared to delight in keeping things as they were. Never mind, happy days were here again and it looked as if they would go on for ever.

Wartime working conditions (all-round-the-clock shifts) had given way again to pre-war hours – 8 a.m. to 6 p.m. for the workers, 9 p.m. to 5 p.m. for the office staff. Banks still closed at three o'clock and all schools came out at four. Most ordinary people worked on Saturday morning but for everyone, at least for men and boys, Saturday afternoon was sacrosanct. Saturday afternoon meant only one thing – the match. Life for many – then and now – began at 3 p.m. on a Saturday and ended 105 minutes later.

Some footballers were unlucky that wartime coincided with their best years and by the time that peace came so did their decline. One, however, who began in the blackout came into his own when the lights went on again. His name was Billy Liddell.

William Beveridge LIDDELL (1922–2001)
Outside-left for Liverpool

51

A two-footed Fifer and a miner's son, Billy Liddell came from Dunfermline, but a pre-war appearance on the left wing for Scotland Schoolboys led him directly to Liverpool where he began his professional football career and where he remained to the end. His first landlady was the widow of Ned Doig, the old Scotland goalkeeper, so young Billy was never far from a football influence. Sensibly, however, he was apprenticed to an accountant and so laid the basis of a very successful business life after football. He first played for his country during the war, in the 5–4 game at Hampden against England and was a regular on the wing until he broke his leg the following year. He returned in 1945, but this time on the losing side against England at Villa Park. Altogether, Billy made eight wartime appearances in addition to his twenty full caps, and he and Stanley Matthews were the only players to feature in both of the two Great Britain teams against the Rest of the World in 1947 and 1955. Always popular, he drew a crowd of almost forty thousand for his testimonial at Anfield. He was the mainstay of Liverpool FC during their barren years – so much so that they were dubbed 'Liddellpool'. He never won an honour with them, but no player could have been more honoured by the city and its supporters during a long and admirable career. He was noted for his work among the youth of Liverpool. He later became Assistant Bursar of Liverpool University and a Justice of the Peace. It is odd to think that such a daring winger should become such a respectable citizen. Billy died of Alzheimer's disease aged 79.

1947 was an *annus mirabilis* for Scots footballers of quality. No fewer than twenty players received their first cap in that year, including most of the Rangers first team, which then featured returned war hero Willy Thornton at centre-forward. Others like Frank Brennan (Airdrie), Billy Campbell (Morton) and Andy McLaren (Preston North End), were recognised in addition to those illustrated in this chapter. And yet the future Sir George Graham, Secretary of the SFA, thought we couldn't make up a team for the 1950 World Cup in South America. Scotland and England had been invited by FIFA to appear at the World Cup Finals in Brazil to mark the British Associations' return to the international body and also as a mark of respect for their contribution to the game since its inception. However, the SFA, or rather Sir George, said that Scotland would only go as Home Champions, but a Bentley goal at Hampden decided that that was not to be, and a great chance was lost to enter onto the world stage at an honourable level. We have had to struggle to get to the Finals ever since. Graham's contention was that 'We hadn't the stuff.' In the wider context, he may have been right, yet we could boast players like Billy Campbell, Jackie Husband, Jimmy Dougall, George Hamilton and Willie Miller – who were all capped in that first season of 1946. Miller of Celtic is remarkable in that he is one of the few players who won international honours without ever winning a medal in *any* domestic competition.

William MILLER (b. 1924)
Goalkeeper for Celtic, Clyde and Hibernian

52

The tragedy of Willie Miller, in the football sense, was that he was at his best when his team, Celtic, were at their worst. He joined them in 1942, at their nadir, and left them in 1950, just when it looked as if they might finally turn the corner, but Willie Miller was not to see the glorious view that awaited that fateful corner-turning. Much to the Celtic supporters' fury, and despite passionate demonstrations outside the ground, which he himself had to come out to pacify, he was put on the transfer list. He went on, nevertheless, to give four good years to Clyde, and even though he was waning by his own standards by 1954, he went on to give a reasonable season to Hibernian before handing in his gloves and going on the road as a whisky rep. Willie Miller was brilliant. There is no other word for it. Season after season, week after week, time after time, this slim, handsome, courageous, curly-haired acrobat held out alone against team after team all around Scotland, while the defence in front of him dithered dismally. The only time he played with good players was when he was picked for Scotland. He said it made him nervous. Playing with Celtic, he knew that everything depended on him. Their League position was determined by how few games they lost rather than by how many they won. Playing at the top level, however, he could rely on a little help. He was unlucky, however, in that recognition was delayed because of Bobby Brown in the Scotland goal, and he was denied further caps by the emergence of Jimmy Cowan, but there is no denying that his six games for Scotland during 1946 and 1947 were feats of valour as well as skill. Who can forget his blood-bandaged head, thrown back as his body arched like the letter 'C' to tip over yet another English volley at Wembley? Once again, he had kept a mighty English forward line at bay despite a severe head injury. Scotland snatched a 1–1 draw, but it was Miller's victory.

Celtic, however, at last managed to get their act together enough to win the Scottish Cup in 1951 and, in keeping with their unique tradition of winning one-off trophies, they also won the St Mungo Cup donated by the Glasgow City Fathers as part of the celebrations for the 1951 Festival of Britain, beating Aberdeen in the final, thanks to the antics of Charlie Tully. To add to the comedy, when the Cup was presented to Celtic in a ceremony at the Kelvin Hall, one of the handles of the Cup fell off. It turned out to be second-hand silver, being a previous award given to the Provan Gas Company. This tournament was followed in 1953 by the Coronation Cup, in which Celtic were involved with Rangers, Aberdeen and Hibernian as Scottish representatives, and Arsenal, Tottenham Hotspur, Newcastle and Manchester United from England. Celtic had a disastrous season again and were in the tournament merely to make weight. Rangers were there as Scottish champions and the other teams were in on merit but, to everyone's astonishment, Celtic beat Arsenal and Manchester United to face Hibernian in the final at Hampden which they won, thanks to the goalkeeping of John Bonnar. Celtic had once again stolen one of their finest hours out of a barren year and against the best forward line in Britain – Hibernian's Famous Five: Smith, Johnstone, Reilly, Turnbull and Ormond. Celtic's captain was a certain John Stein.

When, in 1946, Winston Churchill spoke to America from Missouri, he coined the phrase 'The Iron Curtain' to describe the hold that Russia was taking in Eastern Europe, but all Scotland thought he meant the Rangers' defence which let in only twenty-six goals in winning the first Championship of the new era and drew 2–2 with the celebrated Moscow Dynamo, a match that was *not* in aid of Mrs Churchill's 'Aid to Russia' Fund. Before he retired in 1954, Struth had left a legacy of excellence that would last throughout another decade. Despite his undoubted influence, he would have been the first to state that at Ibrox the players were the thing. Rangers had defenders in the Drummond tradition like Jock Shaw, midfield men in the Meiklejohn tradition like George Young and Willie Woodburn, forwards in the Hamilton and Cunningham tradition like Alec Venters and a goalkeeper who owed more to the Queen's Park tradition, Bobby Brown, but who became the man to replace the legendary Jerry Dawson. All of these players were very conscious of belonging to an Ibrox tradition by which they lived and played and had their being. They were told they were the best so often that they began to believe it, and this self-belief showed on the field. We shall now consider three of this pride of players.

Three Rangers who could be said to be the linchpins of the all-conquering Rangers team of the first decade after the war and the forerunners of those who would keep their grip on Scottish silverware until that hold was broken by Stein's Celtic in the mid-1960s. But that is to anticipate. The day, meantime, belonged to Rangers and Rangers belonged to the likes of Willie Waddell, Willie Woodburn and George Young. Ibrox giants in every sense of the word.

William WADDELL (1921–92)
Outside-right for Rangers

53

Yet another Lanarkshire lad, Willie Waddell made his first appearance for Rangers at Highbury in 1938 and scored the only goal of the game. He made his Scotland debut with Liddell in 1942, and he and Jimmy Delaney made the right wing their own throughout the war. Both players had that knack of enthusing the crowd as soon as they received the ball, but the surging runs of the well-built Waddell along the touchline almost always produced results, especially in club games when he crossed to the head of Willie Thornton. Their partnership became famous, but it was too rarely called on by Scotland. Willie Waddell was idolised at Ibrox and when he returned there as manager, after an eight-year spell as manager of Kilmarnock, he took Rangers successfully into Europe by winning the Cup Winners' Cup in 1972. He was perhaps the nearest thing to the great Bill Struth in the influence he had and the authority he enjoyed. He then followed Alan Morton's example by being moved onto the Rangers' Board. Waddell can be said to be the mainspring behind Rangers' move into the modern era and what they have done since then owes much to his forceful and direct manner. He was not afraid to be blunt to the point of rudeness, but the Rangers' management since has built on what he began.

William Alexander WOODBURN (1919–2001)
Centre-half for Rangers

54

Willie Woodburn ought to have been a rugby player. He went to that kind of school in Edinburgh but Musselburgh Athletic offered him football of the soccer variety. It was from there he graduated via the Queen's Park Victoria XI to Rangers. He first appeared for Scotland in a drawn game at Wembley in 1947 and went on to win twenty-four caps as a strong but stylish centre-half who could play a bit. He was as skilled as any forward in his use of the ball, which did not always endear him to diehard defenders. His one lack on the field was self-control. His international career might have been greater had he been able to control his temper on the field. He was sent off no fewer than five times in his career and on the last, in 1954, the SFA suspended him *sine die*. Many considered him a dirty player, but by today's standards, his offences can only be seen as a vigorous application of his defensive duties. The SFA sentence seemed unduly severe at the time but it effectively killed his career. The sentence was lifted two years later, but Woodburn never came back to the game. Rangers had big George Young in possession of the centre-half position by then, and Willie decided to give all his time to his family garage business in Edinburgh and to take up golf. It was football's loss. He was called 'Big Ben' by his Rangers team-mates because he kept raising his glass to toast 'Viva Benfica' at the banquet after their game against Rangers in 1948. The name stuck, and so does the memory of this fine, footballing centre-half who played as a 'libero' before the word was thought of in the game.

George Lewis YOUNG (1922–97)
Right-back and centre-half for Rangers   55

George Young was a giant of the game in every sense. His sixteen years in the top flight, from joining Rangers from Kirkintilloch Rob Roy until he left to become manager of Third Lanark, are sufficient proof of his consistency and ability. The big man, however, would have preferred to give the reason as a matter of luck and give the credit to the champagne cork he always carried into the dressing-room. Corky made more than thirty-eight consecutive appearances for Scotland, and was captain for a record-breaking forty-eight times. In 1955, he was Scottish Player of the Year. He was at the heart of the famous Rangers 'Iron Curtain' defence for years, either at right-back or centre-half, and did the same sterling work for Scotland. He richly deserves his place in the SFA's official Players' Portrait Gallery at Park Gate. Yet, despite his lucky cork, George had some bad luck too. He was inexplicably dropped for the 1958 World Cup in Sweden and was the unwitting victim of shady commercial underdealings when he was manager of Third Lanark. He watched helplessly as that famous old club was raped and then murdered by ruthless commercial interests and resigned in protest against the increasingly suspicious activities of the Board, or rather those of the chairman at the time. Much to the disgrace of all involved, the valiant old club went under in 1967. Young went into the hotel business and made the same big success in that as he had done in football. He was a big man in every way, and is the only famous Ranger to be guest of the world-famous Kearney Celtic Supporters' Club in New Jersey, USA.

The game was growing up and the players were beginning to realise the power they had but as far as the clubs were concerned they were still bound by the Retain and Transfer system, which meant that players had all the freedom in their profession of a slave on a Virginia plantation. The rumblings were heard in every dressing-room but so far no one had taken a stand and players went on being regarded as so much livestock, the property entirely of their respective clubs. The Players' Union was getting stronger all the time, but at this time was not strong enough and things just went on as before. Rangers continued their winning way in Cup and League while Celtic languished in mid-table, with only Hibernian offering any real competition. Israel was founded and the Russians set up the Berlin Blockade but that did little to alter the state of Scottish football, where, even if Hibernian had set up a new kingdom in the east, it made little difference to the blockade Rangers had set up in the west. It was the status quo and there seemed little hope of ever altering the balance of power as long as Rangers ruled. Don Bradman bowed out of an illustrious cricket career with a duck at the Oval, twelve-year-old Lester Piggott become the youngest-ever winning jockey, and Gorgeous Gussie Moran shocked Wimbledon with her lace panties. At least it brought a bit of colour to drab days.

However, to the football fan there was colour enough on the pitch as the players spilled their blue, green, red and black and blue onto the pitch. The final two players of the class of '47 were Gordon Smith and Billy Steel, the one graceful and lithe, the other chunky and dynamic. They were the two faces of Scottish football, the first smiling and unruffled, the second, scowling and determined, but they both expressed the very best of the Scottish game and the crowd loved one as much as the other. The next pairing in this section, but from 1948, bracketed Jimmy Cowan of Morton with Bobby Evans of Celtic. Goalkeeper Cowan had first made his mark in a British Army side when they played Scotland in Germany after the war, but he was to become famous for what came to be called Cowan's Wembley in 1949. Evans dominated the Coronation Cup final in much the same way, and he played in front of Cowan at Wembley, but it was as Celtic's mainstay in their mediocre years that he is best remembered. He was one of those players who got better as he got older, yet he was so consistently barracked by some supporters when he played for Scotland that he asked at one point not to be considered for selection. Fortunately for Scotland, the selectors ignored the request. The last of the footballing '40s were Lawrie Reilly and Jimmy Mason, a centre-forward and inside-forward of an old and much-respected school, the one an opportunist, the second a schemer and both relying on the other to do their best work. Reilly's reflexes were quicksilver, Mason's guile was deadly and between them they represented a worthy Scottish football tradition in their positions, even though Reilly often featured at outside-left. They too were at Cowan's Wembley, both scoring, and significantly, they were never on a losing Scottish team together. So here they are, six of the best from the austere '40s, to show that however strict rationing still was, Scotland, if nothing else, was rich in football talent and in a superabundance of supporters. Loyal, stoic, full of fun and wisecracks as their feet froze on decrepit terracings and water from leaking, rusting roofs dripped down their necks. The supporter put up with much in the barbaric conditions he endured, but like his father before him, and his father before that, he thought it was worth it. A great goal covers a multitude of inconveniences – or a lack of them.

Gordon SMITH (b. 1924)
Outside-right for Hibernian, Hearts, Dundee and Drumcondra 56

Gordon Smith, known in his day as the Gay Cavalier (unfortunately, not an epithet that would be appreciated today), had a wonderful football career that spanned twenty-three years in all. Like Alex Jackson, he had an attractive style and he also looked good on the field. Beneath the superficial attraction, however, was true football steel, as his three hundred goals showed, and as his three Scottish Championship medals with three different clubs amply demonstrate. The stamina and concentration required to maintain such a high standard for so long and to make it all seem so effortless, indicates his class. His grace on the run, cloaking a deceptive speed, allowed him to seize on half-chances around the goal area, hence his high tally of goals. He once scored five against Third Lanark – still a record for a winger. Lawrie Reilly remembers him running along the touchline keeping up the ball on his head against the same club. 'Yet the Third Lanark players didn't hack him down,' he said. 'The old supporters talk about it yet.' Gordon was Scottish Player of the Year in 1951. On moving to Hearts in 1959 after recovering from injury, he fell back into the role of playmaker, a position he continued in until he joined Dundee in 1961. This made him the architect rather than the builder, but all the old rhythm was still in his play, as was evident from the success these teams achieved while he was with them. He played first-class football until he was nearly forty, when he turned out for

Drumcondra in Ireland until 1964. This was a tribute not only to his easy style but to his fitness and professional attitude. He might be taken as a model type of player and deserved more caps than he got during his career, although he did captain the side against Hungary in 1955. There were many good wingers at this stage – Willie Waddell, Jimmy Delaney, Johnny McKenzie, Graham Leggat, etc. – but there was only one Gordon Smith. The game is not the same without him.

William STEEL (1923–82)
Inside-forward for Leicester City, St Mirren, Morton, Derby County, Dundee and in USA

57

Billy Steel came from Denny, where Jimmy McMullen had also come from. Small, strong and tricky, Steel was in the long tradition of Scottish inside men and arguably the most skilful Scottish footballer of the immediate post-war generation. He also packed a lethal shot in his size five boots. Always a handful for defenders, he came into wide prominence as a member of the Great Britain team against the Rest of the World in 1947. He scored a memorable goal and from then on 'Mr Perpetual Motion', as he was called, was on the move. First to Derby County for a then-record fee, the first five-figure sum to be paid for a Scot, and then on through a series of transfers that caused Dundee to pay a Scottish record fee for him and finally took him to Hollywood of all places. Appropriate too, for this little fellow was always a star, despite his caustic tongue on the park and his controversial antics off it. Nevertheless, he was an automatic choice for Scotland, much as Alan Morton was in his day. At one point, Billy played in nineteeen consecutive internationals and it would have been more had he not been sidelined by an ankle injury. He was also the first Scot to be sent off in an international match. Unlike so many, his game didn't deteriorate as he went on. He went out as he came in, with a bang – and a Hollywood bang at that. That was Billy Steel, one of the greatest inside-forwards of all time.

James Clews COWAN (1926–68)
Goalkeeper for St Mirren, Morton, Sunderland and Third Lanark

58

Everyone has their five minutes in the sun, but on the afternoon of 9 April 1949, Jimmy Cowan of Morton had forty-five, if not twice that, as he single-handedly defied the English forward line to allow Scotland a win at Wembley. He was carried off the field as a hero, the first time that had happened since a Scottish team carried off Harry McNeil at Hamilton Crescent in 1874. Skipper George Young had told his forwards, 'You get on with the scoring. We'll hold these fellows without your help.' Cowan did just that on the day, while Mason, Steel and Reilly got the goals. From that day it was known to the fans as Cowan's Wembley. Even his start in the senior game was dramatic. He had signed first for his home team, St Mirren, but had been given a free transfer to Morton while in the Army. On leave on one occasion, he had been hurriedly called into the side to replace regular keeper Archie McFeat, and, just like Jimmy Brownlie, saved two penalties on his debut. He was again the hero in the Scottish Cup final of 1948, holding the mighty Rangers to a replay. Not long afterwards, he broke his arm but recovered to make his own little bit of Wembley history. He was transferred to Sunderland in 1953 following eighteen consecutive appearances for Scotland, but returned to his homeland to play out his career with Third Lanark. He died aged only forty-two, following a sudden illness, but he will never be forgotten in Scottish football.

Robert EVANS (1927–2001)
Half-back for Celtic, Chelsea, Newport County, Morton, Third Lanark and Raith Rovers

59

Bobby Evans began as a left-winger for Celtic, but fell back to right-half to accommodate team problems in 1948 when Celtic faced relegation for the first time in their existence and had to beat Dundee at Dens Park to stay up. They did so thanks to a Jock Weir hat-trick and a towering display by Evans in defence and attack. He had found his real position at last, and this was acknowledged when he was voted Scotland's Player of the Year in 1953. Later in his career with Scotland (he won forty-eight caps) he moved to centre-half and remained there till the end of his long career in 1967, when he was almost forty years of age. He twice captained Scotland against England and he was never to appear in a losing Scottish side. His enthusiasm for the game never waned, despite increasing pain from a back injury sustained in 1958. Although not tall, he was good in the air, and his stocky frame lent weight to his terrier-like tackling. He kept good wing-halves like Ian McColl and Tommy Docherty out of the Scotland side for season after season, and his red-headed spirit was worth at least a goal in any match. He had an outstanding football career, because he got back from the game almost as much as he put into it, in game after game, at every level, for season after season, and not only with Celtic, but with his many clubs thereafter. All in all, he was a credit to the sport.

Lawrence REILLY (b. 1928)
Centre-forward for Hibernian

60

Lawrie Reilly, like Willie Woodburn, went to Boroughmuir, an Edinburgh rugby-playing school, but that didn't prevent his becoming one of Scotland's great centre-forwards and the most capped Hibernian player, with thirty-eight in all. He led the Famous Five, that Hibernian forward line of the '50s – Smith, Johnstone, Reilly, Turnbull and Ormond – that did so much to decorate the Scottish game of that time, and win so much for their club. The story is that whenever the defence let in a couple of goals, Reilly would quip, 'Oh, don't say we have to score four again?' And often, they did. He was the leading Scottish goalscorer for three successive seasons and only a bout of illness in 1954 prevented his adding even more and beating Hughie Gallacher's scoring record. In 1957, he played for Scotland at Wembley with stitches in his leg, and also helped Scotland to reach the World Cup Finals in Sweden. What he is best known for, however, was his ability to score vital goals with almost the last kick of the ball, as he did in 1951, 1952, 1955 and 1956. He never gave up, whether for Hibernian or Scotland, and so earned himself the name 'Last-Minute' Reilly. He was a painter by trade and a publican by profession, but most of all he was Hibernian's most famous centre-forward. He turned down a chance to become a director of the club, choosing instead to sit in the stand in a reserved seat. He reverted to being a supporter again. That says much for the man – and the club. Incidentally, Lawrie made his Scotland debut at outside-left with Jimmy Mason as his inside partner. 'Jimmy made it so easy for me,' he said. 'I couldn't fail.'

James MASON (1906–71)
Inside-forward for Third Lanark

61

Jimmy Mason played for a much-respected but unfashionable club and paid the penalty in lack of appropriate recognition at international level. The little Glasgow trickster had his pick of senior clubs in 1936 when Tom Jennings signed him for Third Lanark. Leicester had made the unique offer of paying for him to attend university if he joined them, but at seventeen that held no great attraction for Jimmy, nor did offers from Arsenal and Rangers either. Yet how different his career might have been had he signed for either of these. And how different, too, his international career if he hadn't come into his full football maturity during the war years when he guested with Portsmouth and Charlton. He had to wait until 1948 to get his first full cap, when he played against Wales at Cardiff, but he stamped his mark on the inside-right position and nine further honours came his way by 1951. Lazio tried to lure him to Italy with a house and a car and a convent education for his children, but despite long appeals, Jimmy refused to sign. He said he had a house and a car, and his four children already went to a good school. In 1952, he suffered a groin injury and was forced to retire at thirty-four after sixteen years with the Thirds. A Scotland Select played for his testimonial in 1953. The proceeds assisted him to become licensee of a popular bar in Bridgeton.

The time had now come to go out into the world – the World Cup – and in 1954 it was held in Switzerland. Scotland had its first-ever manager, albeit temporary, Andy Beattie, and it was typical of the situation he found himself in that he threatened to resign before he even met the players. The selectors chose only thirteen players for the trip. No Rangers players were included because they were on a trip to the USA. They were lucky. Scotland landed in the group which included Austria and Uruguay and lost by one to the first and by seven to the second. One of the selectors commented fatuously, 'Never mind, just as long as we beat England.' It was time to get off the park – and quickly.

Chapter Eleven

Foreign Fields

In 1953, the beginning of the second Elizabethan Age, Hungary came to Wembley and gave England a lesson in the old Scottish football methods. It was evident that the old 'Professors' like Jackie Robertson had done their work well. Which is more than can be said for the Scotland team of 1955. Poor Freddy Martin of Aberdeen froze in goal at Wembley in 1955 and Stanley Matthews made a right Harry Haddock out of Clyde's normally reliable left-back. Reilly had his usual goal a game and Tommy Docherty got one from right-half, but England scored *seven*. It was Davidson of Partick Thistle's eighth cap at centre-half and his last. Big George Young resumed as captain as Scotland tried to make the best of a bad year. Martin had some consolation in that he won a Cup medal with Aberdeen in the same season. 1955–56 was also notable for the fact that Accrington Stanley, founder members of the Football League in 1888, set a record in that League by fielding a team for the current Third Division season composed entirely of Scotsmen. The 'Scotch Professors' were obviously still in demand. They were unable, however, to prevent Accrington Stanley going out of existence not long afterwards. The second Elizabethan Age was by now two years underway and floodlights made their first appearance. What was more ominous was that television made its first approaches to the football authorities. They were not well received, but it wasn't the end of the matter. Before a year was out, viewers at home would watch Celtic lose to Clyde in a Scottish Cup final after a replay. What made it all the more galling for Celtic was that Clyde's winning goal which took the cup to Shawfield was scored by their outside-left, Tommy Ring, a self-confessed Celtic supporter. It appears that when Tommy went to his mother's for the usual Sunday lunch, his brothers wouldn't speak to him. Loyalties go deep in Glasgow. The football fan has two families, and it's a question which one has the priority. The Ring brothers made it up, of course, but there was no denying it was a tense lunch.

A lot of things were changing in football. The groundswell of player-power was rising but was just being held in check. The game was becoming less and less parochial and insular and was being forced to look out and beyond its historical borders. This didn't suit officialdom, which cherished small authority spread wide instead of taking a wider and longer view, which would have allowed them to see the way that football was going. And it was going more and more out of Scotland. Paradoxically, it was reaching into more homes as *Match of the Day* became a match nearly every other night, and Scottish viewers were able to see Manchester United and Real Madrid and AC Milan from their armchairs instead of watching Albion Rovers and Cowdenbeath and Ayr United from prehistoric terraces. A revolution was afoot, and even if it were bloodless, it was not going to be silent. The premier clubs talked openly about Super Leagues and players had a sense of horizons other than Scotland's Division One. Football was never more popular but it was in the process of changing from a national sport to an international entertainment industry. Some closed minds couldn't open up to this fact. There would have to be a lot of thinking done, and quickly, before the people's game was lost to the media moguls with a greed for money-power. Football Scotland had to get herself out into the world and play with the big boys.

William Russell Logan BAULD (1928–77) 62
Centre-forward for Hearts

Had Willie Bauld's thunderbolt gone in instead of hitting the crossbar in the Hampden game against England, Scotland would have won the Home Championship and gone to the World Cup in Brazil in 1950. As has been mentioned previously, both England and Scotland might have been there as of right. They were formally invited but the SFA, in its high-handed way, had decided that Scotland would only go as champions or not at all. This short-sighted and idiotic decision robbed Willie Bauld of a World Cup chance and put Scotland back, in world football terms, for years. England, however, did go and were sensationally beaten by a United States team that happened to contain two Scots. Willie Bauld's cap chance never came again and the three he won in this one year were his only international recognition. And yet, at the time, he was perhaps one of the most effective centre-forwards in Scotland, at the spearhead of that deadly Tynecastle trio of Conn, Bauld and Wardhaugh who performed so heroically for Hearts. Unfortunately, Bauld was contemporaneous with Reilly in much the same way as McGrory was with Gallacher, and his appearances for Scotland suffered accordingly. But not his almost mythological status with Hearts supporters. He continued to delight them with his swashbuckling style as he, the D'Artagnan, flanked by his Porthos and Athos, led Hearts towards that long-awaited League Championship of 1958. At the very start of his career, when playing with Musselburgh Athletic, he had signed forms for Sunderland but there was some kind of irregularity and the registration was cancelled. He was then free to sign for Hearts – as Fate no doubt had intended.

It is sobering to think that Willie Bauld died when still comparatively young. Sadly, so did Wardhaugh and Conn. So many footballers go out quickly once they've left the playing pitch, or survive as cripples to rheumatism and lumbago. The price that young men pay later for the requirement of being constantly fit is not often considered. The records show that only four Scottish players have died *on* the field: John Thompson, of course, full-back James Main of Hibernian at Firhill in 1909, goalkeeper Josiah Wilkinson of Dumbarton FC at Ibrox in 1921 and big Bob Mercer, a centre-half who had a fatal heart attack while playing for a Hearts XI against Selkirk in 1926. The number seriously injured in play is happily in the minority, but it is salutary to think of those many more who have succumbed to lingering illness soon after their playing days are over. They are late victims to the accumulation of injuries and the effects of stress and tension arising from continuing competition at the highest level. Some, of course, thrive on it but others don't and it is good to remember them too. There is of course the rare case of football martyrdom, when Columbia's Andres Escobar was shot by vengeful supporters because he had let in an own goal during the 1994 World Cup. There may have been gambling ramifications here, but it is still a terrible price to pay. Even worse is that his three assassins called out 'Goal!' as thy pumped their bullets into his chest. Escobar is well remembered, but so many of football's real heroes go unsung.

Similarly, many of our better players do not get the rewards, either financial or in public recognition, that their talents deserve. Whether by personality or character, whether by fashion or custom, a good player is bypassed in favour of others who are patently not as good but satisfy some other criterion then in vogue. The better player, if he is a good professional, accepts the situation and gets on with his game. He builds a good career for himself at club level, winning the respect of everyone in the game, except the press perhaps – and the selectors. A good example of two such players, vastly different in temperament but similar in the international neglect of their talents, is the case of Celtic's Bertie Auld and Willie McNaught of Raith Rovers. The volatile Celt and the phlegmatic Rover may seem an odd pairing, but between them they represent what is finest about the old-fashioned Scottish game – abundant skill allied with poise and assurance and the inborn ability to read every game fluently.

Robert AULD (b. 1938)   63
Winger and inside-forward for Celtic, Birmingham City and Hibernian

It is hard to believe that the astute and guileful Bertie Auld, the arch-schemer of inside-forwards, began his football with Partick Thistle youth club as a full-back and it was when he joined the junior Maryhill Harp that he became a left-winger. He joined Celtic as such the first time around but his individual style did not suit the autocratic regime existing at that time in Parkhead and he was sold off to Birmingham like hot coals – being too hot to handle. Luckily for Scottish football, one of the first things Jock Stein did when he became manager was to fetch a shovel and bring the hot coals back promptly. Stein was quick to recognise the value of a firebrand to the team he was slowly building and he moved Bertie inside for even greater effect. He had only three caps in all but that didn't detract from his impact on Celtic and the Scottish game. Bertie Auld was too hot for a lot of people to handle, including defenders, and the stuffy SFA of the time wouldn't think him ideal team material for what was often a stuffy Scottish side. What they needed, in fact, was the Napoleonic touch that only Bertie could provide, but perhaps he was too dangerous to trust. Celtic fans adored him for that very daring and his tandem touch with Murdoch was the basis of the legendary Lions. At the end of his playing phase, he became manager of Partick Thistle. He had turned full circle but it was only the start of a somersault which took him to Hibs as their manager, complete with cigar. The fires were by no means extinguished, but too many people couldn't stand the heat Bertie generated in the kitchen. He was 'fired' several times.

William McNAUGHT (b. 1922)   64
Left full-back for Raith Rovers

The handful of caps won by Willie McNaught between 1951 and 1955 did scant justice to this classy full-back's ability and influence. At a time when backs were required to get rid of the ball at all costs and when in doubt, kick it out, McNaught took the time to be constructive, and in the manner of Celtic's McNair, he played the ball forward to a team-mate whenever posssible thus starting an attack rather than merely spoiling one. His long passing was quite uncanny and he had good on-ball skills. McNaught had many admirers (he was Scotland's Footballer of the Year in 1956) but he played for a provincial club to whom he was totally loyal, and the lack of the larger arenas and continued experience at the highest level told against his regular international selection. He was one of that admirable band of one-club players and belonged to an era when club loyalty meant something. It had no financial incentive whatsoever, the player could only look forward to his testimonial match as any kind of reward. This was the kind of player Willie McNaught was, the kind of man he was. A further service he did for Scotland was that he brought forward the talents of the very young Jim Baxter. He taught the youngster to play it cool, that ninety minutes was long enough to win any game. It was the time on the ball that mattered.

Meantime, Celtic made one of their geyser-like emergings from the still pond of their own mediocrity to thrash Rangers 7–1 in the final of the 1957 Scottish League Cup at Ibrox. No one knows where this flash of fine football came from, nor the record-breaking score, but the *Glasgow Herald* had no doubt that the architect of the win was Willie Fernie, the Celtic and Scotland inside-forward playing that day at right-half.

> This wonderful footballer who achieves his purpose without the merest suggestion of relying on the physical, and who suffers the crude, unfair attempts to stop him without a thought of retaliation.

This reads much like a notice this same paper would have given to a Victorian player. As indeed, Willie Fernie was. A timeless, classy player of consummate skill, who might have been in these pages in his own right had space permitted. His style and self-control roused Celtic to a one-off display of attacking football which delighted the purists and gave one hope for the essential Scottish game carried by the early 'Professors' around the world. It had nothing to do with stamina and aggression and power, but with subtlety, incisiveness and skill with the long pass. It depended on a certain kind of player and Scotland has always had this type. They are as stereotypical of Scotland as the ship's engineer, Highland gillie or gruff but kindly GP. All the world recognises the breed – small in stature, slight in physique but big in football brains. Willie Fernie was one, John Mudie of Blackpool was another, Wardhaugh of Hearts too. There was also Ian McMillan of Rangers, Pat Quinn of Motherwell and many others in every level of football and in every generation. Two more can be added from this period, who amply illustrate that the strain continues, the two Bobbies – Messrs Collins and Johnstone.

Robert Young COLLINS (b. 1931)   65
Forward for Celtic, Everton, Leeds United, Bury, Morton,
Oldham Athletic, Shamrock Rovers and in Australia

Bobby Collins was almost an Everton player from the start. He and his father travelled down to Liverpool by train but nobody met them at the station, so they just about-turned and went back to Glasgow where Celtic were more than happy to sign him up. He may have been pint-sized, but he got an extraordinary mileage per gallon out of his football journeyings. He had a longer than usual international career (six years) and even then it was halted only by a broken thigh. This still did not prevent his turning out for Oldham Athletic as player-manager in 1973 – twenty-three years after his debut for Scotland. He developed from a cheeky little winger with Celtic into an astute inside-forward with Everton and a chunky little midfield man with Leeds. He was the first Scot to have been elected Footballer of the Year in England (1965) and like a true Scottish forward he was always greedy for the ball, but he could be just as tenacious defending as in attack. He played a large part in taking Leeds to Division One in 1963, and wherever he played, at whatever level, he had the same indomitable influence on his team-mates, and therefore on the result. Jack Charlton, the Leeds and England centre-half, summed him up exactly:

> A very, very strong, skilful little player, but what marked him out, what made a difference to the Leeds sides he played in, was his total commitment to winning. He was so combative, like a little flyweight boxer. He would kill his mother for a result.

Bobby's nickname in his Parkhead days was 'Lester' after Lester Piggott, the champion jockey of the day, who was renowned for his ability to win and the dedication and determination that went with it. The little footballer had exactly the same attitude. He expected to win every game and resented when he didn't. Latterly, Collins took his football know-how to Australia. It was just the size of country that suited his huge football talent.

Robert JOHNSTONE (b. 1929)
Inside-right for Hibernian, Manchester City and Oldham Athletic 66

Bobby Johnstone was the baby of the Famous Five, yet he had an old football head on those young shoulders and he operated with some guile behind the fleet-footed Gordon Smith on the wing and the spearhead provided by Lawrie Reilly. Coming as he did from Selkirk, in the heart of Scottish rugby country, his football skills were perhaps surprising, but nonetheless he made rapid progress from Newton-grange Bluebell via Hibernian and Manchester City to the Great Britain side against the Rest of Europe in 1955. He was the first man to score in successive Cup finals at Wembley with Manchester City and was also in six successive internationals against England between 1951 and 1956. The whole is no greater than the sum of all its parts, but Johnstone's part in the best-ever forward line Hibernian ever had, also his part in the two Cup final sides for Manchester City and in his many games for Scotland, ensure that his place in the Scotland football story is not inconsiderable. He concluded a very successful career at Oldham. Bobby Johnstone was noted particularly for his mastery of the long, defence-splitting pass.

The decade had begun with someone stealing the Stone of Destiny from Westminster, but before the decade was out Scots felt someone had stolen their scone – in football terms, at least. The SFA was finding it hard to adjust to foreign fields. In 1958 Scotland qualified to go to Sweden, but they went without George Young, who for some reason was coldly passed over as captain and player. It was as if a large mountain had been removed from the skyline in the Scottish camp. The resulting draught of chilly air was anything but bracing and the atmosphere among the players was not comfortable. Big George had been a shelter from some of the bureaucratic bungling, he could read the official mind and had the ear of George Graham, but now he was gone, and already he was missed.

A trainer (Dawson Walker) was appointed as yet another temporary manager and every error made in 1954 was duplicated in 1958. It would seem as if Scottish football did not travel well. The lightweight players, for all their skill, were no match for the brawn and muscle of World Cup encounters, and Scotland, after losing to France and again to Paraguay, finished up last in their group.

Yet they had the players. It was as if all the ingredients were there for the feast but there was no chef – or else, there were too many, and as a result the Scotch broth was well and truly spoiled. *The Goon*

Show was then all the rage on the radio and the Scottish road show was going some way to rival it for laughs. The team needed a strong character in charge. The irony was that they had two players in the squad who were later to make excellent managers in their different ways – Tommy Docherty and Willie Ormond.

Thomas Henderson DOCHERTY (b. 1928)
Wing-half for Celtic, Preston North End and Arsenal

67

Born in the Depression years, Tommy is the ex-baker's boy who has made a lot of dough, not from football but from talking about it. He is one of the most sought after-dinner speakers on the celebrity circuit because he is opinionated, direct and funny. He says himself he's had more clubs than Jack Nicklaus. Starting with Celtic in 1947, the club he supported as a local East End boy, he had the first of his many clashes with management and moved on to Preston North End in 1949. It was while he was at Deepdale with such as Bill Shankly and Tom Finney that he won his first cap. Being Tommy, he immediately asked for a rise, if not in his playing wage then at least in his close season figure. 'I want the same as Tom Finney,' stated the Doc. 'You're not as good as Tom Finney,' he was told. 'In the close season, I am,' he replied. He got his raise. In 1958, he transferred to Arsenal, and finally, to Chelsea as a player-coach in 1961. His first managerial job was with Rotherham in 1967. It only lasted a season but it could be said that it was from this point that his second career really started. The hard-tackling wing-half, with twenty-five caps for Scotland, a Scotland captain and manager in his time, gave way to the hard-talking, wise-cracking, inspirational manager who worked as hard on his own image as he did on his players, whether at Rotherham United, Queen's Park Rangers, Aston Villa, Hull City, Manchester United, Derby County, Preston North End, Oporto FC, Sydney Olympic or even as manager of Scotland. His volatile second career, studded with litigation and controversy, as critics have noted, ended in 1982 when his third career began – as a professional talker. This was immediately successful and he's still talking. He'll talk on anything – as long as it's football. He is more than an after-dinner entertainer, however. He was too good a footballer to be merely that.

William Esplin ORMOND OBE (1927–84)
Outside-left for Stenhousemuir, Hibernian and Falkirk

68

Willie Ormond was the shy man of the Hibernian Famous Five. On the other wing was the debonair Smith, inside, the mischievous Johnstone and robust Turnbull, and at the front the mercurial Reilly, but Ormond went about his business in his usual unassuming way and just as effectively got results. With the same quiet efficiency he became a successful Scottish manager when he followed Tommy Docherty into the job in 1973 and led the finest-ever group of players to represent Scotland to the 1974 World Cup Finals in Germany. They were the only unbeaten team in the tournament but, in the end, goal difference prevented their reaching the knockout stages. There was only one goal in it. Despite this, a crowd of ten thousand supporters met the team on their return to Scotland, and no one was cheered louder than their modest manager. Much was expected of this Scottish team but the very next year they were soundly beaten by England. Some critics blamed poor discipline off the pitch rather than lack of ability on it but Ormond retired to his Musselburgh pub, giving way to the flamboyant Ally MacLeod as Scotland manager. He was awarded the OBE for his services to the game in Scotland. It was no more than he deserved.

Among the same pool of players at this time was a future president of the SFA, Tommy Younger.

Thomas YOUNGER (1930–84)
Goalkeeper for Hibernian, Liverpool, Falkirk, Stoke City and Leeds United

69

Tommy Younger's personality was as large as the goalmouth he inhabited. Expansive and gregarious, he embraced all aspects of the game and it is significant that he returned to Hibernian to become their public relations officer at the end of his playing career. He was as right for that job as he was for the last line of defence, although he was no mean outfielder too. Once, in an Army game, he bet one of his team-mates that he could score a hat-trick if he played at centre-forward. He was taken on – and he did. He joked his way through all his clubs, but that didn't hide the fact that he played in goal for Scotland for twenty-four successive matches between 1955 and 1958, which is still a record for a goalkeeper, and only six of those games were lost. He captained the side at the 1958 World Cup and, although this wasn't the happiest experience for him, especially against Paraguay, he could look back on a good run for his country. He was prone to injury due to his remarkable daring in the goal area and once played against England with a bandaged hand. Ironically, he made his money after football from a franchise in one-armed bandits. There was no putting him down and when he was invited onto the Hibernian Board he proved an unexpectedly able administrator. So much so that in 1983, cigar in hand, the other waving to all and sundry, he succeeded Willie Harkness as President of the SFA – the youngest man ever to be appointed to this office. Then, early in 1984, not long after the death of his wife, Diana, he suddenly died. It was if a very large tree had been abruptly cut down.

Rangers won the Scottish First Division in season 1958–59 but strangely contributed only one player to the Scottish team – their captain, Eric Caldow.

Eric CALDOW (b. 1934)   70
Left-full-back for Rangers, Stirling Albion and Corby Town

Heroic and gentlemanly, Eric Caldow missed only two international appearances from his first selection in 1957 until his final appearance in 1963. He won forty caps for Scotland, but on his fortieth appearance he broke a leg in a collision with England's Bobby Smith and never appeared for his country again. He had always been quick on the turn and though wingers might pass him, they never succeeded in getting their crosses over. Caldow was an automatic choice for left-back from the beginning of his international career, and had he not been injured, would certainly have won even more caps. He succeeded Bobby Evans as captain of the Scotland side and took special responsibility for penalty kicks, at which he had some skill. What is remarkable about Caldow's international career was that he partnered such an array of full-backs such as Bobby Shearer, Dunky McKay, Alec Parker, John Grant and Alex Hamilton. He had seen them come and go, but he had remained constant on the left flank – until he broke his leg. That says it all. He went on to Corby Town to play out his career but he is still remembered as the gentleman footballer who broke his leg at Wembley. Today he graces the hospitality rooms at Ibrox and recently his medal collection was auctioned at Christie's.

*

In England, Arthur Rowe was building the famous Tottenham Hotspur, captained by Ireland's Danny Blanchflower, which would win the FA League and Cup double with their push-and-run tactics. (This form of triangular progression was adapted later by Holland in their revolving form of Total Football. What is less well known is that it echoes the close passing game initiated by Queen's Park.) At the heart of that great Spurs team were three Scots – Mackay, Brown and White.

David Craig MACKAY (b. 1934)

Right half-back for Hearts, Tottenham Hotspur, Derby County and Swindon Town

71

Dave Mackay was in the ferro-concrete tradition of Scottish defenders who made their name by their iron dependability in the face of whatever odds. Mackay won every honour in the game and at every level from schoolboy caps to full international, from Scottish League Cup (with Hearts) to FA Cup with Tottenham Hotspur and joint Footballer of the Year when at Derby County. He was the first player to represent the Scottish Football League against the Football League and in the next season, the Football League against the Scottish League. He could score with either foot and was especially effective at long range – witness his two goals against Norway in 1963 and his special skill at the long throw. However, it is as a steely defender that he is best known. A twice-fractured leg put him out of contention for nearly two years, but he came back again as strong as ever, in the heart if not the leg, and won for himself a place as one of Scotland's sturdiest defenders. He didn't always appear on the winning side, but he never let you believe that. As long as the ball was in the air and players were on the park, to Dave Mackay there was always a chance of winning the game, whatever the score. This very Scottish attitude was one which he exemplified to the full in every game he played. The only irony is that he didn't win often enough. He may have had two broken legs, but never a broken heart. His career in management has taken him from Swindon to Walsall and, in 1978, to the Arabic Sporting Club in Kuwait.

William Dallas Fyfe BROWN (b. 1931)
Goalkeeper for Dundee, Tottenham Hotspur, Northampton Town and Toronto Falcons 72

Having been for so long bridesmaid to Tommy Younger's bride, Bill Brown at last got his chance against France in 1958 while he was with Dundee. He took it to such effect that by the time he played his last international game, against Italy at Hampden in 1965, and was Tottenham Hotspur's regular keeper, he had beaten Jimmy Cowan's record of caps for a goalkeeper and set a new one – twenty-eight. Long and lean, he was the very acme of consistency. During Spurs' famous double year in 1960–61 he never missed a single game in either League or Cup. So prized was he at Tottenham that they wouldn't release him to tour with Scotland in Europe and so further caps were lost, but it did not in any way lessen his status as an international goalkeeper and it could be said that he had made his mark all the way up from Dundee Schoolboys to the Toronto Falcons at the end of a distinguished and rewarding career. Bill Brown's schooldays were only the start of it but they laid a firm foundation for all the football to come. He retired to a successful business career in London.

John Anderson WHITE (1937–64)
Inside-forward for Alloa Athletic, Falkirk and Tottenham Hotspur 73

A first-rate cross-country runner, and a golfer with a handicap of fourteen, John was known by football fans as the 'White Ghost' because of the way in which he flitted over the park, almost as if he were keeping out of the way, until he suddenly appeared to send through a telling pass, or score, when everybody seemed to have forgotten all about him. Yet John White was a shrewd and skilful inside-forward, who from his first international appearance (in which he scored) against West Germany in 1959 suggested a long international career ahead. He was part of the Spurs famous 'double' team along with Brown and Mackay, who were also his international colleagues. White missed several international calls because of club commitments, but then a game of golf at Crews Hill Golf Club in 1964 put an end to more than a career. He was sheltering under a tree during a thunderstorm and was struck by a bolt of lightning. He was found sitting with a towel around his shoulders, and medical opinion is that, had he received immediate resuscitation, he might well have recovered, but he never regained consciousness. He was only twenty-seven years of age. Bill Nicholson, his manager at Tottenham, was convinced that we had not seen the best of John White. 'He hadn't yet reached his peak,' he said. We can only imagine the heights he might have attained, and regret that one game should accidentally lose so much to another.

Billy Wright, of Wolves and England, was the first player to win a hundred caps, and did so in the 1959 game against Scotland at Wembley which England won 2–1. Scotland next lost to Austria and then to Poland, but then, to everyone's surprise, drew with the mighty Magyars of Hungary, who had so soundly beaten England. Thus finished the football '50s, but before they did, one Scottish player made his debut (in 1958, against Wales at Cardiff) in the same game as Matt Busby made his as team manager. The player concerned was Denis Law, and, as far as Scotland is concerned, he almost deserves a whole chapter to himself.

Chapter Twelve

Swinging Soccer

At the beginning of the '50s, there was no such thing as a teenager. By the start of the '60s, however, there were more than five million of them in Britain alone, with (it was reckoned) more than five hundred million pounds to spend. That made them a market force to be counted. In 1950 it was a world without Elvis Presley, but by 1960 there were at least a hundred third-rate impressionists of him making a good living from him with a guitar and a head of hair. We had Tommy Steele and Bridgeton's own Lonnie Donegan, both incidentally quite good footballers too. In the early '50s, only the favoured few had a television set. By the end of the decade, nearly every home had one. Similarly, around 1951, a young Aberdonian schoolboy had to get a note from his mother giving him permission to take off his spectacles to play football, but by 1958 he had become a professional footballer and received the first of his fifty-five international caps, being selected to play for Scotland against Wales at Cardiff. His name was Denis Law.

Denis LAW (b. 1940)
Forward for Huddersfield Town, Manchester City, Torino,
Manchester United and Manchester City

74

One of the great forwards of all time, one of the first strikers in the modern game, Denis Law ran the whole gamut of the Scottish game from A (for Aberdeen Schools) to Z (for Zaire, his final opponents in the 1974 World Cup). Such was his impact on the game internationally that a Mr and Mrs Bergkamp of Holland named their son after the great Scot. This was something of a gamble as the young Dutchman may have turned out to have a talent for snooker! The original Denis always gave the impression when playing that he was, literally and metaphorically, a Law unto himself. His style was all-out attack with flair and a genius for the unexpected. He was often as much of a surprise to his own team-mates, but there was no denying his 101 per cent commitment to the team on the day. Huddersfield Town took on a gangling, fair-haired Aberdonian with a squint in his left eye on the recommendation of the manager's brother. They put him up in digs, corrected his squint, gave him an English accent, and threw him into the first team at sixteen. The boy revelled in the challenge and in 1959, when he was just eighteen, he became the youngest-ever Scottish football internationalist. He was not the greatest dribbler with the ball, or the best passer in the game, and hardly a feared tackler, but what he was was a snapper-up of unconsidered trifles around the penalty box, and he had a leap and twist of that blonde head that any ballet dancer would envy. He was 'Denis the Menace' to any defence and his record-breaking tally of goals for Scotland (thirty) shows that. He scored seven in one eleven-game streak.

Denis Law did everything at speed – changed clubs, countries, defied trainers, coaches, managers, team-mates at times, but always with the same grand end in view – to win. Bill Shankly, who took over from Andy Beattie as manager of Huddersfield, underlined this attitude in the young Denis Law. He said:

> He would have died to have won. He would have kicked you to
> have won. He had a temper and he was a terror – a bloody terror
> with ability.

Law's difference to many other players was that he wanted to win with joy. If ever a player made football seem a game, Denis Law did. Matt Busby nearly signed him for Manchester United in 1960, but was beaten to it by Manchester City who paid a British record fee to get him. In the same year, he was chosen to play for the Football League against England, the first Scot to be so honoured, and he acknowledged the compliment by stealing the show. In 1961, he chose to play for Scotland rather than his club, so Manchester sold their crackerjack to Torino in Italy for yet another British record fee. Despite his great popularity with the Italian fans, and his riotous friendship with fellow Scot, Joe Baker, who had been signed from Hibs, Law was not really happy in Italian football, and was viciously double-marked in every game. Thanks to his superb athleticism he managed to remain unscathed. Indeed, the only time he was in any real danger was when he was a passenger in Joe Baker's brand new Alfa Romeo and Joe crashed it at a roundabout. However, the Law luck held, especially when he walked out on the Italians in 1962 to sign for Matt Busby and Manchester United at last. He had come home in the football sense and his true football destiny awaited him at Old Trafford. He did not waste the opportunity and when he was joined by Pat Crerand and George Best by 1968, another great United team was created. By this time he was married to Diana, whom he had met in an Aberdeen dance-hall, and he was ready to live life to the full in much the same manner as he played his football. He had a series of commercial posts, which traded on his name, but for the most part he maintained his football connections as a radio and television commentator and darling of the after-dinner talks circuit. Like Hughie Gallacher, he was capped by Scotland while with four different clubs, and he also set about Gallacher's scoring record, which stood till Kenny Dalglish equalled it. Law might have ended his playing days under Matt Busby, but when Tommy Docherty took over at Old Trafford in 1973, one of the first things he did was to hand Denis Law a free transfer, so he took his two pairs of football boots and crossed the city to Maine Road. When City played United, it was Law, in back-heeling a typically cheeky goal that sent United into the Second Divison. His whole career was a rollicking, roller-coaster ride of great moments and terrible times – the England defeat by 9–3 in 1961, being elected European Player of the Year in 1964, his tandem display with Jim Baxter at Wembley in 1967, being handed a free transfer in 1973 – not to mention the laughter-making antics like the whole comic-opera sequence of his flight from Italy. The theatrical image is not misplaced. This Danny Kaye look-alike was always the star performer in his own play and Scottish fans loved him for it. For a start he did not look Scottish, he didn't sound Scottish and he had a very un-Scottish extroversion that showed unashamedly and at all times. It didn't burn a hole in his soul as it did for so many Scots who have crossed the same border to look for lucre under their muddy bootlaces.

Law was even larger than his own life, which was large by any standard, but what endears him even yet to all Scots, even those with no great interest in football, was that he made himself into his own successful product off the pitch. While he roamed the playing field, his jersey wrapped around him like a banner, arms flailing like rapiers, he had all the swashbuckling panache of an impudent pirate. Then one remembers he was a fisherman's son.

His greatest catch, however, came in December 2000 when he pipped Jim Baxter and Kenny Dalglish in the *Daily Record*'s 'Hampden Heroes' poll to be named as the 'greatest ever Scotland player'. It was the fans' choice. He would have accepted no less.

If Denis Law personified the theatrical in football, then Alec Young was his screen equivalent. It was no accident that this Midlothian man with the flaxen hair was the subject of a television play called *The Golden Vision*. He was the darling of the Merseysiders (at least the Everton half) for almost a decade, and only injury put paid to what had been a glittering career.

Alexander YOUNG (b. 1937)
Centre-forward for Hearts, Everton, Glentoran and Stockport County

75

A golden-haired football aristocrat, virtually deified in his time at Goodison Park (Everton fans called him 'The Golden Vision'), Alec Young was every schoolboy story's idea of a centre-forward – lithe, alert, subtle and beautiful to watch. He was a throwback to the Corinthians' G.O. Smith, or Preston's John Goodall. Players who weren't battering rams like Jimmy Quinn, or high fliers like Joe Jordan, but silky footballers who could give as well as receive a telling pass and used their heads in more cerebral ways than connecting with crosses. Like all great players, he always seemed to have plenty of time. If ever a player had vision, he had. He seemed to have a picture in his head of what was going on around him at all times. In that way, he knew how many playing options he had, with the extra gift of being able to decide which to choose in a flash. He was perhaps a mite too delicate and far-seeing for his times. That would explain his ridiculously low cap count. It remains one of those Scottish selection mysteries. There was no doubt he was the most popular Scot ever signed by Everton, and considering the number of Scots who have played for them down the years, that is indeed a testimony. After an ankle injury finished his playing career at Goodison in 1969, he became player-manager of Glentoran, then of Stockport County, but he soon retired fully to found a wholesale furniture business, although he had originally been apprenticed, like Alan Morton, as a mining engineer. It can only be assumed that his golden touch didn't leave him once he entered the world of commerce. Football still runs in the family, however. Not so long ago his son, Jason, also signed for Hearts. Jason? Is he too in search of a Golden Football Fleece?

Alec Young, for all his success, modestly disdains a status on a level with such as Denis Law in the Scottish football pantheon. Most would. Except perhaps our next candidate for immortality, a player who is not at all afraid to follow the Lawman. This Scottish great is considered by many to be in the same class as Law, an opinion disarmingly shared by the player himself. Indeed, some would think him in a class of his own. If, however, Jim Baxter's candour could hardly be considered self-effacing or modest, it is certainly honest. And true.

James Curran BAXTER (1939–2001)
Left-half-back for Raith Rovers, Rangers, Sunderland
and Nottingham Forest

76

The facts about wing-half Jim Baxter are simply stated. He was born in Fife, played his first football for the Halbeath Youth Club, then Crossgates Primrose. In 1958, he was called up for his two years' National Service in the Black Watch during which time he had signed on as an amateur for Raith Rovers. Incredibly, he considered giving up the game at this stage, being quite content to support Hibs, and Gordon Smith in particular, but then in 1960 Rangers signed him as a full-time professional. The move through to Glasgow was something of a culture shock for the ex-pit boy and he never forgot how he was laughed at for his broad Fife accent and his provincial clothes. Oddly enough, he made an exceptionally smart soldier. He was to take ample revenge in the years to come for being ridiculed, using a famous wit to cut a swathe through any dressing-room, and he saw to it too that no one would ever laugh at him again because of his clothes. He spent five years with Rangers, winning three League titles, three Scottish Cups, four League Cups and twenty-four international caps. Former Rangers wing-half, Ian McColl, signed him for Sunderland with whom he stayed for three seasons before moving to Nottingham Forest, who gave him a free transfer in 1968. He returned to Rangers but he was already bored with the game. Suddenly, to everyone's consternation, he decided to hang up his boots and open a pub. He was just thirty years of age.

But anyone's life is more than the mere facts of it and Jim Baxter's life in Scottish football is one of its abiding legends. Arguably, he was the finest left-sided ball-player Scotland has ever produced. This was evident to Willie Butchart, the secretary-manager of Crossgates Primrose, when he signed Jim as a sixteen-year-old. 'For fifty shillings in old money,' laughs old Willie today. 'Just enough to buy him a new Teddy Boy suit.' Crossgates Primrose, a junior side, owed their name to their Rosebery colours rather than their dainty football ways, but they are proud of the fact that they are the only team in Fife to rear a player who went on to play for the Rest of the World, which Jim Baxter did at Wembley against England in 1964. When he signed for Raith Rovers in 1957 he got enough to buy his mother a new washing machine. Subtly coached on the park by Willie McNaught, the Rovers' cultured left-back, wisely left alone by Scot Symon at Ibrox, he came to speedy maturity shielded by such as Eric Caldow behind him, and Ralph Brand and Ian McMillan in front. This protective framework allowed him to play at his own pace. His precocious football maturity was the only thing that was speedy about him. Like all great players, 'Slim Jim' as he was called, seemed to have plenty of time for everything. This was especially seen in his debut for Scotland at Wembley in 1963 when he scored the only two goals of the game. At the end of the match he had not only stolen the show but the ball as well. He went off with it stuffed up his jersey. Typically, the SFA demanded it back. He sent them an old deflated ball and nothing was heard of the matter again.

Jim always enjoyed his trips to Wembley. He regarded it as his rightful stage. The bigger the occasion, the better he played. Never more so than for Rangers against Rapid Vienna in Austria in the 1964 European Cup. He enthralled the 70,000 Viennese the way that Bobby Templeton had delighted the Danes, until an exasperated tackle from behind broke his leg. He knew he had taunted the opposition too much, and he got his due. Jim Baxter was never really the same again but he had done enough in half a career to become immortal. Matthews, Puskas, Pele, Cruyff, Beckenbauer, Best and Law were his rightful peers in the world game. He was good and he knew it and when he had the opportunity he played his part to perfection. He was an out-and-out performer who realised the sheer entertainment value of class on the football field and he gave the Scottish fans their full money's worth – especially against England. 'If you're good at something and you're paid to do it, then why not give value for money?' Nobody can say that Jim Baxter didn't do that.

Trevor Brooking, in his *100 Great British Footballers* (Queen Anne Press, 1988), writes that he believed that Baxter 'saw it almost as his duty to entertain – with his showbiz routine of feinting and pirouetting and neat little drag-backs'. In many ways, Brooking goes on, Baxter was victim to his own personality. His antics certainly did not please everyone, however, and there were those who saw his behaviour as eccentric and self-destructive. They were probably right in the short term but, in the long run, it is the myth that is maintained and it is the legend of Jim Baxter that is imperishable in Scottish football memories. This is greater than the sum of his three international goals in thirty-four appearances. He had an emperor's assurance on the park. His talent had the carat-stamp of the finest quality. His careless authority hung on his shoulders like a matador's cape as he taunted the opposing bulls before putting through the final pass like a sword-point between the eyes. Yes, Slim Jim was a classy act and a hard one to follow. The theatrical allusion comes easily because he saw the pitch as a special kind of theatre. It was his stage and he strode it majestically, taking his time, making his mark. Without question, his football gifts, like those of George Best and Jimmy Johnstone, were God-given. So he was arrogant, outrageous, irresponsible and, in the end, self-defeating. He doesn't have the big house, the big car, the big business. He doesn't even have a big head. So what? He still has the big name and in any Scottish Football Hall of Fame Jim Baxter would have a room all to himself – with a bed, of course – and a well-stocked bar. His death from cancer on the fourteenth of April 2001, was a day of mourning in Scotland. Whole pages in the press were devoted to his feats, on and off the field. The general consensus was that it was the passing of a legend, who might have been greater still had he not been his own worst enemy. He could have played in any team or at any time, but with the ball at his feet, it was always going to be the Jim Baxter show. There were few like him and 'maist o' them are deid'. Now so is he.

Baxter was introduced to the Scotland team to make up the left-wing triangle with club-mates Ralph Brand and Davy Wilson against Northern Ireland at Hampden. Part-time manager, Andy Beattie, had walked out on the team again, this time for good, and his place was taken by ex-Ranger, Ian McColl. He restored Denis Law immediately and the order of the day was five goals for the Scottish forward line. For the next game, the big one at Wembley in April 1961, changes were made because of injury and Baxter and Brand did not play. They were lucky. Poor Frank Haffey, the Celtic goalkeeper, who could be so brilliant on his day, did not have a happy time in the Wembley sunshine and Jimmy Greaves, the cheeky England forward, had a great time among the goals, helping his side to a rare 9–3 victory. This gave rise to a mordant joke among Scottish fans on the long way home.

'Time is it, Jimmy?' was the question.

'Nine past Haffey!' was the mournful reply.

Yet the truth was that the Scottish team wasn't as bad, nor the English team as good, as that scoreline suggests. Many Scottish teams have scored three goals and won well, but everything seemed to go against them on the day and the more experienced English players were not slow to take advantage. There were too many players in the Scottish side who had not the same playing time at international level and, unlike the Wembley Wizards, who had the same problem, the Scots didn't rise to the occasion. Perhaps they might've done better had it rained? Ironically, one of the best players on the park, making his debut in the Scottish team that day, and playing at the centre of the embattled defence, was another young Celt, centre-half Billy McNeill. Not many defenders start their international career by losing nine goals.

William McNEILL, MBE (b. 1940)
Centre-half for Celtic

77

Billy McNeill is another Bellshill boy but not in the Gallacher or James mould. He is more like Stein, tall, commanding and highly articulate. He was made to be a captain and not for nothing was he nicknamed 'Caesar'. Another of that loyal band of one-club men, he was happy to remain with Celtic throughout his entire career and had little cause to complain. He ended up as the most honoured footballer in Britain, with medals in every competition available in the then European football calendar. He was the first British captain to receive the European Cup when he led the Lisbon Lions, as that Celtic side came to be called, to victory in Portugal in 1967. This was the home-grown Scottish team that won nine successive League Championships, from 1965 till 1974, a record that stood till Rangers equalled it in 1997. Billy still holds the record for most League appearances in a Celtic jersey – 486 – and was the first Scottish Footballer of the Year in 1965. He made a speciality of heading vital goals in the late stages of a game and his winning strike in the 1965 Cup final is now seen as the turning point in Celtic's fortunes of that time and the beginning of that remarkable decade in which they were virtually unbeatable. He might have had more caps for Scotland, but injuries caused frequent withdrawals and eventually he ceded his place to Ron McKinnon of Rangers. He retired from Celtic in 1975 to become a highly successful manager with Clyde, Aberdeen, Manchester City and Celtic. He was awarded an MBE for his services to football but left the game in 1991 to pursue his many business interests and become a media pundit. To anyone watching, his love of the game still shines through. Hail Caesar!

McNeill's replacement in the Scotland line-up was lanky Ian Ure of Dundee (and later Arsenal). That Dundee should be recognised in the international selection was only appropriate. In 1962, the north-eastern club won the Scottish League Championship by three points over Rangers and eight over Celtic. This caused nearly as much excitement as American John Glenn's orbiting of the earth, and as much surprise as the Tories' losing of the Orpington by-election. Dundee, after all, was only supposed to act as goal fodder for the Old Firm in Glasgow and the other Old Firm in Edinburgh or, when the occasion arose, that other branch office in Aberdeen. However, Dundee had taken everyone aback, even the phlegmatic Taysiders themselves, by comporting themselves well in Europe as well as taking the home title with style. It is to be remembered that Bill Brown was a Dundee goalkeeper, the crew-cut Alex Hamilton became a regular Scotland right-back, and that they had inside-forwards of the calibre of Charlie Cooke, and foraging Alan Gilzean at centre-forward. They were no push-over for any side, as their success at this time showed. Celtic were still stagnant and Rangers, under their new manager, Scot Symon, showed only glimpses now of their former omnipotence. Jock Stein had gone to Dunfermline as manager and taken them to the Scottish Cup final, where, thanks to the goalkeeping of Eddie Connachan, another Celtic supporter, they defeated Celtic and made their first foray into Europe. Celtic may have realised then that they may have erred in letting Stein go, but then being Celtic, or rather being Robert Kelly, perhaps they saw the threat he might be.

The winter of 1962–63 was a bitter one and everyone had a hard time of it. A Pools Panel was introduced, whereby a group of football pundits met in a hotel in London and pontificated on how the games might have gone had they been played. It was a cushy number for the panel, if a little irritating for the clubs and the punters at home, but it showed that people would accept any kind of football, even if based on hypothetical results. There were moves to change the game to a summer pursuit for the benefit of the television cameras, and make the season from March to November (which still seems very sensible) but the radical nature of this proposal frightened the powers-that-be into their normal stupefied inaction. Rangers became so impatient with the attitude of the Scottish Football League that they even proposed, in 1964, that it should be wound up and the proceeds divided up among the clubs. This was only avoided by the granting of an interim interdict in the Edinburgh Court of Session against Rangers and Others. It was a near thing, however, and it gave a sound indication of the way the wind was blowing. The big clubs were no longer content to carry the minnows. It looked as if it would be sink or swim for everyone, but Rangers were eventually persuaded to withdraw their action, and the little clubs heaved a hugh sigh of relief. Changes would come, but not yet.

Meantime, Scotland won a thrilling game at Wembley in 1963 with ten men, although one of them was Jim Baxter. In one of the most exciting finishes ever in the League Championship race, Kilmarnock, by this time managed by former Ibrox idol, Willie Waddell (who had taken over from Malcolm MacDonald, the ex-Celtic star), won the title in a photo-finish with Hearts. It showed that life did exist in Scottish football outside Ibrox and Parkhead. Rangers were fith in 1964–65 and Celtic out of sight. It was so rare a situation that it only emphasised how splendid had been the little provincial club's feat. Kilmarnock had been runners-up four times in five seasons and certainly deserved their moment of glory.

Then, to confound the purists, England won the World Cup in London in 1966 and set back the idea of attacking, free-flowing football for a generation at least. The idea behind Sir Alf Ramsay's machine team was that, above all, they should not lose, and consequently everything was geared to preventing the other teams from playing. Exuberant spontaneity was anathema, and a drilled discipline took the place of imagination and self-expression in play. Baxter and Law would never have played for England, and if they had done, it would have been a very different England. Scotland continued its habit of snatching defeat from the jaws of victory (in Willie McIlvanney's famous phrase), and only seemed to play really well when it didn't really matter – although when they had the chance of beating England, they beat the World Champions with arrogance, as is the Scottish way. Baxter and Law ruled supreme as only they could. Goals didn't matter when style was in charge and sheer class showed up the sterility of the English industrial approach. What Baxter and Law did that day was to announce that the real champions of the world were Scotland – if only for a day. That was sufficient. Their swinging soccer made merry with Ramsay robots and another memory was made, another legend created. This is something more meaningful than the mere statistic of a 3–2 victory. There is a time when football is more than figures. On the home front, the Rangers assembly line of players still continued to serve a great tradition, and if all didn't touch the heights, it still managed to produce Willie Henderson and John Greig.

William HENDERSON (b. 1944)
Outside-left for Rangers, Sheffield Wednesday,
Hong Kong Rangers and Airdrie

78

Willie Henderson is so small one would think he would hardly stretch to a footnote in any history of the game in Scotland, but this little, bouncing-ball of a man measured large in any football context. What he lacked in height, he more than made up for in dynamism. Born in Baillieston, on the fringe of football's Holy Land, Lanarkshire, he had a prodigious start, breaking into the Rangers team as a seventeen-year-old and was a Scotland player only a year later – one of the youngest ever. Like Jackson, Delaney and Waddell, the crowd roared in anticipation as soon as he touched the ball, and his crosses had much to do with Scotland's record 8–0 win against Cyprus in 1969. Like Bobby Templeton, Jim Baxter, Jimmy Johnstone and Charlie Cooke, he was one of football's natural crowd pleasers. Ironically for a footballer, he suffered badly from bunions and this cost him caps as well as medals, but he was fit enough to make twenty-nine international appearances for his country and score a handful of goals in the process. He left Glasgow Rangers to join Hong Kong Rangers near the end of his career in 1975.He finished up captaining the Hong Kong national side, but came home to Airdrie. The little ball still had lots of bounce left.

John GREIG, MBE (b. 1942)
Wing-half and full-back for Rangers   79

John Greig MBE can only be described as stalwart. For almost twenty years (his whole football career) he was a faithful servant to the Rangers Football Club, first as a player, then as manager and he serves it yet as its public relations officer. His heart is still at Ibrox even though as an Edinburgh boy he supported Hearts, and had hopes to play for them. However, once Rangers came for him, the commitment was mutual and lasting. He made his debut against Locomotiv Moscow as an inside-forward, then with Scotland he had an uninterrupted run of twenty-one internationals as a wing-half before finding yet another lease of life at right-back. He succeeded Harold Davis in the Rangers side as a hard-tackling balance to Baxter's attacking game, but the difference was that John Greig could score goals, as he did so dramatically for Scotland against Italy at Hampden in November 1965 when he was playing at right-back. It was as a full-back, and Scotland captain, that he was twice elected Scottish Footballer of the Year, in 1966 and 1976. Sixty-five thousand spectators turned out for his testimonial against a Scottish Select. His MBE was part of the Jubilee Honours List in 1977. When he retired in 1978 as captain of Rangers he was immediately appointed manager, a post he held until 1983. But he couldn't stay away from the ground so they made him PRO – which could also mean a Professional Ranger Only. Nothing could sum up John Greig better.

Irvine Welsh, in his foreword to the *The Greatest Footballer You Never Saw* by Paul McGuigan and Paolo Hewitt (Mainstream, 1997), writes:

> At the first Hibs–Hearts game I ever attended, the mighty Greens were firm favourites to win. They lost 3–1. The reason was this decrepit-looking guy in the middle of the park whom nobody could get the ball from. I remember booing this geriatric Jambo bastard and subsequently getting into a row with my Dad who told me this guy was Willie Hamilton, and that he was The Man . . .

William Murdoch HAMILTON (1938–76)

Inside-forward for Sheffield Wednesday, Middlesbrough, Hearts, Hibernian, Aston Villa and Ross County

80

It is hard to think of Willie Hamilton, a man of many clubs, as a 'failure'. He, at least, had a cap to show for his career, (a 2–1 victory against Finland in 1965), and he also played twice for the Scottish League, but he would have had many more had his off-the-field antics matched his erratic on-field genius. Had his temperament matched his ability, he would indeed have been a world-beater, for Willie Hamilton had everything – speed, guile, stamina and two great left feet. To many educated observers of the Scottish game, like Bob Crampsey for instance, Hamilton was a marvellously gifted footballer with a real and original vision, but everyone who had anything to do with him in football couldn't deny that he had his faults. He had his own view of what was required from a day-to-day professional. His foibles defied all attempts to make him conform and it was this, rather than a lack of skill or recognition, that caused him to be labelled a failure. But his failure was only in failing to live up to the vast potential of his enormous football talent.

Tragically, the basis of his unrest might have been the fact that he was continually plagued by stomach ulcers. One wonders why this wasn't medically treated at the time. He was constantly drinking milk to assuage his stomach pains. Unfortunately, he was also given to more potent beverages on other occasions, and was known to leave the team bus on more than one occasion to be sick at the side of the road. Yet his condition might also have been psychological – a reaction to stress for instance, a sense of social incompetance; any of a hundred things that could cause a young, Scottish working-class man thrown into the public eye to be dismissed with the damning phrase: 'He takes a drink.' Willie deserved better than that and his 'illnesses' ought to have been investigated.

He had never imagined he would ever be a professional footballer and served out a full apprenticeship as a bricklayer. However, being brought up in Airdrie, in Lanarkshire, he couldn't help but play football and it was while playing for Drumpelier Amateurs that he was spotted by Joe Mercer and taken by him to Sheffield. Willie did not enjoy being out of Scotland, and it was here the stomach pains started. After only a season, he was so unsettled he was reluctantly transferred to Middlesbrough. He was six years in the north-east before Tommy Walker bought him for Hearts in 1962. He was an immediate sensation and helped the Tynecastle club to win the League Cup. His troubled physical condition reasserted itself, however, and after a period of suspension and a cartilage operation, he was tranferred to city rivals Hibernian. Things did not improve for either club or player.

It must be admitted that Willie Hamilton had his eccentricities and stories about his quirky behaviour began to abound around the training grounds. Selected for the Scottish League to play Italy, he turned up at the Scottish team's rendezvous in Glasgow without a coat – in freezing mid-winter. In Canada, on tour, he won the Man of the Match award, a huge silver salver. Unable to get it into his holdall, he simply bent the tray in two and stuffed it in. Another story told about him concerns a conversation he had in an Edinburgh pub much favoured by the football fraternity. John Fairgrieve, the well-known Edinburgh sports journalist of the time, was there and recounts it in *We'll Support You Evermore* (Souvenir Press, 1979). He writes:

> Willie was asked about the finest players he had known. He paused for a moment and then said: 'Well, there was Pele. You must have Pele, right? Then there was di Stefano. Aye. And Tom Finney.' Someone then asked if there was anybody else in that class. Willie grinned. 'Sure. There was *me*.' Nobody scoffed. Willie wasn't a modest man, but he wasn't boastful either. He was very like Jim Baxter – too much alike. Neither believed in the virtues of a retiring nature. They needed to think – to know – they were the best. And in both their short careers neither found any grounds for self-doubt. On the field, Willie was languid, elegant, arrogant. He never believed in hurrying, he could beat a man gently. He always had time, and when Willie Hamilton passed a ball, it stayed passed. Having Baxter and Hamilton on the same park would have been like having Olivier and Gielgud on the same stage, but I don't know who would have played the lead.

Poor, wayward Willie ended his career in the Highlands playing for Ross County but his heart wasn't in it, and he and his wife, Carol, with young son, Billy, emigrated to Canada in 1974, after Willie had shown the authorities that he could still lay bricks. He died in Calgary a year later, aged only 38, of a heart seizure (just like Bobby Templeton) but in reality, a victim of chronic ill-health. Willie Hamilton died of himself. The parallel with Willie Groves, another great Hibernian, is uncanny. It would seem that football genius comes at a high price. Yet the memories they leave are priceless. For Willie Hamilton, they are the tantalising glimpses of greatness he showed in every game, when this sometime bricklayer from Airdrie made soccer bricks without straw. If he had met Jock Stein first instead of Joe Mercer, it might have been a different story. At any rate, we can only leave the last word on this tragic football enigma to Jock Stein, who said simply that Willie Hamilton was the best footballer he had ever seen.

Ian McColl was summarily dismissed as the Scotland manager after a training session with the team at Largs. Bobby Brown, another Ranger, was persuaded to take over. He did so, heavily influenced by the Ramsay syndrome. The old Scottish way, relying on individual flair and sudden inspiration, gave way to a drilled, disciplined approach based on the English 4-3-3 system. Players were described as 'ball-winners' and 'ball-players' – or 'strikers' – instead of being just players. They were selected for a specific function, to obey managerial instructions, to play a tactical game. Luckily for Scotland on the 1967 Wembley occasion, Baxter (ball-player) and Law (striker) were playing and they relied as always on the inspired whim or, when required, sheer impudence. As a result, England, the World Cup winners, or ten of them at least, were taken aback by the Scottish verve after Law had scored early on, and were on the back foot for most of the game. Had it not been for Gordon Banks in the English goal, Scotland would have scored five. Once again, when playing England, Scotland, and especially Baxter and Law, seemed to like to rub it in by tanner ba' expression on the park rather than by number of times the ball went in the net. It is not the most attractive side of Scottish football, but it seems to be ingrained in some of our better players. Ronnie Simpson of Celtic earned his first cap at thirty-six that day. However, the man who took the eye on this occasion was the selected ball-winner, Billy Bremner of Leeds, earning only his ninth cap, and already playing like a veteran in midfield. He was small and stocky, with choir-boy looks that belied his all-out aggression on the field. For Billy Bremner, every field he played on for Scotland was a Bannockburn. A fitting attitude for a boy from Stirling.

William John BREMNER (1942–97)
Right-half for Leeds United and Hull City

81

Billy Bremner was small but big-hearted, red-haired and dynamic, and was Scotland's captain for nearly half of his fifty-four international appearances. As a boy he was Celtic-daft, but on his father's advice he opted for a professional career in England. He began on the right-wing for Leeds, but it was when he moved inside and then back that he came to wider notice and began a representative career that saw him only very rarely on the losing side. He was English Footballer of the Year in 1971 and his very success with Leeds militated against his winning even more caps, as he was so often involved with his club at the final stages of almost every competition at that time. He captained his country at the 1974 World Cup and his display against the world champions, Brazil, brought him right to the fore as a player of world class. Unfortunately, his temper often got in the way of his talent and several incidents on the park cost him money in fines and eventually his Scotland place. At that time, he was only one cap short of Law's then record total (forty-five) but Billy Bremner had done enough by 1975 to put him into the Scottish Football Hall of Fame, where he deservedly figures among the best who have ever pulled on the dark blue shirt. To many, he epitomised the Scottish footballer down the years, both in his virtues and in his faults. He had the fiery spirit that exemplified the best of the Scot in times of danger, allied with a lack of control that marks many Scots at other times, but a team of Billy Bremners would beat the world – or self-combust.

Billy Bremner died suddenly of a heart attack at fifty-four. He must have been looking the other way to have been caught so off-guard. Not even death would have beaten Billy in a fair tackle. His book, *Billy Bremner's Scottish Football Heroes* (Breedon Sport, 1997), had just been published. He was certainly one himself, but he could never have guessed it was to be his own epitaph. He had quite simply played his heart out.

A chapter concerning itself with the twin greats of modern Scottish football, Baxter and Law, should conclude with reference to the third member of the trinity. If they are twin pillars, he is the crossbar, although it must be said that even if stretched full out, he would have difficulty in connecting with either. For in the great tradition of Scottish forwards, there wasn't much of Jimmy Johnstone. He was as wilful as Baxter, as flamboyant as Law, but he had none of the essential ego of these two, that streak of ruthlessness needed in anyone with great gifts on the field. Off the football field, Jimmy was an amiable little chap, but on it he was a demon who could dribble a ball like Wilf Mannion and torment full-backs in the manner of a Matthews at his George Best, if one may coin the simile. Just at a time when individuality was going out of football fashion, Johnstone emerged as a one-off, a throwback to the golden times when skill with the ball was all that was required of a footballer, not stamina, or work-rate or a capacity to follow instructions. He had his faults certainly.

When the Victorian press railed against 'the moral and physical shipwreck inseparable from the life of a professional footballer' they could not have foreseen wee Jimmy's rowing-boat exploits at Largs which have now passed down into Scottish football legend. Or his tormenting of Terry Cooper at Hampden in the European Cup semi-final, which caused Jim Baxter to remark: 'That should be prohibited by an Act of Parliament.' When AC Milan offered a hundred thousand pounds for him, Jock Stein replied that that would only get the wee man for one game. Yet he was to end up as a lorry driver, all his money gone. It is almost the norm in this money-mad game of today. He was not the ideal team man (none of the greats is) but he was a wonderful man to have on your team. All the same, he could talk himself out of a game just as easily as he could play himself into it. His was a rare talent, but it had to be carefully nurtured. He was a miniature orchid in a field of overgrown daisies. He needed just that little bit of extra care, as Jock Stein knew, and the SFA officials didn't; and, given trust, he repaid it a hundredfold in the games he won virtually single-handedly. Not everyone understood him, least of all Jimmy Johnstone himself, but he gave extra colour to a game which was rapidly becoming monochrome in its dull efficiency. We didn't have him at the top of his game all that long, but we were lucky to have the little imp at all. Everyone in Scottish football should thank God for small mercies down the years – like Alan Morton, Hughie Gallacher, Alex James, Billy Steel, Jimmy Mason, Bobby Collins, Bobby Johnstone, Billy Bremner, Gordon Strachan – and Jimmy Johnstone. We don't seem to make them like that anymore. Is the famous Scottish forward type yet another casualty of the National Health Service and better council housing?

James JOHNSTONE (b. 1944)

Outside-right for Celtic, San Jose Earthquakes, Sheffield United,
Dundee, Shelbourne and Elgin City

82

'Weejimmyjohns'on.' Only Glaswegians seem able to say the phrase as one word and convey in it the almost mythical response they have to this little fellow who was also known as 'Jinky', and represented in himself a compact, self-contained one-man rebellion against all established order and reasonable expectation. He was the first soccer anarchist, some would say nihilist, for he had no awe of expectancy. Wee Jimmy Johnstone was, in fact, a one-off and he is unlikely to be repeated in our time. He had every football skill imaginable with a temperament that diligently worked against his every expression of extraordinary ability. He was so in tune with the ball that he could virtually make it talk. Celtic team-mates used to say that in training, when the mood was on him, it was impossible to get the ball off him, and the key phrase there is 'when the mood was on him'. There is no doubt that when on his game, Jimmy Johnstone was world-class, and when it wasn't he was still unique, because he was incalculable. He could turn up with the unexpected in a flash and turn the game round with a swivel of hips and a twinkle of toes. He appeared to beat full-backs without touching the ball, which was only another part of his on-the-field mesmerism.

He was the mascot for his age, talismanic and emblematic, the last hurrah for individualism in an increasingly mechanical football epoch. He was not a team man, because he was a team in himself. He had more tricks than any conjurer and he wasn't above showing them off when they were least required. There were those that thought wee Jimmy Johnstone not 'mentally attuned' to the demands of modern international football, but the truth was that his critics were not on the same football field as this little magician with the wands in his feet. He began his international career brilliantly against Wales in 1974, but he only lasted four matches before he was in trouble for training escapades and trivial, laughable misdemeanours. He was *always* in trouble.

He had begun as a ball-boy at Celtic Park and nothing could have prepared him better for his great days to come, for it was what he could do with a ball that made him the player he was. He was world-class but, in many respects, other-worldly. Of course he had personality problems, but they seem so little compared with his giant football gifts. He was a Gulliver beset by Lilliputians and only a fellow giant like Jock Stein understood him enough to let him be himself.

All right, he was not 'wholly mentally attuned', but neither was Van Gogh nor Beethoven, so why should Jinky Johnstone worry? He made his mark on the Scottish football psyche and despite a mere twenty-three caps he will be remembered when the uniformists and regimentalists are long forgotten. He existed as an antidote to conformity. He reminded ordinary people that it was still their game, if they would throw off all their hang-ups and just play. (It was a game, after all, long before it was an industry. Although it must be said that the first professional footballers were, in fact, urban refugees from an industrial world. However, it is necessary to remember that it *is* a game when results rule in our strictly mercenary world.) Every court needs its jester and Jinky was just that. He treated the ball like a bauble, and toyed with it as if it had bells on. When on form, the rectangular football arena became his three-ring circus, and he clowned in it for our delight. Football was child's play to him, which is why he so appeals to the child in all of us.

A poignant postscript to the end of the supposedly Swinging Soccer '60s was supplied by the abrupt and tragic end of Third Lanark in 1967. This great old club, the favourite of many, had paid its way since its founding in 1872 as the 3rd Lanark Rifle Volunteers Football Club – 'proposed by Sergeant Ralston and seconded by Private Taylor' – and now, because of a deliberate policy of running down the club and its assets by an unscrupulous chairman, Third Lanark was no more. Cathkin Park was sold as a building site, but it is still a sports ground, owned now by the City of Glasgow. Who knows, it may become a football park again one day. A training ground for young Glaswegians, perhaps? The scheming entrepreneur was foiled and the grass is still green on the pitch, even if the team is no more, but seventy seasons is a lot to be lost for the sake of a quick profit. Harry McNeil, 'Reddy' Lang, Walter Arnott, Jimmy Brownlie, Jimmy Carabine, Bobby Evans, Jimmy Mason, Ronnie Simpson and Ally MacLeod – all mentioned in these pages – had worn the famous military red jersey in their time, as had many other fine players, but now Third Lanark is gone from the field as they are gone. Be that as it may, the 'Hi-Hi' battalions, keeping their fighting formation on the terraces to the last, were laid low, and as Bert Bell, the Third Lanark historian, says so aptly in his book on the subject 'We're still seeing red.'

But as one old club faded into history, another was about to rise again.

Chapter Thirteen

A Giant Re-awakening

'It's all yours now.' With these words, uttered by chairman Robert Kelly and accompanied by a firm handshake with former player, John Stein, a revolution took place within the Celtic Football Club that was to have reverberations throughout Scottish and European football over the following decade. A Protestant had become the fourth manager of a Catholic club (or at least, a club that had been founded by Catholics), and the news was trumpeted to the sporting world at a press conference held at Celtic Park on 31 January 1965. What was also being announced, although not in so many words, was that the autocratic reign of the chairman, meekly assisted by a compliant coach and a diffident manager, was now over and the managerial reins of a faltering organisation were now firmly in the hands of a professional. Jock Stein had learned about life and a life in football the hard, slow way and the lessons were now to bear fruit. The supposed youth policy of the once-supreme Celtic had stuttered and spluttered, occasionally throwing up excellent players but more often than not leaving many to die, in the football sense, with that deadly epithet 'promising' cold on their lips. A Glasgow giant had shrunk to a near-pygmy in less than a decade and it was Stein's task to restore it to its former stature – and quickly.

Almost as if they knew something was afoot in the boardroom, the self-same team beat Aberdeen 8–0 on an icy pitch at Parkhead, and the winds of change blew coldly through the musty corridors of Celtic Park. Stein must have regretted the loss of Paddy Crerand, a wing-half of real class who, much against his will, had been sold off to Manchester United; but any move which substituted Matt Busby for Bob Kelly could not upset any quality player for long. Willie Fernie had been similarly traded to Middlesbrough. Bertie Auld, too, sought exile in Birmingham and the places of these irreplaceable talents were taken by players who were hardly heard of then and haven't been heard of since. No doubt with the best will in the world, but with blatant and continuing amateur mismanagement, the club had been brought to the brink of ordinariness. So far was management thinking removed from reality that they even sent Jimmy McGrory to Spain (with player John Cushley as interpreter) to try and sign the Real Madrid legend, Alfredo di Stefano. At least they both came back with a bit of a tan, as opposed to the tanning the team was taking at eighth position in the League table. Something had to be done, and that something was called Jock Stein.

Because of his commitment to Hibernian, to whom he was contracted, he could not actually join up with Celtic until March, but his influence was already being felt and the team picked up the sense of excitement that affected players and supporters alike. Good progress was made through the Scottish Cup, and with that irony that pervades so many football stories, their opponents in the final were to be Dunfermline Athletic, the very team Stein had coached to the famous 1961 final, when they beat a dispirited Celtic in the replay. It was a very different Celtic now. Chairman Kelly was puzzled about Stein's selection of the young Bobby Murdoch at right-half instead of his normal inside-right.

'He's a forward, not a half-back,' pointed out the autocratic Kelly, expecting Stein to accede and change the team accordingly, as McGrory might have done, but all the big man would say was: 'Just watch on Saturday and see whether he's a half-back or not.'

More than a player's position had been made clear in this exchange and the future Sir Robert retired to his chairman's chair to let his new manager get on with it. Celtic won that final thanks to their young captain, Billy McNeill, who headed the winner in the last moments of the match. It was almost as if destiny had demanded it, because this win, the first trophy for seven years, signalled the beginning of a remarkable phase. Even Jock Stein admitted nearly twenty years later: 'It would not have gone so well for Celtic had they not won that game.' By the way, Bobby Murdoch played at right-half in that final, as Stein had insisted, and did so well that he played in the same position for Scotland less than a year later.

Robert MURDOCH (1944–2001)
Right-half-back for Celtic and Middlesbrough

83

Bobby Murdoch was the engine-room of the famous Celtic team known worldwide as the Lisbon Lions. He was the tenacious workhorse, who was nonetheless a quality footballer himself and his cross-field dialogue with inside-left, Bertie Auld, was the basis of the teamwork which won Celtic everything in sight during their tremendous decade from 1965 to 1975. This consistent excellence for his club was not reflected in his international career, mainly because Scotland had so many fine half-backs like Crerand, Bremner and Stanton available at the same time and Bobby's cap total suffered as a result. He made only a dozen appearances in all, but this archetypal half-back, strong-tackling and quick-thinking, did not need international recognition to highlight his abilities. He was a footballer's footballer and was recognised as such in his time. He was Scottish Player of the Year in 1969. When a foreign journalist was asked to sum up the Celtic team of the Lisbon era, he smiled, shrugged and replied in one word – 'Mur-dock'. In his latter years, he had besetting weight problems and finally he was persuaded to cart off the extra poundage to Middlesbrough, where he added considerable weight to that team until he retired. Latterly, Bobby Murdoch was to be seen limping into Celtic Park leaning on a cane, but even then he carried his head high, for here was a lion that once roared. That lion heart gave out in 2001, but it was a heart that had driven a remarkable team.

Famous players sometimes find it hard to deal with the eclipse of playing fame but if they have attained any heights at all they never really forget the view from the top. Those who have never attained the summit of their professional activity can only regret it but for those fortunate few, like Murdoch, and the ninety-nine others in this volume, it is something that once gained, nothing can spoil, and not even time can take away. It has nothing to do with medals or trophies, and certainly not money. It lives in the memory somewhere. Or in the heart. At any rate, thanks to players like Murdoch, McNeill, Bertie Auld and Jimmy Johnstone, responding as they did to the inspirations of Jock Stein, Celtic, in 1966, were once again on their way. The slumbering giant had wakened and was beginning to flex his muscles. More games were being won than lost and the Championship was attained for the first time since 1954. It seemed that they could win anything they played for.

During that halcyon era from 1966 to 1974, a great side had come into being that would take its place with the great teams of football history. Every player in the squad was conscious that he was going to be part of something special – and unforgettable. This was largely because a particular group of players had come to manhood and fruition just when the mentor they required arrived to lead them. The time had found the man. Celtic's extraordinary success from this time was not due solely to their gifted manager or to any individual in a very talented group of players, or even to the mass of their relieved support who had been patient for so long. No, the reason was that each player was exactly right for his position at that exact time and such a happy congruence doesn't happen often. Their time was right, and no matter what they did, they couldn't prevent what was to happen, happening. As always, Shakespeare has a quote for it:

> There's a divinity that shapes our ends,
> Rough-hew them how we will . . .

Stein planned the greatest year a Scottish club has known during a close season tour of Bermuda and North America. He tinkered with team selection, experimented with positional changes and gradually found the formation that was founded on each player's particular strength. Like Bill Struth earlier, he insisted on the best hotels wherever they went. The players got used to feeling good. Pace and flair became their hallmark on the field and they returned to Scotland like hungry lions. It was clear that something exceptional was happening at Celtic Park. Domestic honours were won as a matter of course and Rangers, now going through a succession of managers, could only look on amazed, like the rest of Scotland. It was time now to look outwards. The Glasgow boys from Parkhead were about to play with the men. As Celtic progressed through the European Cup during 1966–67, an English journalist described them as 'An exhilarating team that sought to blend athletic speed and combativeness with imagination, delicacy of touch at close quarters, and surges of virtuosity.'

There was fun in the team as well. Each player had his nickname, from 'Faither' Simpson in goal (because of his seniority), 'Cairney' Craig at right-back (because of the BBC series of the time, *This Man Craig*, in which I had played Craig when everyone knew I'd rather have played for Celtic), 'Caesar' McNeill for obvious, leadership reasons, 'Whispy' Wallace at inside forward (for his initials W.S.B.) and for his breathy voice, and so on right through the side. As these young men stood in the tunnel of the National Stadium in Lisbon waiting to play Internazionale of Milan in the final of the European Cup, and with all Scotland glued to their television sets, they were already the winners of the Scottish League Championship, the Scottish Cup, the Scottish League Cup and the Glasgow Cup. The European Cup would make it the Grand Slam. As they waited, they sang the Celtic songs with gusto, astonishing the grave *signori* from Milan who didn't respond with anything from Verdi. Celtic knew they were going to win. It was in the stars. And win they did, thanks to goals from Tommy Gemmell and Steve Chalmers. Nothing could have stopped this Celtic side of Scots and they returned to Glasgow as heroes and to dancing in the streets of Parkhead. The legend was born on that night. Their return from Lisbon was a huge event in every sense, and from that moment they become known as the Lisbon Lions.

Whether this was from the usual press preference for label alliteration or from historical links with the Lion of Scotland, one can only guess. The red Lion Rampant on its yellow field owes its origins to the royal House of Stuart, and further back to William the Lyon in 1165 – and even if an actual lion has never been seen north of Gretna, except as part of a travelling circus, Lisbon Lions there are. We might look back on the team that Stein made as being the finest of the twentieth century, but any group of players which maintains such a level of consistency over nine seasons, from Beatlemania all the way to Watergate, must be held to be unique. Rangers have repeated the feat in recent years, but not with the same innocence somehow. Rangers are to be congratulated, of course, but they bought their success, and expensively (just as the first Celtic had done) whereas these Lisbon Celts were unostentatious, mainly Protestant, local Scots with Scottish names, whose total transfer value then would hardly buy a single name player today. It's a sobering thought. It was perhaps the only sober element in the celebrations afterwards. Seven thousand Celtic supporters had taken over Lisbon and they had to be persuaded to give it back to the amiable Portuguese. There were *no* arrests or fights or ugly scenes. On the contrary, it was fiesta time for everyone, especially the ecstatic Glaswegians. Much of what happened over that day and night, and the morning after, is part of football folklore now . . .

There was the British Embassy man who complained that every time he opened a cupboard a Celtic supporter fell out . . .

The supporter who woke up on the plane back and suddenly remembered he had gone by car . . .

The lone hitchhiker, trailing his green and white scarf, wanders somewhere on the road outside Lisbon when a Scottish car draws up alongside him with room for one.

'Where are yous gawn?' he asks, as the door is opened for him.

'Edinburgh.'

'That's nae use. Ah'm fur Glesca.' And he slams the door and staggers on . . .

The mother who received her son at the door, supported by two policemen, but still bedecked in Celtic colours and still smiling: 'But he wis supposed tae be on his honeymoon in Morecambe . . .'

Of course the honeymoon was soon over for all of us but the memory lingers on.

In the following week, Rangers lost to Bayern Munich in extra time. It was a pity, as it would have made for a unique Scottish European Double – the Old Firm goes continental – but it was not to be. Rangers did win the Cup-Winners' Cup in Barcelona in 1972, but their supporters let them down in the after-scenes. It was not a Lisbon story and FIFA suspended Rangers from the following year's competition. The Glasgow giants were determined, however, to put their house in order again and after a quick succession of managers had eventually settled on their former star, Willie Waddell, who had steered Kilmarnock to its Championship in 1965. However, he would need time to do at Ibrox what Stein had achieved at Parkhead, but that time would come. Meantime, Celtic had got back to the bread and butter of winter football in Scotland and the new threats posed by Aberdeen, who beat them in the Scottish Cup final, and by Partick Thistle, who beat them in the League Cup final to everyone's surprise – including Partick Thistle's.

Worse was to come. Their second European Cup final, in 1970, was to be held in Milan. Celtic were firm favourites to win, especially after beating Leeds at Hampden in a classic semi-final, but they were narrowly beaten by Feyenoord, the Dutch champions, by a goal in extra time. All of which served to show that nothing in football can ever be taken for granted. Nevertheless, Celtic continued to dominate the era as players came and went through the following seasons but, paradoxically, attendances at Celtic Park declined. Could supporters be jaded by success as much as they are made despondent by failure? Sponsorship entered football and names like Texaco and Drybrough became familiar.

The close season was now threatened by an overspill of fixtures. The Home Internationals, for so long the lifeblood of the British Associations, were in gradual decline. All eyes were fixed on Europe, for that's where the pot of gold was to be found. The Scottish game couldn't afford to be insular or parochial. Celtic had started something by winning the European Cup, the first British club to do so. They had effectively ruined the old Scottish football set-up forever. Who would want to see Hamilton Accies after they'd seen Ajax? It was a difficult time for the smaller clubs. The bigger ones only got bigger and the little ones went to the wall. A free-market strategy had little to do with football sentiment and many famous names were in danger of extinction. All they could hope for was a decent Cup run and four games a year against Rangers and Celtic. It was not a balanced picture, but it was the view of football in the '70s as seen through a TV camera's lens. The future was now and it was harsh. Teams were hurrying to merge, meetings were held, panic signals were sent out and Scottish football dithered typically in the face of the media monster. 'Something's got to be done,' was the cry that went up all round, but nobody knew quite what.

The better players saw that the playing fields were greener in England and more and more nipped over the border much as they had done ninety years before. Even Celtic and Rangers were losing good players to England; and other Scottish clubs, who could ill afford to lose their star players from the field, were happy to see their sale as an item in the treasurer's report. Charlie Cooke was just such an entry in Dundee's books. It was proof that the player was still a commodity, still part of the goods and chattels, marked up much as livestock would be in any market sale and knocked down to the highest bidder. Even a classy player like Charlie Cooke. Of whom Jim Baxter, in his inimitable way, once said: 'See that Cookie. If he selt ye a dummy, ye had tae pey tae get back oan the park.'

Charles COOKE (b. 1942)
Inside-forward and outside-left for Aberdeen, Dundee, Chelsea and in USA

84

Today, Charlie Cooke runs a soccer academy in the United States teaching young Americans the skills of soccer. No one could be more entitled or better equipped to do so than this dashing, stylish, extro-vert player who was the nearest thing to a Brazilian Scottish football has produced. Although a Fifer from St Monan's, he made his name in the north-east, first with Aberdeen then Dundee, before moving to London to join Chelsea, a club well suited to his flamboyant instincts. Charlie Cooke was so gifted as a footballer, on a par with fellow Fifer, Jim Baxter, that like him he was often careless with those same gifts and infuriated the less gifted but influential men who are so much a part of modern football. Men who know all about work-rate and commitment but very little about ball-skills and flair. Charlie had these last in abundance but his attitude was variable to say the least. However, when he was allowed to give rein to his instinct, he was able to take his place among the very best and it is among the best of his era that he will be remembered, for he represented bravura and panache, the quality of glamour that belongs to the true star in whatever field, even a football field. He could beat his man, just for kicks, one might say, but he had the skill to evade the flailing, vengeful legs that followed him at all times. Somehow it seems right that he should finish up in America, where his kind of appeal is admired and respected. Not like in his native Scotland, where any kind of fun front is regarded as suspect and frivolous. Bonnie Charlie's noo awa' perhaps, but why is his type, the great footballer-entertainer, so rare in the game today? We can't have too many Cookes. It is time to pry the sport away from the money-men, if it's not already too late, and give it back to the players so that, once again, they can play.

Ronald Campbell SIMPSON (1930–2004)
Goalkeeper for Queen's Park, Third Lanark, Newcastle, Hibernian and Celtic

85

If Ronnie Simpson didn't begin his goalkeeping career in the cradle then he certainly began it in short trousers, for he was only fourteen when he played as an amateur with Queen's Park in the Scottish League. He then went on to have a career that stretched almost thirty years to culminate in a European Cup winner's medal with Celtic as part of the legendary Lisbon Lions. Goalkeepers are famous long-livers in the football sense, but Simpson's record at the highest level is surely unique. Not that it is surprising. His father was the celebrated Rangers centre-half of the pre-war years, but wags said that Ronnie's initials prevented his following his father to Ibrox. (Although that didn't stop R.C. Hamilton in 1897.) Third Lanark signed Ronnie while he was doing his National Service in 1951. Though not tall, he had an extraordinary agility and was said to have the safest pair of hands in football. What is remarkable is that he had to wait until he was thirty-six to play his first full international (against England at Wembley in 1967) and even then had only a handful of caps to show for a sterling professional career. His late success with Celtic and Scotland surprised him but he accepted it happily and in 1970 the man his Celtic team-mates nicknamed 'Faither', retired to a good job and a comfortable home in Edinburgh until his death in 2004

With his sure sense of theatricality, Stein chose the retired Simpson to lead out the Celtic team on the final day of the 1970–71 season. The League had been easily won and the last game against Clyde was a mere formality but Stein, with his sure showman's touch, turned it into an occasion. He fielded the Lisbon Lions. It was the last time they would be seen together. The young cubs – Connelly, Hay, Macari, Dalglish and McGrain, etc. – were already snapping at their heels. Thirty-five thousand spectators turned out to watch their 'pride' win 6–1 without breaking sweat and see Bertie Auld carried off on the shoulders of his team-mates. He was transferred to Hibs a week later. Stein had written in *The Celtic View*, 'You'll be able to tell your grandchildren about this game.'

I have done and still do.

Celtic were to win three more Championships in their amazing run, three more Scottish Cups and suffer four defeats in four League Cup finals in four successive years before the new Premier League restored Rangers to the forefront in 1976 – but everyone knew that a special epoch had just ended. It ended where it began, with Jock Stein. The same Stein, still sitting at his desk, still on the phone, still talking football, still finding time for anyone who has his enthusiasm for his beloved game. John Rafferty, the late *Scotsman* football correspondent, a shrewd and perceptive writer on football men and their ways, described a typical Stein day:

> He took the training every morning, stayed on for special coaching of individuals, was interminably on the telephone at the ground and in his home. Talking to football people, to managers, to contacts, becoming saturated with the current news on the game. He was ever available to the press, providing the routine news of the team, arguing, trying to influence opinion, putting the club's case and at times winning press friends by helping with a story on a dull day.

The Big Man had his failures too. When he was with Dunfermline, he had great hopes for Alex Edwards, an inside-forward who played for amateur Scotland, but was never capped as a professional. For no reason that was obvious, his immense promise as a seventeen-year-old was never realised and he faded from the game. Another enigma was George Connelly of Celtic, perhaps the most naturally talented player Celtic have had since the war. Stein brought him into the side in 1968, into a team that some thought even better than the Lions. They won the domestic treble with new signings like Harry Hood and Tom Callaghan – and included young George Connelly. He made an immediate impact on the team and on the fans on the right-wing, then later at inside-forward. He also starred in what was called the greatest club match ever seen in Britain – that between Celtic and Leeds in the semi-final of the 1970 European Cup at Hampden. Latterly, he took over from Auld, and moved back to wing-half, right or left. By 1974, he had won two caps for Scotland but all was not well with the young Fifer. A shy, intensely private young man, he found the demands of the footballer's life a constant strain and, on occasions, he just couldn't cope. He once walked out of Glasgow Airport when he was about to fly off with the Scotland party. Later, in 1974, he walked out of Celtic Park just as suddenly. Stein tried his best to reassure the troubled player, but he never settled and just walked away from football altogether. What a real shame. He had so much to give the game. Another example of a prodigal waste of genuine talent was Jimmy Smith.

James SMITH (b. 1947)
Inside-forward for Aberdeen, Newcastle and Whitley Bay   86

Lanky, skinny, pallid and awkward, Jimmy Smith looked anything but the splendid footballer he could be when the mood was on him, but that he was touched with genius on the ball there is no doubt. He was also gifted with a generous measure of indolence which sapped his natural authority on the field and this, on occasion, made him look ordinary when in fact he was quite extraordinary. As a Parkhead boy, he had hoped that he would one day play for his favourite club, Celtic, but Aberdeen nipped in early and the easy-going Jimmy signed on for the Dons. He was an instant success with that club because they allowed him to play his own idiosyncratic game. Significantly, he never seemed to play well against Celtic. There was something special about the young man and Newcastle recognised this in 1969 when he was transferred to them for a very large fee. Football writer, Brian Glanville, acutely described him as a 'an authentic star'. Ian Archer called him 'poetic', a view which puzzled the more pragmatic around St James' Park, who looked for goals and effort rather than poetry. After losing in the Cup final to Liverpool there was a mutual loss of interest and one of Scotland's finest natural football talents had himself reinstated to play out his time in the Northern League with Whitley Bay. He had that certain something, but he never really made anything of it, just like Willie Hamilton and George Connelly. When Jimmy finished playing, he just stayed on in Whitley Bay. Perhaps it was too much trouble moving. He doesn't even bother going to see a game at the nearby St James' Park. 'There's nobody worth watching. Is there?'

Well, no one quite like 'Jinky' Smith at least.

No such problems beset Archie Gemmill.

Archibald GEMMILL (b. 1947)

Inside-forward for St Mirren, Preston North End, Derby County, Nottingham Forest, Birmingham City, Jacksonville and Wigan

87

Archie was a suitcase footballer who plied his trade like any professional journeyman and followed wherever the work was. He was in the tradition of J.J. Lang, Fergus Suter and the rest of the Scots pioneer professionals who sold their boots for cash and made a living from their football skills. It is said that Archie began running in August and did not stop till May. He was a tireless worker in the midfield, a fetcher and carrier of the ball rather than a playmaker, but he had his inspirational moments and was a zealous captain for all his club sides and for Scotland. One of Archie's smaller claims to fame was that he was Scotland's first substitute, being brought on during the St Mirren *v* Airdrie game in 1966. He had an exceptional career in terms of medals and trophies, especially with Derby County and Nottingham Forest, but what he will always be remembered for is his wonderful individual goal against Holland in the 1978 World Cup Finals in Argentina. He took on the whole of the Dutch defence single-handedly and in a brazen display of cheeky Scottish tanner-ba' virtuosity astounded the Dutch and the world with a goal that would have done credit to the very greatest football masters. It was Archie's, and Scotland's, hour in the sun. His son Scot has followed him in the trade. Yet another football son with a father to live up to.

And for another Scottish inside-forward of the time, the problem he had seemed at one point to be insurmountable – but that didn't stop Asa Hartford.

Richard Asa HARTFORD (b. 1950)

Inside-forward for West Bromwich Albion, Manchester City, Nottingham Forest, Everton, Norwich City and Bolton Wanderers

88

Asa Hartford was a Drumchapel amateur like Kenny Dalglish but the difference was that Asa (after singer Al Jolson, real name Asa Yoelson, who died on the day Hartford was born) went straight to join the ground staff at West Bromwich Albion at sixteen and by twenty-one he was playing for Scotland. However, in November 1971, when he was set to join Leeds, a routine medical examination discovered he had a hole in his heart. The transfer was cancelled and Hartford withdrew from the Scottish team to play Belgium. It seemed as if his career might be over but in less than a year he had won his way back to full fitness and continued in a distinguished career with a whole host of clubs. He also regained his international place. He played in most of the Scottish teams during 1972 and again in 1975 and 1979, but he was unfortunate in coinciding with many other excellent midfield playmakers and had to take his turn as it came. Nonetheless, Asa Hartford did enough over a decade to justify his international status and to deserve a long and successful career marked by his exceptional control and a remarkable ability to read a game. He finally retired in 1985, having shown everyone that his Clydebank heart was in the right place after all.

Asa Hartford represented a kind of Scottish forward that is now almost extinct. With the emphasis now on speed and work-rate, and reliance placed more and more on tactics and overall team effort, there is little need now for the player who takes his time in the middle of the park and lets the ball do most of the work for him. This chapter has rightly celebrated the play of men like Willie Hamilton, Charlie Cooke and Jimmy Smith because their like, unfortunately, may not be seen again in the modern game. They are a luxury that result-obsessed, points-driven managers and coaches can no longer afford. Yet how much poorer the game is without this kind of player, who goes his own way because it's the right way, the only way, for him. There have been many players in the game who never fulfilled their promise because their talent was systematically drilled out of them, and there were some who never even bothered to try. Puck Ure was one of these. He lived and worked and played his football around the Lanarkshire village of Baillieston, in the hard times just before the Second World War. Puck's football skills were legend in the area, with a cap turned the wrong way round on his head, playing with his braces showing, trouser legs twisted into his socks and his working boots used to great effect on any open space where he was shown a ball and someone to play against. He could easily have become a professional. It is said that he drank several signing-on fees, but it's true that he played on Sundays for money – a shilling a head per man, winner take the lot. Puck usually won. Once, when reminded that one of the players in the other team had only one eye, and a bad arm as well, Puck, who had a bit of a stutter, was unmoved. 'He's got t-two f-f-fuckin' f-f-feet, has he no'?'

Yes, they don't make them like Puck Ure any more.

*

On 26 September 1973, Scotland beat Czechoslovakia at Hampden to qualify for the World Cup Finals in Germany for the first time in sixteen years. The new Scotland manager, Willie Ormond, was carried from the field on the shoulders of his team, led by captain Billy Bremner, and including the wayward George Connelly. The SFA had played the usual musical chairs with team managers. Bobby Brown had left under a cloud, Tommy Docherty came and went like a hurricane, blowing hot and cold, then left to manage Manchester United. Now the quiet, likeable Ormond had tiptoed into the hot seat with a winning team. He put together the best squad ever taken to a World Cup by Scotland, Bremner, Law, Johnstone *et al* – and they didn't let anyone down. It was a typical Scottish triumph in that we never won anything, but ended up the only unbeaten team in the tournament. On their return to Glasgow they were met as if they had won the Cup, which to the Scottish psyche now seemed immaterial. They had played with a bit of class and some style and had given some of the big names a fright. The only difference was that we didn't frighten the little names enough, and lost out on goal average. Scotland had still to learn that you can play badly and win, and that it's no use playing brilliantly and losing. However, two names now appeared on the international team lists and they were to remain there longer than any others. They were two of Jock Stein's charges – Kenny Dalglish and Danny McGrain.

Kenneth Mathieson DALGLISH, MBE (b. 1951)
Inside- and centre-forward for Celtic and Liverpool   89

At the time of writing, there are only fifteen players in the world who have played more than a hundred times for their countries, players like Pele, Gylmar, Santos and Rivelino of Brazil, Bobbies Charlton and Moore of England, not to mention Billy Wright, Sanches of Chile, Nordquist of Sweden and Deyna of Poland. Scotland's own Kenny Dalglish numbers among this elect. 'One of the finest footballers to come out of Scotland since the War – tactically and technically outstanding,' writes Brian Glanville in his 1997 survey of world players. 'King Kenny' he is called on the terraces of Parkhead and Anfield, yet it must be said his presence is a little less than sovereign when viewed in an off-the-pitch situation. The face one sees there is often sombre and morose, whatever the result, but the truth is that, like most Scots, Kenny Dalglish is two people, or at least he has two faces. The first, the public image, may appear dour, even taciturn and the speech monosyllabic, but the second, the real face of Kenneth Dalglish MBE, is gleeful, boyish and impish, for that is how he plays his football. He smiles as he plays, for he is doing what he knows he does best.

Kenny Dalglish is, in reality, a shy man who prefers to let his feet speak for him on most occasions, but there have been times when it might be said he put his foot in it. If he lacks guile with the media, it cannot be said that he is in the least unsophisticated on the football field. As a player, he had that gift that all the football greats have, of making the game seem effortless, and he played it much as he would have done as a boy, instinctively and naturally and with endless enthusiasm, just as he did at Cumbernauld United. When Sean Fallon, the then assistant manager of Celtic, came to the Dalglish home near Ibrox to sign the young man, the family had to hurriedly remove the Rangers pennants and favours decorating the boy's room in order to hide the fact that he was a life-long Rangers supporter – but nevertheless Kenny went on, under the guidance of Jock Stein and Billy McNeill, to become a Celtic legend and then to become the same and even more at Liverpool. He was bought in 1977 to replace Kevin Keegan but in effect he became his own man at Anfield, and it was no understatement on the Kop when supporters' banners read 'Kenny's from Heaven!' It was his goal that won the European Cup final in 1978 and he was twice elected English Footballer of the Year. In the same year he became Scotland's most-capped player, having made his debut in 1971 at the age of twenty, and with 102 caps he is likely to remain so. He was awarded the MBE in 1985.

In March 1986, he completed his century of caps, and as an acknowledgement of this feat, he was the first professional footballer to be awarded the freedom of the City of Glasgow. He has since had success as a manager with Liverpool and Blackburn Rovers but inexplicably walked out of each post. Moving to Newcastle, he was frustrated in his attempts to build a youth policy. They didn't even have a reserve team. Mounting pressure from the board for instant success and a more 'entertaining' style of play resulted in Kenny's dismissal from the club. Nevertheless, Dalglish has more medals than a South American general. Of course, it is as a player that he will be best remembered. When asked what was Kenny's best position on the team (he had begun in midfield) Jock Stein said simply: 'Ach, just let him oot on the park.'

Daniel Fergus McGRAIN, MBE (b. 1950)
Full-back for Celtic, Hamilton Academical and Rochdale
Rovers (Brisbane)

90

His name sounds Irish, which he isn't, and suggests a Catholic, which he isn't, but that was probably why he signed for Celtic instead of Rangers in 1967. For Danny, like his friend Kenny Dalglish, was a keen Rangers supporter when he played for Maryhill Juniors, but Celtic at that time were on their Lisbon high and no one could refuse Jock Stein so Danny joined up with Kenny at Parkhead on the same day. Neither regretted it, although on the day he took his boots from Parkhead for the last time in 1987 nobody even said goodbye or thanks to Celtic's most-capped player of his day (sixty-two between 1973 and 1982). Danny had made his own niche at the club as the finest attacking full-back in the country, with a cap collection second only to Dalglish's. It would have been more but for a terrible clash of heads with Falkirk's Dougie Somner, which resulted in McGrain's suffering a fractured skull in 1972. By 1973 he had recovered sufficiently to make his international debut against Wales. In 1975 it was found that he had diabetes, yet by 1977 he was voted Scottish Player of the Year. This was typical of the tenacity of purpose that gave him a telescopic tackle in either leg, yet allowed him the speed and skills of an old-fashioned winger. He was proclaimed 'The Best Footballer Ever Seen in Australia' but he will be remembered as McGrain of the Celtic. (Well, it's hardly likely to be McGrain of Arbroath FC, even though he was manager there for a season.) His autobiography, *Celtic My Team*, was published in 1978. The title is more than apposite because for a number of seasons, especially after the departure of Dalglish, Danny McGrain *was* Celtic. Glasgow awarded him a Civic Medal for services to sport and the Queen gave him an MBE. Yes, Danny Boy had class – world class.

In the summer of 1975, Jock Stein was driving back from holiday with his wife and two friends when he was involved in a head-on collision with another car on the notorious A74 just beyond Gretna. The other car was on the wrong side of the road. Jock was the most seriously hurt of those involved, but thanks to his splendid pitman's physical condition, he recovered from horrendous injuries. Effectively, however, he was lost to Celtic from then on. They would have to get on without the Big Man who had given them a fantastic decade which constituted an entire chapter of Scottish football history.

Chapter Fourteen

One Over the '80s

By the end of the '70s, the bad news was that Mrs Thatcher had nosed her way to the leadership of the Conservative Party and that meant that there was to be no such thing as society any more. Britain had voted to go into the Common Market and at a throw had jettisoned a century or so of Commonwealth trust. Inflation was rampant and the pound sank like a stone on the foreign exchanges. The good news was that the West Indies won the first cricket World Cup, Bjorn Borg won his first Wimbledon singles title to the squeals of excited little girls, and Edson Arantes do Nascimento (otherwise known as Pele of Brazil) had signed a seven-million-dollar contract to play for the New York Cosmos for three years. Police were still looking for Lord Lucan and Scotland were still hoping to get to Argentina for the 1978 World Cup. Willie Ormond had resigned as team manager 'for personal reasons', Jock Stein was not available and Ally MacLeod, a better player than he pretended, and a better manager than most people thought, stepped into the tartan breeches. He cued the curtain on what was to become a football farce which simultaneously reflected what was so good and so awful about Scotland and football.

Scotland had qualified for the Finals thanks to a goal against Wales at Anfield, scored by Dalglish, already celebrating his fiftieth cap. From then on, a ludicrous hysteria seemed to build up around our expectations for Argentina, and the effervescent MacLeod revelled in the euphoria which swept through Scotland like a hurricane. Anything was better than dwelling on Mrs Thatcher and her all-for-ME ideology. The northern part of the United Kingdom was on 'MacLeod Nine', as it were, and false hopes were raised as high as the Lion Rampant and St Andrew's flags that suddenly appeared everywhere. Scotland went to the Argentine with hopes held high, but higher jinks among the players, low morale among the 'Anglos' and the expulsion of Willie Johnston, the Rangers winger, for drug-taking put paid to any real Scottish chances on the field. Poor results against Peru and Iran did nothing to help, and then, typically, with everything lost and with the team the butt of everyone's jokes, Scotland turned on a scintillating display against Holland, beating them in style and having the best goal of the whole competition scored by Archie Gemmill. It was too much too late. It was also typically Scottish to be brilliant when it didn't matter. It was almost a relief to get back to home fare.

Celtic had won their first Premier League title and their last Scottish Cup under Supremo Stein. Billy McNeill, having been groomed by Clyde and Aberdeen as a manager, was all set to return to Paradise as Stein's successor. Rangers were picking up the pace again rapidly under manager Jock Wallace, with Willie Waddell at the top, but the '80s began with the unfamiliar sight of Dundee United at the top of the League and with victories over such as Borussia Moenchengladbach in Europe to their credit. They had also won the League Cup under their dour manager, Jim McLean, and this only emphasised how far they had come since they were the Dundee Hibernians. Aberdeen, under their young manager, Alex Ferguson, also had their successes in the new decade, taking the title in 1980, the Scottish Cup in 1982 and, wonder of wonders for Scotland, the European Cup-Winners' Cup in 1983. Aberdeen 2, Real Madrid 1. Where's your di Stefano noo?

The New Firm from the north-east was making a realistic takeover bid for the Old Firm of the south-west. Attendances were rising again in the Premier League and Scotland was beginning to feel good about itself. Good players were coming through again. Here are just four of them, for example, starting with Joe Jordan.

Joseph JORDAN (b. 1951)
Centre-forward for Morton, Leeds United, Manchester United,
AC Milan, Verona, Southampton and Bristol City   **91**

Joe Jordan combines the dash of the old-fashioned centre-forward with the subtlety and sophistication of the modern target-forward, who can play off to colleagues from a more deep-lying position. He had a formidable heading ability and his gap-toothed charge into the penalty area indicated that he also had the courage and daring every spearhead player must possess if goals are to be won. Only Kenny Dalglish has scored more goals but Joe has the added distinction of having scored in three World Cup Finals: 1974, 1978 and 1982. It was in these World Cup forays that he made his name and from that time he was a sought-after striker with a reputation to match his transfer fees. He earned fifty-two caps in all, which is a very healthy figure in these competitive times, and he more than earned his keep as a

Scotland scorer in vital matches. Given his daredevil style of play, he surprised the football world by emerging on his retiral from playing as an astute and thinking manager for Bristol City and Hearts. It was seen that the head which had scored so many goals in its time had its supply of brains. He also has a winning smile when he puts his front teeth in.

It cannot be said that any of the following trio lacked bite, either – Souness, Rough and Robertson.

Graeme James SOUNESS (b. 1953)
Midfielder for Tottenham Hotspur, Middlesbrough, Liverpool,
Sampdoria and Rangers

92

Graeme Souness didn't get off to a good start in football. Although an Edinburgh boy, he had trained with Celtic but it was a London club, Tottenham Hotspur, which signed him up in 1967. However, by 1970 he felt he was making little progress and was very homesick, so he returned to Scotland uncertain about his whole football future. Then in 1973 Jack Charlton signed him for Middlesbrough and within two years he was in the Scotland side. In 1978 he was transferred to Liverpool and linked up with Kenny Dalglish. This was the crucial axis that made a good Liverpool side into a great one and a huge wave of success ensued for Souness and Liverpool at home and in Europe. It was obvious that Graeme Souness could play a bit, but his early experiences may have embittered him and his time at Middlesbrough under Charlton had hardened him. A spell in Italian football with Sampdoria toughened him further and it was a teak-hard professional who returned to Scotland to join Rangers. He became their player-manager and it may be said that his influence at Ibrox precipitated their astonishing run of nine seasons' League success. However, he left Ibrox suddenly (after a storm over a teacup) to rejoin Liverpool as their manager. This was either the best or the worst decision of his life. He later left Liverpool abruptly for Turkey to manage Galatasaray in Istanbul. After winning their national cup, he came back to England to save Southampton from relegation. As soon as this was accomplished he returned to Italy to manage Torino, but this time he was promoted to Head of Football at the club – at which point, astonishingly, he left once more, this time to manage the Portuguese giants, Benfica. There is no doubt he has a winning way even if it doesn't seem to win him friends. This seems to be Graeme's thing. He is seeking his own particular grail, and only he will know when he's found it. Perhaps in the end he will come back to Edinburgh. After all, they say that deep down a man seeks to return to his beginnings, and he was always homesick for the place.

Alan Roderick ROUGH (b. 1951)

Goalkeeper for Partick Thistle, Hamilton Academical, Hibernian, Celtic, Ayr United and Orlando Lions (USA)

93

Alan Rough joined Partick Thistle from a Glasgow amateur side; when he made his international debut he was the fifth choice named to face Sweden in 1976, but he went on to miss only ten games in the next six years and establish himself as a goalkeeper of the highest quality. He had that essential quality required in all the great custodians, flair combined with reliability and a confident unflappability, and this showed in almost every game he played. In 1981 he was voted Scottish Footballer of the Year and in 1986, now a Hibernian player, he was still Scotland's choice as reserve to Jim Leighton. Alan has the distinction of having played at three successive World Cup Finals – Argentina in 1978, Spain in 1982 and Mexico in 1986. One needs special high-altitude training to maintain consistency at such a level, and it says much for Rough's quality that he lasted so long at the top. He was a second-half substitute at Cardiff on the night Jock Stein died. It is a night he will never forget. 'I think we spent two hours in the dressing-room before anyone moved,' he said. It is not generally known, but he was a good outfield player too and could dribble with the best of them, as he showed once at Hampden when he beat Kevin Keegan on the ground, with the aplomb of a Kenny Dalglish.

John Neilson ROBERTSON (b. 1953)

Outside-left for Nottingham Forest, Derby County, Nottingham Forest, Corby and Grantham

94

John Robertson was in that long tradition of Scottish wingers who do their own thing. Bobby Templeton and Alan Morton come to mind, Alex Jackson and Jimmy Johnstone are others. Players who are regarded as being slightly different, even eccentric, but are so prized as individual talents that they are allowed to go their own way. John Robertson was such a player. Brought as a schoolboy international to Nottingham Forest, he blossomed under the equally idiosyncratic Brian

Clough and played a leading part in that club's two European Cup triumphs. Clough let the baby-faced Robertson play his own game and the results more than justified the freedom given to the stocky little winger. Trevor Brooking included him in his *100 Great British Footballers* in 1988, and made this comment about John at the time:

> John Robertson played so wide as a winger that he could have swapped places with the linesman. Superb close control allowed him to virtually run on the line itself and his sudden acceleration let him dart inside at will. Most of all, he knew just when to release a ball. Not every footballer does. He could also entice defenders to commit themselves and when they did he could twist clear to put over yet another goal-making ball from the left, curling it away from the goalkeeper.

He was not a great worker on the pitch, but he didn't need to be. He only ran when necessary, but was a lethal taker of penalty kicks and rarely missed. It was his kick that won the match at Wembley in 1981. He was transferred for a time to Derby County and continued to win honours while with them but, like so many football players, he returned to his first club, and to his mentor, Brian Clough, thus rounding off a completely satisfying professional career in football.

John Robertson's penalty goal at Wembley in 1981 set the seal on the Home Championships which were becoming more and more meaningless in the welter of European and World Cup ties. Soon even the famous annual Scotland *v* England encounter would go the way of the Inter-League fixtures and become a matter more for the record books than for the avid spectator eager for his football thrills. The world was changing too fast and some things would never be the same again. John Lennon had been shot outside his New York flat, and such was the world now, his murderer would become nearly as famous. President Reagan and the Pope were both shot at but nobody attempted to assassinate Kenny Dalglish when Liverpool beat Real Madrid in Paris to win the European Cup for the third time. If King Kenny had ever been killed, Merseyside would have erupted. He and Souness now ruled, one with a sceptre, the other with a rod of iron. Jock Stein was now Scotland's manager by general acclaim, but he was a changed man. The quips and wisecracks were fewer, his manner was guarded and cautious but there was no denying his continued passion for the game. Calmly, he steered Scotland to Spain in 1982 for yet another unsuccessful bid at world honours, but if they won no prizes they achieved the same general measure of acclaim as that accorded their manager and came home quietly satisfied if not elated. They had thrown away a lot of goals against New Zealand, given Brazil a harder game than the score suggested and they drew with Russia. The football-wise Spaniards applauded the Scottish party in the street. This was fitting, as that is where many of the Scots had first learned their football. One could be sure that John Robertson did in Uddingston, much as Jimmy Johnstone did in the same streets. Whether Davie Cooper was street-wise in the football sense, one is less sure, but he had exactly the same kind of insouciance that made them both such memorable ball-jugglers – the kind that has *Made in Scotland* written all over them.

David COOPER (1956–96)   **95**
Outside-left for Clydebank, Rangers and Motherwell

Davie Cooper was in the very first Under-21 Scottish team which drew in a no-scoring game with Czechoslovakia in 1976. He kept his place throughout the next year but it was not until 1979 that he made his first full international appearance against Austria as substitute, and seven years later he completed his total of twenty caps with the game against Brazil in 1987. He was everybody's favourite left-winger and graced the position with his three clubs – Clydebank, Rangers and Motherwell – but especially Rangers. His footwork was a joy to watch and he harked back to another era with his dribbling skills. Some thought he lacked drive but with his ability he had little need of it, and if he were supplied with the ball sufficiently he could turn a game on his own. Towards the end of his career he returned to his first club once more. It was as if he were coming home again. The homecoming was all too brief. Davie Cooper died suddenly after a heart attack in 1996 and another little bit of colour went out of the Scottish game.

Gordon David STRACHAN (b. 1957)   **96**
Inside-forward for Dundee, Aberdeen, Manchester United and Coventry City

As an Edinburgh schoolboy, Gordon went to be part of the ground staff at Dundee and by the time he was nineteen he was captain of the first team. His was always a kind of worrying authority and for a small man he made a large impact on any side he was on. Billy McNeill bought him for Aberdeen just in time for their Championship season of 1979–80 at the end of which Strachan was named Scottish Footballer of the Year. In the same year, he made his international debut against Northern Ireland and seemed set for a lengthy run in midfield, but a hernia operation and intestinal problems put him out of action for some time. He came back the following year against Sweden and didn't look back until he had played on forty occasions for his country. Gordon Strachan is everybody's idea of a Scottish football player – red-haired and vociferous, diminutive and pugnacious. On one occasion, in a reserve game with Dundee, he was playing against a set of twins. One of them fouled him, he wasn't sure which, so he punched both just to make sure. His twinkling feet on the ball were seen in two World Cup Finals and he was rare in that he could both make and score goals on the big occasion. Like a lot of little men, he thrived in the big time. His tongue, however, was a coruscating weapon and he used it both on and off the pitch to withering effect. He was dreaded in the dressing-room. Colleagues called him 'King Tongue' – but never to his face. In 1984 he was transferred to Manchester United and won an FA Cup medal with them in 1985. After an Indian summer with Leeds United, he was sent to Coventry City in the final phase of his career and became their player/manager. He was later manager of Southampton when, in 2004, he abruptly retired – to have a hip replacement. Who knows what he'll do once he's on his feet again – walk right into 6 Park Gardens as the next Scotland manager? I wouldn't put it past him.

Goalkeeper Jim Leighton could not have been more contrasting but Leighton's phlegmatic temperament was as right for his job in football as Strachan's mercurial disposition was for his.

James LEIGHTON (b. 1958)   97
Goalkeeper for Aberdeen, Manchester United and Hibernian

Jim Leighton is a patient and philosophical man. It is not a bad attitude for a professional goalkeeper and one that has stood the Renfrewshire man in good stead. As a schoolboy he played in every outfield position before landing up in goal, but once there, he stayed. Alex Ferguson signed him for Aberdeen in 1976, and once with him, he stayed for most of his career, first with Aberdeen and then with Manchester United. He had to wait for nearly five years to take over from Bobby Clark in the Aberdeen goal and for nearly three years to do so from Alan Rough for Scotland, but he took his chance on both occasions and established himself as first choice. It was the same Alex Ferguson who took him on with him to Manchester United then astonishingly dropped him on the eve of their successful 1985 Wembley Cup final replay. It was Jim's football nadir, but he shrugged it off eventually and returned to Scotland and Hibernian. He had a brilliant World Cup in Mexico and his Scotland career continued in France '98. After achieving his ninety-first cap, against Estonia in October 1998, he decided to retire from international football at the age of forty. What remarkable durability – or is it just ability?

Group Seven in the 1986 World Cup qualifying competition was a tough one for Scotland for it contained Spain, a World Cup favourite, as well as Wales, always a tough proposition, and Iceland, who might spring a surprise as Zaire, Iran and New Zealand had done. Scotland never played well as favourites. It must be something to do with a national complex about always having to come from under or behind that brings out the best in us. At any rate, three wins in a row at Hampden set Scotland up for Mexico. Alex Ferguson remembers:

> Scotland are always best as the underdog. Three months before, Spain were in the European Championship final against France, and were unlucky not to win, in many people's eyes. The press were talking about this great Spanish team and that gave us a wee bit of incentive. It's difficult for me to assess that performance in relation to other Scottish performances but it was a marvellous night for job satisfaction. I was totally elated. At the time you keep calm and sane . . . but I felt like going round a corner and shouting and screaming . . .

At heart, every Scottish manager and player is a fan. The team had everyone excited. Souness was captain, maintaining his club axis with Dalglish, the defence was virtually Aberdeen's and Davie Cooper was inspired out on the left wing. Scotland then won the Sir Stanley Rous Cup by beating England at Hampden on the Whitsun weekend, an event that would have thrilled all of Scotland a few years before, but it passed scarcely noticed. Much more important was the World Cup game against Iceland three days later. Yet another indication of the change in football values. Later, an emotional night in Cardiff saw Scotland draw with Wales thanks to a Davie Cooper penalty. It was enough to see Scotland through to Mexico but it was at the cost of Jock Stein. The terraces were stilled, the floodlights switched off and a pit darkness descended on Scotland's playing field.

His death, coming as it did only months after the horrendous events at the Heysel Stadium in Brussels when forty-one Italian and Belgian supporters were crushed to death behind wire netting after Liverpool supporters had run amok among them, showed the darker face of football. Results were becoming too important, as rewards became greater for success and penalties more onerous for failure. Every team had to win every match in every competition. It was an impossible position and an impossible strain on everyone concerned, most of all the growing number of spectators. Police in every country, fearful of riots when such numbers assembled in restricted areas, insisted on segregation and retention fences. These were hurriedly added to football grounds already years out of date. Stanchions were attached to rusting railings, concrete was poured into deteriorating foundations, so that when excessive body pressure was applied, railings and fences and walls gave way and innocent people, intent on a sporting occasion, died painfully. A respected Law Lord, Lord Taylor, was appointed to look into the whole position of football stadia and their accommodation in the modern age, and his findings were to change the look of every football ground in the country.

Aberdeen were the first to make their ground all-seated, although a large part of it was in the form of spartan benches bleakly exposed to winds off the North Sea, and such a setting was quite in keeping with Aberdeen's unfrivolous efficiency in all aspects of their organisation. Rangers were next to make a palace out of their fortress, and to rid the terraces of the sad traces of two Ibrox disasters. It took Celtic longer to blink into the glare of modernity but they have eventually got there after running as near to bankruptcy as any large concern needs to go. Hearts have a splendid home at the new Tynecastle and when Hibs do climb down the slope from Easter Road, they too will come into line with their peers.

St Johnstone have shown the way at Perth, Clyde at Cumbernauld and Livingston at Livingston New Town, but there is still a long way to go before Albion Rovers can accommodate Benfica in appropriate style. The new football world will have fewer but richer clubs, fewer but more comfortable fans, but it will still have at its centre a flat, green rectangle of grass with a goal at either end where twenty-two young men will pursue a round ball for ninety minutes. As long as the game is kept as simple as that, it will survive everything – even death.

Scotland was the last country to qualify for the 1986 World Cup, the last country to arrive in Mexico for the June games, and the last country anybody expected to win, and yet it was hoped that we would at least get to the later, knock-out stages, but it was not to be. Despite spirited games in the heat against Denmark and West Germany, Scotland, true to international form, wilted before the thug tactics of a ten-man

Uruguay without either side scoring and another wishful-thinking World Cup was over on Friday 13th. Scotland and Northern Ireland went home, leaving England to be beaten by Diego Maradona and the 'Right hand of God' in the semi-final. Argentina and Maradona went on to win the Cup by beating West Germany, the team Scotland nearly beat in the earlier rounds. If only Strachan's shot near the end had gone one inch to the left of the post instead of an inch to the right. *If only* – the perennial Scottish legend. Never mind, there was always 1990 to look forward to, even if it was going to be held in Italy. That's the saving grace of football-following, the one thought that keeps everybody going – there's always next Saturday. However, one blessing from these far-flung outings was that they helped to blood young players coming through the system – Charlie Nicholas, for one. In Mexico, Charlie stole his fifteen minutes of fame, which still continues happily today.

Charles NICHOLAS (b. 1961)
Inside-forward for Celtic, Arsenal, Aberdeen and Clyde

98

Charlie Nicholas was the 'Cheekie Chappie' of Scottish football in the latter part of the twentieth century. He was a direct throwback to Alex James, a snappy dresser with a throwaway line and an eye to the main chance both on and off the field. As a former motor mechanic apprentice, he knew the value of clean hands and appreciated the luxury of a well-cut suit, but again like James, he could also play and he proved it time and time again for club and country. Charlie first played for Scotland against Switzerland in 1983, but his contribution to the Scottish game was greater than his match statistics. He had that rare commodity, *personality*, as evident on the pitch as off and immediately recognised by punters on the terracing. They are quick to recognise their own and to applaud them when they rise above their given level and represent them at the highest levels of sport. If Kenny Dalglish was the idol of the terracings, Charlie was the darling. He was as revered at Highbury as much as he was at Parkhead and Pittodrie. It is this wide generality of appeal that marks him out as a seminal figure in the cavalcade of Scottish players since the end of the last century. Charlie Nicholas remembered that football should be played as a game. He was the epitome of the modern player. He had his agent and his hair-do and he sold his image adroitly to the highest bidder but, like all the greats, when he came to play the actual game on the park, he played it as if he were still a boy. The same impishness informs his current work as a perky TV commentator.

*

Four successive World Cup Finals up to 1986 had given Scotland a remarkable ground base of experience at so many levels (literally and metaphorically) and had provided data of enormous value in preparing a future generation of football players for an international career. Carrying on from Jock Stein's example, both with Celtic and Scotland, preparations and planning were now exemplary. Andy Roxburgh, the SFA's Director of Coaching, took over as manager of Scotland, with Craig Brown as his assistant. Neither of these men was more than a moderate player, but they applied themselves as coaches to an extent where nothing was ever left to chance – except the big chance itself, perhaps. No amount of careful planning, however detailed, or training facilities, however ideal, or hotels, however luxurious, can prepare the young player for the furnace-heat of the game and the taking of chances. Scotland hasn't had a goalscorer since Jimmy McGrory, and not even Lawrie Reilly (who came nearest to him) or Denis Law or Kenny Dalglish, who were the modern equivalents, could guarantee a goal whatever the conditions or occasion.

Playground skills were being forgotten in the over-coaching of the soccer seminar, and natural instincts were being subjugated to the requirements of the team effort. Why has Scotland never produced its own Pele, its own Beckenbauer, its own Puskas today, when it had so many of just that quality a hundred years ago? Where has all the prowess gone? Or is it that we are no longer hungry enough? Scotland were the acknowledged world champions then and we have been in pursuit of that impossible grail ever since. We taught the world to play our game but then forgot how to play it ourselves. We have had, and still have, so many skilful players. Why do we not have a winning team? No expense has been spared recently in training young boys from the earliest years through all the grades of football from primary school to Premier League, but perhaps what the coaches should be teaching them is something that money can't buy.

What is increasingly obvious is that a traditional winter game is being played more and more in summer conditions. Players from the northern hemisphere drag thick thighs and muddy boots through the quagmire of a wet pitch or skate gingerly over ice and snow using more control to keep their feet than to manage the ball. It's often safer to rely on the long ball and chase, than to try any close control or formation passing. These only function in Britain during August to November and from March to May. Billy McNeill has long been an advocate of summer football, with the season ending before Christmas and resuming at or around Easter. The close season would then include the often unplayable months of January, February and March. This makes more sense as fixtures congest year after year and clubs are required to travel into other hemispheres to meet the demands of global competition.

Players from the softer climates are like ballet dancers compared with the dreadnaughts of the north, but things are changing all the time and each is learning from the other. The northerners are learning to be lithe, the southerners are toughening up every season, and soon there will be a universal footballer, fast, clever, full of style and with stamina, and he will probably perform more for the camera than for the spectators around the ground. They will attend free merely to provide atmosphere and the real audience will be the millions gathered by the handful round their respective television sets or in the sports cinemas specially devised for the big occasion.

That time, however, is not quite yet, and football still remains a live experience. The spectator is still held by the sheer drama of the confrontation on the field, the cut and thrust of team exchanges, the gasp at the daring of the unexpected move, the thrill that skill provokes, the emotion that wells up into exaltation or down into tears. One can get all that at a football match. Some people may go through their whole lives without knowing even one of these peaks or depths. This is why football can never die. It has so much of life in it.

Chapter Fifteen

Bosman and After

The man who made so many millionaires out of so many modern footballers lives frugally with his parents in a working-class apartment in a workaday district in a nondescript mid-European city. He himself is mid-height, not quite middle-aged, and is middling good-looking, with an athlete's cropped hair. This is Jean-Marc Bosman, professional footballer, but whether victim or martyr, hero or saint, idiot or prophet, depends on your point of view – or how he feels about himself at the time. In reality, he is rather a sad player who gave up his last club, Fourth Division Vise, in Belgium, to ponder on the fame which cost him his career, his home and his wife, but brought him telephone calls from Johann Cruyff, Eric Cantona and Diego Maradona and newspaper reporters who want to know if he's got his money yet. What had caused all the attention?

He shrugs. 'A principle,' he says quietly.

Bosman was a very promising young player who won more than a score of caps for Under-21 Belgium when with his home-town club, Standard Liège, as well as European Cup experience. An intelligent youth, he had given up his studies to become a professional footballer because, ever since he was a boy, football was all he ever wanted. However, at a crucial stage in his career, aged twenty-five, his form slumped and he was transferred to RFC, the other team in Liège. In 1990 his form hadn't improved and he was offered only a one-year deal from the club, which he rejected. He pointed out: 'The ordinary player is given five years to show that he is good, then he is given another five years to make a living. It was exactly at this point in my life I was deprived of the chance.'

Bosman then retreated to Dunkerque in northern France at an agreed transfer fee, but Liège then withdrew from the deal and Bosman's clearance papers were withheld. He was suspended in the meantime and thus denied an opportunity to earn a living while the two clubs wrangled. Bosman sued FC Liège and the Federation. This resulted eventually in his being allowed to sign for the French Third

Division side, St-Quentin, but then his case was thrown out on appeal so Bosman decided to take it to Europe, claiming that his freedom to work was being threatened by the existing rules. While waiting for the lawyers he played for Charleroi, but his career was sliding as clubs heard about his litigation and very soon he couldn't get a game anywhere. Nor could he even get unemployment benefit, because he had played out of the country, and when he was destitute he had no option but to return to his parents. Meanwhile, he was offered a lump sum by the president of FC Liège to drop the case. He was tempted but refused – on principle.

> At first it was a private affair, but as the case went further, I realised that it was a problem affecting the whole football profession. For five years, I wasn't taken seriously by the clubs, but I wasn't going to be bought off by peanuts. As soon as they saw they were going to lose, it was only the money that mattered to them, but for me it was personal. I wasn't going to walk away now. It wouldn't be fair to the other players.

The case reached the European Court of Justice in Luxembourg in 1995 and support began to come in from the other European federations – France, Spain, Portugal, Denmark, but not, oddly enough, from his own players' union, FIF-pro. Then eight days before the final ruling, after twenty-five meetings with them, a retrospective contract was offered guaranteeing support payments and suggesting a special benefit match be arranged. The case also challenged the use of foreign players and the limits imposed, as well as a footballer's right to the worker's freedom of movement under the Treaty of Rome. Bosman said:

> I don't think football learned anything. Look at the flow of money through the game and yet the rights of the players are despised. I didn't give up my career for others. I didn't want to lose my way of life. It was just the position I was forced into. I had to defend myself. I had no means, and they had everything but I had to go on. I suffered, sure, but that's life. Because of the ruling, every player now gets his money, but I'm still waiting for mine. And it looks as if I'll have to organise the benefit game myself.

Bosman has been totally upheld and justified, yet he has little to show for it. He is due the thanks of every man playing football for a living today and at least he has achieved a kind of football immortality, even if it is only legal. The ghosts of W.C. Rose, the Wolverhampton Wanderers goalkeeper who first proposed a professional union for footballers in 1893, of Charlie Roberts, the Manchester United centre-half and chairman of the union in 1908, of Billy Meredith, the Welsh winger and players' champion throughout his long career from 1894 to 1924, and of Jack Bell, the Scot who spoke out for players' interests before the First World War, would surely applaud the determined Belgian. He has certainly changed the game for ever, and for more than just the players.

These pages have already told of how the old-time internationalists like Jimmy Brownlie of Third Lanark would do half-a-day's normal work on a Saturday morning, have a light 'dinner' as they used to call lunch, wash their faces, put on their only suit and take a tram to Hampden an hour or so before the match. They would meet up with their team-mates in the dressing-room, some they knew and some they didn't, nod to the selectors and then would go out and play like a team that had been playing together all season. There were several reasons why they could do this. One was that there were many fewer international fixtures in the season. An international was a rare article, generally the best player in his position, so he could therefore fit in with most players, adapting the game plan as they went along. He was respected as an individual talent and for the most part he was allowed to follow his own instincts. It is very different today. The modern player is noticed at school, signed on as an apprentice at sixteen, and by eighteen he has been through the international system so thoroughly that he knows his Scotland colleagues better than his fellow club players. Under-16, Under-17, Under-18, Under-19, Under-20, Under-21, Under-22, Under-23 – step by step, rung by rung, the young player goes up the ladder, watched at all times, screened for faults or special aptitudes, exposed to heat and cold, large stadia and tiny grounds, vast crowds and a knot of strangers – he gets everything thrown at him. Some can't take the continuing stress. Some say that the system breeds only marionettes who have their individuality drained out of them, others that it is the only way to cope with the demands of total football.

Some revel in it, and mature steadily and unforcedly. It plays to the strengths of the team man rather than the soloist, but then football is a team game. A good example of the benefits of the system is Celtic wing-half, Paul McStay.

Paul Michael Lyons McSTAY, MBE (b. 1964)
Wing half-back for Celtic

99

Paul McStay, of the famous Lanarkshire footballing family, has been a Celtic man all his life, just like his uncles before him. Similarly, he has been brought through the Scotland ranks from a schoolboy through every stage until the senior side and is one of that generation of footballers who have been educated gradually to be the leaders of their profession. Paul captained the Under-18 Scotland team which won the European Championship and led virtually the same group of players to Mexico for the World Cup in 1986. Billy McNeill, his manager at Celtic, once joked that the SFA should pay Paul's wages since he played more often for Scotland than he did for Celtic. Paul had come through the system with flying colours and many more would follow in his talented footsteps. Before he was a man himself, he had played man-to-man with the world's best at the highest level. He may have been tempted to Italy or Spain at the height of his career, but his heart was with Celtic and he remained with them until an injury cut short his career. He left football with regret and an MBE. He was a good man, Paul McStay, in every way worthy of his lineage. His brothers were fellow professionals and his uncles were famous. Uncle Jimmy McStay was a Celtic player and manager, and his Uncle Willie was a Celtic and Scotland player of some standing between the wars. Uncle Willie's hobby, typically for a mining area, was breeding pedigree dogs. From a football point of view, their own pedigree could not be bettered and Paul is only the latest product. Paul is now a coaching advisor for the Scottish Professional Footballers' Association.

The other kind of player is that type who makes his own way in the football world without the advantage of day-to-day coaching. He learned his trade much in the way that previous generations did, on the park, with older players around him, shouting encouragement or bawling abuse. In the heat of the action, rather than in front of a blackboard, this kind of young player grows up in the sweat of the game, in the frolics of the training session, the banter of the dressing-room. He learns the football business from the inside and by keeping his eyes and ears open. His is not the college approach, he is among the dirt and the scrapes and the missing teeth from the start and if he survives it all he is as capable of taking his place in a commando platoon as much as in a football team. He learns to value the support of team-mates. Things don't always go according to theory or as the textbooks would have one believe. It's rough-and-tumble from the moment the whistle blows and it's a question of taking it and giving it back until it's time to skip or trudge back to the pavilion. Character stamina is as important as physical stamina, a strong personality can assist a weaker talent. The ideal player is he who can combine the best of both worlds, the calm assured composure of the well-schooled and well-coached professional with the survival instincts of the street-fighter in the coloured jersey. Scotland boasts quite a few of these bi-talented players, and one that comes to mind, and who is still playing at the highest level as this is written, is the final player in our century of caps, the veteran striker and 1986 internationalist, Ally McCoist.

Alistair Murdoch McCOIST (b. 1962)
Centre-forward for St Johnstone, Sunderland, Rangers and Kilmarnock **100**

Ally McCoist was always an entertainer and it is no surprise that he has ended up with a flourishing career as a personality on television. He had a personality on the field too and a ready wit to go with it. He also had charm and this linked him to Bobby Templeton and Alex Jackson as an athlete who had immediate appeal to female spectators – but Ally had a sterner side, at least as it applied to the scoring of goals, which he was hired to do. To indicate that he applied himself thoroughly is the fact that he broke Bob McPhail's scoring record at Ibrox and he now stands as Rangers' highest goal-getter. Yet another Bellshill football product, he took some time to get going after a promising start at Perth with St Johnstone. He then moved on to Sunderland for a time but the only good thing he found there was a wife and it wasn't until he joined Rangers (and manager Jock Wallace) that he began to make his mark as a calibre player. He made his first international appearance in 1986, and in 1992 and 1993 he won the Golden Boot award for the highest goalscorer in Europe. He was at his zenith at this time yet he has only a handful of caps to show for his proven goal-scoring talent. This was largely due to his breaking his leg against Portugal in 1993. He was out of action for more than two years, but like Jimmy Delaney after his broken arm, Ally played for Scotland again. He made his comeback by scoring the winning goal at Hampden against Greece. The smile was back on his face and even today, in the Indian summer of his career, he is still smiling – even though it is increasingly into a television camera. 'Super Ally' they call him, and Graeme Souness calls him a lucky bastard. Ally agrees but as he points out: 'You can be lucky once or twice but you can't be lucky forty-nine times. It's gambling, it's instinct, it's timing. A goal's like a good joke, like delivering the punchline at exactly the right moment.' Once again, the analogy is that of the entertainer. Billy Connolly, an admirer, says of him: 'He's handsome, he's rich, he's funny and he's happy – my envy knows no bounds.' Billy speaks for thousands there. During his high times at Rangers, Ally himself said:

> I wake up every morning and I think I'm the luckiest man alive.
> I'm coming in here [to Ibrox]. It's not work, is it? I'd be doing it
> anywhere, just training and playing with my mates for fun. I love
> it. I really love it.

Admirable sentiments for a thoroughly professional sportsman and what a good taste in the mouth it leaves at the end of this football survey. In the summer of 1998 he was transferred to Kilmarnock, with whom he has continued his goalscoring ways. Scotland needs its Alistair McCoists.

Here ends this catalogue of one hundred Scottish international footballers. Just over a century of caps to mark the hundred great players that represent the Scottish game at its highest level. These men are the accepted elite of the sport, but they are only the tiniest fraction of the footballers who have played in and out of their home country since the first ball was kicked in earnest. The great general mass of players has never been acknowledged. It is a team game after all and it takes ten others to make up the side, for no star, however great or gifted, can play the game on his own. So an extra page has been added to accommodate A.N. Other – the Unknown Player, the Twelfth Man, as it were, the Travelling Reserve, the one who doesn't always make the team but makes a living. There have been many more than a hundred great Scottish players playing the great game, but not all of them were capped. Some played before caps were issued, some when caps were suspended, some played for unfashionable clubs and escaped notice and some others had faces that didn't fit with the powers-that-were at the time. Whatever the reason, they ought not to be neglected and so, to complete the full story of the Scottish footballer from the beginning to date, the one-hundred-and-first place in this collection will go to all these others in the person of A.N. Other.

A.N. OTHER

101

This was one of the names given to the extra man brought on to the side when neither party was sure that he was going to make it on the team. He was also known as 'Junior', 'Trialist', 'Newman' or 'A. Centre' – it didn't matter, he was anonymous until he made his name. Alan Morton, one of the all-time greats, started in this manner as did so many others.

Alexander Tait of Preston North End and the first Tottenham Hotspur team is quite forgotten today but he became a big football name when the game began in England nearly one hundred and thirty years ago. Little is known of Sandy Tait from that faraway football epoch except that he came from Ayr and graduated from the football academy that was Preston North End in those days. Although nominally a full-back, he played all over the place for the Spurs, in every position as required in the course of any one game. He virtually comprised a one-man team in the manner of those days and played till he was almost fifty. For the rest of his long life, this 'honest man frae the toon o' Ayr' remained a hero of north London.

Archie Hunter also came from Ayr, where he had played for Ayr Thistle. In 1874 he left to work in Birmingham. Keen to continue his football, he enquired at the Birmingham City ground and instead was directed to the newly founded Aston Villa, who couldn't believe their luck in having such a player walk in and ask for a trial. He began as 'A. Centre', but rapidly became known throughout the Midlands and was finally dubbed 'The Prince of Dribblers'. He would often score straight from the kick-off, working his way right and left through an entire defence then rounding the goalkeeper to place the ball in the empty net. He was also skilful in the long pass while on the run and in 'laying off' to team-mates in the modern manner by shielding the ball with his body while his back was to goal. '*Now, lads!*' was his only exhortation on the field and the Villa would respond to a man. Unfortunately, his employer was not so easily coaxed and would not always release Archie, who had to work a full day on a Saturday. So, on match days, workmates would cover for Archie as he slipped out by a side entrance and ran to the brake waiting around the corner. He would come onto the field to a great ovation. The papers that evening would report on the splendid performance once again by A. Centre, but everyone – except his employer, perhaps – knew who it was. Yet this football paragon never played for Scotland. He was only one of many who were missed. Billy McPhail, brother of Celtic's John, was another. He was injured on each of the many occasions he was selected to play and never won a cap.

Nicholas John Ross (1863–94) was another uncapped Scottish player who nevertheless was a giant of the early game and was perhaps the greatest full-back of his time, on a par with Queen's Park's Walter Arnott, John Forbes of Vale of Leven or Dan Doyle of Celtic. He could kick as artistically as Walter Arnott, tackle as hard as Forbes and go forward like Doyle, yet he never played for Scotland. He was born in Edinburgh, played first for Edinburgh Rovers and in 1874 signed as a professional for Hearts and became their captain. He joined Preston North End in 1883. Nick Ross was neither big nor strong but he 'read' the game so well that he could play on the weaknesses of the opposition. He laid the foundation of the famous 'Invincibles' Cup and League 'double' side, although he didn't play in that particular team due to his death at thirty-one from consumption. A slater to trade, he was one of the first to try his football luck in England. Ross developed the scientific game which that wonderful Preston side perfected. He and Captain Sudell, the North End manager, discussed tactics on a blackboard and played out games with chessmen on a billiard table. It all paid off. He completely dominated the Preston and Everton sides he played for and might have done the same for his country if only the selectors had glanced just across the border, but that wasn't their policy at that time. Ironically, he played in the first Football League representative side in 1891. It was his only honour. He deserved so much more.

The other Ross in the Scottish football story deserves a passing mention, if only for his application to training, an aptitude not shared by too many Scottish players. The Victorian report says:

> This Ross is a sturdy fellow. Rumour has it that he attends training to a ridiculous degree. A run in the early morning is good for any man, but practising charging against railway trucks is completely out of it.

He might be said to have made a laughing rolling stock of himself. Other players were unlucky in coinciding with two World Wars. Like J.G. Reid of Airdrie and Willie Cringan of Celtic, who had their best years during the Great War. A victim of World War Two in that sense was Ephraim 'Jock' Dodds, who came to fame in wartime, leading the Scotland line eight times and scoring eight goals in the process. Yet, officially, he does not exist as a Scottish internationalist, as is the case with so many others of his generation, like Malcolm MacDonald of Celtic, Archie Baird of Aberdeen, Jimmy Brown of Hearts, Jackie McGowan of Partick Thistle, Bert Crozier, Brentford's goalkeeper and wee Jimmy Caskie of St Mirren, Hibernian, Everton and Rangers, who also played eight times for Scotland yet never won a cap. Officially, these international appearances count for nothing in the records because there was a war on. This seems a pity but it is so. A matter of the same unfortunate fact is that poor Tommy Bogan of Hibernian and Celtic had the shortest-ever international career, breaking his leg in under a minute against England at Hampden in 1945. He never played for Scotland again. Leslie Johnstone of Clyde came on as a substitute but that didn't count for a cap. All these fine footballers were unlucky in their dates of birth. In other times, who knows how many caps they might have gone on to earn? This space therefore is given over to them and to the many, many others who also played once for Scotland and never again. Good players like Jock Dodd's Blackpool team-mates Buchan and Finan, Celtic's Willie Corbett, Liverpool's Fagan, Hibernian's Kean; and those whose names are quite forgotten, like Harris of Queen's Park and Harris of Wolves, Pinkerton of Falkirk, Williams of Clyde and McCulloch of Derby – these are only some of the players with a solitary appearance. Their immortality only lasted ninety minutes. Never mind, they are still entitled to say: 'I played for Scotland.' Many would love to say the same.

There are many Scottish players who never played for their country and ought to have done and one that readily comes to mind from recent times in this respect is Ally MacLeod. This likeable, unlucky extrovert was buried in the aftermath of Scotland's unhappy World Cup in Argentina in 1978, but this was more a reaction to the hype beforehand and to the poor performance of the team on the day. Ally was only the manager but the buck stopped there and it's been bucking him ever since. This is unfair, surely. His record got him the job. He had proved himself a good manager with Ayr United and Aberdeen. It was unfortunate that he hit a poor crop with his Scotland pool but the fact remains that he drew 25,000 people to Hampden just to watch a Scotland team line up in their suits. 'Aye,' quipped Ally drily, 'but there was 100,000 waiting for me when we g \t back!' At the time, he was a tonic to the game and to the country. He added to the joy of the nation. He deserved better. He was a brilliant salesman and given the goods he could have done his country proud. As it was, he took all the blame. What is forgotten, too, is that he was a really good (if rather eccentric) player in his time, but then he said, 'If I don't know what I'm going to do then the other fellow won't know either.' This philosophy confused many good defenders, like big George Young who hated playing against MacLeod. Jimmy Mason, who was in the same team with Ally, said at the time, 'I play with him every week, and I still don't know his next move.' Third Lanark was Ally's local club when he began his career as an eighteen-year-old in 1949. He had supported them as a boy and he wasn't long in making himself a 'Hi-Hi' favourite. There was never a dull moment when he played and he relished the big occasion. He only moved to Blackburn Rovers in 1956 because the transfer fee helped pay off the club debt. He had an unquenchable humour. When the stand caught fire before the end of his first game with the club: 'I knew I'd set Cathkin on fire,' he recalled. With the other players, he had to scamper to the dressing-room, grab his clothes and run. He ran from there to Blackburn and back to Cathkin again and then all the way to Córdoba in the course of time, but somewhere along the way he caught the heart of the football population and he should be fondly remembered for that. Football, after all, is more a matter of heart than feet. As anyone who loves the game well knows.

*

Arthur Hopcraft says in *The Football Man* (1968):

> Football matters. As poetry does to some people and alcohol does
> to others; it engages the personality. It is a compulsion.

As the millennium draws nearer, the world is worried about the
gradual extinction of the humpback whale, the Bengal tiger, the white
rhinoceros, the giant panda and the great ape, but also under the same
threat is that even rarer species, the Scottish inside-forward. In this
uniform age where the risks are great because costs are astronomical,
this is a form of football life at risk. No more is he allowed to dwell
lovingly on the ball, stroke it deftly right or left and watch, from a
standing position, the goal that results from his special insights. It
would be a shame if he were run off his feet, for he has much to offer
even in the helter-skelter of the modern game. He gives the spectator
a moment of peace in the mayhem and an opportunity to see the brain
at work among twenty other hurrying legs. Football will not be itself
again until the virtuoso is brought out from among the industrious
orchestral players and allowed his cadenza. It will have a definite
Scotch feel to it, for that is how it all began just over a hundred years
ago, when the world of football was measured in Scottish feet as they
danced over the border to the jingle of coin.

How important is football in Scotland? It depends on how your
team is doing, but how important is it *to* Scotland? The answer is –
vital. In future histories, it might be seen that the most important
Scottish victory was not Bannockburn in 1314, nor in regaining the
right to her own parliament in 1997, but in holding out against FIFA
in 1946 when the world football authority wanted to fuse the four
British Associations into one Great Britain team. Certainly it would
have been lovely to have had John Charles from Wales, George Best
from Ireland and Tom Finney from England in their time, but it
wouldn't have been the same. It wouldn't have been *Scotland*. The
Scotland that has had our pulses racing with pride and passion – and
exasperation. The Scotland that embodied its nationhood in eleven
young men when most of the world thought that Scotland was merely
the northern part of England. Our football team is in our blood and
bone and it carries a bit of all of us with it wherever it goes. Which is
why our hearts go with those eleven men. If the bonnets of the Tartan
Army are ludicrous, their kilts too long, their language too strong and
their singing atrocious, they are there – they are the people, and they
are there for all of us. For the people, to whom the game belongs. For
all those who have gone before and for all who will come after.

Chapter Sixteen

The Way Ahead

We will now consider those who will come after. Those bright soccer hopefuls whose star is still rising and whose tomorrows still exceed their yesterdays by a long way. They are, in many ways, a different breed from the hundred that have gone before, but they still have the same aim – to make a name in the game and, one day, to pull on a Scottish jersey and play their hearts out at the top level. It's very much a matter of heart, an area where their agents, lawyers and accountants have little relevance – or interest. For any sportsman, to represent one's country is still the highest honour the game can bestow and it has little to do with money. By modern standards, the fee is derisory, but when was that ever an issue? It's a matter of heart, and as Burns said:

> Nae pleasures nor treasures can make us happy lang,
> The heart's ay the part ay that maks us richt or wrang.

How many footballers' hearts were in their mouths, I wonder, when, on Tuesday, 23 March 2004, at the SFA offices at Park Gardens in Glasgow, chief coach Bertie Vogts announced the Scotland squad from which he would choose the team to face Romania in the Safeway international friendly at Hampden on Wednesday 31.

Goalkeepers:
Robert Douglas (Celtic)
Paul Gallacher (Dundee United
Craig Gordon (Heart of Midlothian)

Defenders:
Graham Alexander (Preston North End)
Steven Caldwell (Newcastle United)
Christian Dailly (West Ham United)
Jackie McNamara (Celtic)

David McNamee (Livingston)
Graeme Murty (Reading)
Steven Pressley (Heart of Midlothian)
Paul Ritchie (Walsall)
Andy Webster (Heart of Midlothian)

Midfield:
Gary Caldwell (Hibernian)
Colin Campbell (Wolverhampton Wanderers)
Darren Fletcher (Manchester United)
Gary Naysmith (Everton)
Stephen Pearson (Celtic)
Gavin Rae (Rangers)

Forwards:
Stephen Crawford (Dunfermline Athletic)
Paul Gallagher (Blackburn Rovers)
Kevin Kyle (Sunderland)
Neil McCann (Southhampton)
James McFadden (Everton)
Kenny Miller (Wolverhampton Wanderers)
Stephen Thompson (Rangers)

Then, to everyone's surprise, Herr Vogts introduced a further selection by displaying a Scotland jersey with the number 25 on it and the name, The Tartan Army. Yes, the famous (or notorious) Scotland supporters were given a place at the feast – and that was official. This was certainly an innovation, and whether it was in recognition of the Scotland supporters' unquenchable loyalty and the benefit that was to the team or yet another commercial ruse to sell product is open to question. Whatever the reason, there it was, a cap for all those whose fathers wore bunnets. It was a nice gesture – I think. How much did it savour of currying favour, I wonder? Surely not. After all, Aberdeen list their supporters, the Red Army, at No 12. Yet, not so long ago, that same Tartan Army, in long kilts and bare chests, were swinging from the Wembley goalposts and taking over London for the night. More recently, in the European Championships, for the game between England and Scotland, Wembley's booking staff were instructed not to sell tickets to anyone with a Scottish accent. Not that it mattered. Gary McAllister missed a penalty and Scotland lost. Soon afterwards, Gary retired from the international scene after 57 caps because those same fans gave him a hard time. Now they were named as part of the official Scotland squad. Will they be red-carded for invading the pitch? Is the Hampden Roar still worth a goal start? We'll see.

Would the imperious Sir George Graham, former Chief Executive of the SFA, have been capable of such a public relations stroke? I doubt it. That redoubtable martinet had the Scotland team sheet read out with all the solemnity of the Riot Act. Given the mood of the crowds then gathered on the pavement outside the old SFA offices in Carlton Place this was not inappropriate. They were different days indeed. There were no coaches then and supporters wore their own clothes to the game. Football had different values at that time, but what was clearly evident was that playing for Scotland was something of national importance and not a matter to be trivialised by gimmicks or marketing gambits.

That apart, Tuesday was good news day for two of the younger players, Livingston defender David McNamee and Hearts goalkeeper Craig Gordon, but whether they would play on the day would be at the whim of Herr Vogts. This is the man, the 14th Scottish coach in an illustrious line from Andy Beattie in 1947, who, with typical Teutonic efficiency, has masterminded our football decline in the last decade. Despite his own undoubted pedigree as a footballer, starting at seven with his home-town club, VFR Buttgen, near Dusseldorf, and scaling the heights in Europe with Borussia Munchengladbach, Hans-Hubert 'Bertie' Vogts, twice German Player of the Year, has been seemingly unable to bring this experience and expertise to bear on the emerging Scottish players coming under his hand.

Some of them were very good players already. Men like Jackie McNamara of Celtic, and Barry Ferguson, then of Rangers and now of Blackburn Rovers, were star players by any standard. Both captains of their respective sides, each was a credit to the system that produced them. Jackie, the son of a footballer, came to Celtic from Dunfermline in 1995 and won a raft of medals with them as well as the esteem of their vast following for his skills as an attacking defender. Barry, who said he was driven south by the pressures of sectarian abuse in Glasgow, was playing a man's part in the Rangers' team while still a boy. Injury has seriously affected his emergence on the same level with Blackburn Rovers, but given his determination, he will be back. Two much younger players are destined for similar distinction on the field. Edinburgh's Darren Fletcher and Glasgow's Jamie McFadden are already being hailed as Scotland stars after only a handful of international appearances between them. Interestingly, both turned down offers from Rangers and Celtic, despite the fact that Fletcher is a self-confessed Celtic supporter. Buoyant and confident, the midfielder is certainly one for the future, and Everton colleagues predict the same for Faddy, as they call Jamie McFadden. He has all the impishness of his fellow-Glaswegian Charlie Nicholas and should do well in the company he keeps at Everton. Another Scot with high potential is the former 'Jam Tart', Neil McCann, who, after a good spell on the left wing for Rangers, took the eye with Southampton. He was a standout in his international debut while a Rangers player but the best of him may be yet to come. Goalkeeper Craig Gordon, also a Tynecastle product, shows the same high promise. As does Celtic's midfielder, Stephen Pearson. Any of these players are capable of entering the Football Hall of Fame given time. In the present squad, however, there is no pivotal player. No one of outstanding calibre and personality around whom the side can be built. There is a need for such a player in any great team. Just like Murdoch was to the Lisbon Lions or Cantona to Manchester United. The reliable Dailly is there again, of course, but what is needed is the kind of player whose influence is as much in the dressing-room as on the field. Fletcher might grow into it one day. Time will tell.

Then there were players not selected. Like Scot Gemmill. His father was Archie Gemmill, who scored the most famous goal in Scotland's international history when he tanner-ba'd his way through the Holland defence during the 1978 World Cup in Argentina. Father and son are Paisley buddies but Archie went on to Nottingham Forest where Scot also started before going out to play in Japan. He has been with Everton since 1999. Gateshead-born Don Hutchison started with Hartlepools and then played with a string of clubs, including Liverpool and West Ham, then he, too, joined Everton, where there is now quite a Scottish colony. Celtic's Paul Lambert was an established player in the game when he came on the international scene. A former St Mirren and Motherwell player, Lambert had actual German playing experience, winning a UEFA Championship medal with Borussia Dortmund in 1996 before returning to Scotland and joining Celtic. If we add his young clubmate, Shawn Maloney, we can see that a considerable pool of talent was not utilised. Yet, it must be said, their international performances were in no way commensurate with the aggregate skills these players showed in their club form from week to week. They never seemed able to move up an extra gear on the day. Something was wrong. If it were the German influence, which has seen Scotland lose nine of its last games over the last five years, it was another German, assistant-coach Rainer Bonhof, also a notable player in his day, who named the Under-21 squad that day. These were:

Goalkeepers:
Craig Samson (Kilmarnock)
Graeme Smith (Rangers)
Iain Turner (Everton)

Defenders:
Alexander Diamond (Aberdeen)
Andrew Dowie (Rangers)
John Kennedy (Celtic)
Paul Lawson (Celtic)
Jamie McCunnie (Ross County)
Scott Morrison (Aberdeen)

Midfield:
Scott Brown (Hibernian)
Chris Burke (Rangers)
Mark Fotheringham (Dundee)
Simon Lappin (St Mirren)
Peter Sweeney (Millwall)
Kevin Thomson (Hibernian)
Mark Wilson (Dundee United)

Forwards:
Craig Beattie (Celtic)
Kris Boyd (Kilmarnock)
Paul Gallagher (Blackburn Rovers)
David Clarkson (Motherwell)
Robbie Foy (Liverpool)
Stephen Murray (Kilmarnock)
Garry O'Connor (Hibernian)
Derek Riordan (Hibernian)

In all, these two groups of players comprise the 49 best young Scots playing football in 2004. Paul Gallagher was named in both squads, and Zander Diamond and John Kennedy have already moved up to the Under-21s. These upwardly mobile young men are from all kinds of clubs and all parts of the country. At the very least, they are a tribute to the comprehensive scouting system that leaves no stand seat empty in the search for future talent, but still Scotland struggles in the international arena. Before Vogts' coming we were ranked at 20 in the FIFA listings, and when the first edition of this book was published in 1998 we were at 37. We had sunk even lower in 2003, having dipped to 64, so it could be said we were on the up again, but it is surely an embarrassing situation for a country that once so prided itself on its football. What is needed now is a pride of new young lions in the dark blue with the lion rampant on every chest. These cubs are all ready to roar.

As it happened, the Romania game was yet another loss by 2–1 and, clearly, the Teutonic grip on our native game was now put under threat, yet Herr Vogts still insisted that 'the future of Scottish football is very, very bright'. One wonders from which window he is looking? He also expressed himself 'very pleased with the good performance of the team'. But we were beaten, and what was worse, one of our brightest young stars, John Kennedy of Celtic, was seriously injured by a heavy tackle after only ten minutes' play. This is a dear blow for both club and country as Kennedy was just beginning to emerge as a star. However, there were no votes for Herr Vogts. This was succinctly expressed by Graham Spiers, chief sports writer of *The Herald* on 2 April, when he said: 'The sheer tedium of observing Scotland's grinding progress under Berti Vogts is starting to require Benedictine patience and forbearance.' It is hardly an analogy that would endear him to the Scottish football hierarchy who probably only know Benedictine as a drink, but Mr Spiers spoke for an awful lot of people in Scotland, and Scots abroad – even those Scots in Germany.

Their only comfort is that there is a lot of young talent yet to be let loose on the senior playing field and perhaps it is in them our best hopes lie. Who knows if they will ever make it to the top, and if they don't, it won't be for the want of coaching. Old players like Ross Mathie and Tommy Burns now oversee the youth contingents but football is not the coaches, however experienced or skilled, it is the players, and they should always be our first and final concern. In goalkeeper David Marshall of Celtic we might have our next Jerry Dawson or in David Clarkson of Motherwell a future Jimmy McGrory. It's all in the lap of the gods. And not all whom the gods love, die young. They are only injured. These young men have everything to play for.

Goalkeepers:
David Marshall (Celtic)
Andrew Reid (Motherwell)

Defenders:
Mark Baxter (St Johnstone)
Fraser Coyle (Rangers)
Alexander Diamond (Aberdeen)
Gary Irvine (Celtic)
Stephen Low (Celtic)
Paul Quinn (Motherwell)

Midfield:
Charlie Adam (Rangers)
Ross MacLeod (Heart of Midlothian)
Steven Smith (Rangers)
Ross Wallace (Celtic)
Jamie Winter (Leeds United)

Forwards:
Scott Brown (Hibernian)
David Clarkson (Motherwell)
Robert Foy (Liverpool)
Ryan Wilkie (Liverpool)
Kenny Wright (Motherwell)

And then there are the boys of the Under-17 brigade, those with their brand-new boots on the first rung of the football ladder whose only way is up.

Goalkeepers:
Andrew McNeil (Southampton)
Callum Reidford (Rangers)

Defenders:
Patrick Boyle (Everton)
Scott Cuthbert (Celtic)
Alex McColl (Rangers)
Steven McKeown (Leeds United)
Jason Thomson (Heart of Midlothian)

Midfield:
Brian Gilmour (Rangers)
Bryan Hodge (Blackburn Rovers)
James McCluskey (Hibernian)
Michael McGlinchey (Celtic)

Robert Snodgrass (Livingston)

Forwards:
Scott Agnew (Rangers)
Steven Fletcher (Hibernian)
James Graham (Leicester City)
Mark Quinn (Motherwell)
Philip Reid (Motherwell)
Kevin Smith (Leeds United)

At 16, James McCluskey of Hibernian, who has already been mentioned, is the youngest of all the players catalogued in this chapter. Let's hope he may be a talisman for Scotland's new awakening on the park. There are just as many promising young players today as there ever were. My only worry is that we don't let them *play* the game enough. From their first kick of the ball they are made to *work* at it, and this inevitably creates another kind of mindset. Instead of being free to enjoy the adventure of finding out for themselves in the playground or the park or the street, the young boy today is bound to a professional cadetship that drills all the spontaneity out of his game before he really knows how to play it. The fear of error replaces the courage to have a go. The work-rate is instilled too early. What even the best coaches forget is that the great players, even today, revert to the boyish joy in the game that they knew as boys and relish every opportunity to attempt the impossible – and do so with style. Watch Real Madrid's Ronaldo, or Figo or Zidane. They love the ball and want to have it at their feet as much as possible. So did Diego Maradona and Johan Cruyff and George Best in their day. These were all world-class players – and it showed. At the height of their game they went back to playing as boys again. Perhaps that's a lesson we should heed. Lesser talents play as if they were afraid of the ball. They seem to want nothing to do with it. They treat it as if it were red hot and pass it as soon as it comes to them. The players are runners and kickers, not footballers. They may adapt well to the coach's instructions and may be effective tactically and assist the team plan, but it makes for a dull player and a dull game.

Football is not a dull game if played well. It can't be. The tension and excitement are inherent parts of the spectacle, and, if the spectator is more than a celebrity hunter, who only looks for a result at whatever cost, he will be rewarded at some time in the ninety minutes by a sudden flash of skill or an uplifting goal that brings him to his feet. The great game is full of heart-pounding possibilities and this is what brings the thousands upon thousands to the grounds. It is certainly not the corporate hospitality. One goes always hoping that some magic will happen. Perhaps this is best expressed by Eduardo Galeano in his wonderful book, *Football in Sun and in Shadow*:

> Years have gone by, and I've finally learned to accept myself for who I am: a beggar for good football. I go about the world with hand outstretched, and in the stadiums I plead: 'A pretty move for the love of God.'

You always know where you are with football. You either win, lose or draw, whether you're at the game, watching it in the pub or at home. It has its own inescapable logic because it's bound by its own rules. In an uncertain world such as ours, this is its reassuring certainty, and, as a result, makes it more real to many than the real world beyond the turnstiles. It's a comforting thought.

We cannot bring back the past, however glorious, nor can we keep our heads buried in the sands of time. It behoves us, however, now and again, to remember that we, too, once had a pedigree worth boasting about and although there were times when we might have been a little less arrogant, at least we had something to be arrogant about. It's a very different picture today, and our only hope is in tomorrow. Is there yet some undiscovered 'A.N. Other' who, one day, will lead the resurgence towards new glories. Let's hope so. And that there will always be a little boy kicking a football about in the corner of a foreign field that is forever Scotland.

Extra Time for Jonathan

I took my son to a football match
As my father did once with me
To our local club not far from us
A week last Saturday.
We stood in line with the rest of the men
And boys,
And mine whispered hoarsely to me:
'Will we get in all right? Will you lift me over?
How much is it going to be?'
Somehow we force our way in
Climb to the top terracing
Find a spot where he can just see
High on the mound
Engulfed in the sound
My seven-year-old and me.
He was staring straight ahead
Eyes bright, cheeks red,
Draining the scene of its smallest tincture
Drinking it into his blood.
'This is the life, this is life,'
But he didn't hear what I said.
Does he understand
What passion is, what feeling means?
Then I felt him press my hand.
The interval comes like a relief
As thirty thousand men turn about,
A single thought in mind.

Some do it as they stand, into bottles held in hand.
I don't know what to say, I pull my son away.
Some things are better learned late.
We push our way to the refreshment gate.
'Would you like a Bovril?' I ask him,
'They've got hot pies.'
There's a solemn look in the big round eyes.
'I want –' 'What?' 'You know.'
Then I realise he wants to go.
We push our way through the wall of men
In muffled coats, and caps and scarves,
Breathing steam into the winter air
And quickly descend the concrete stair
Into the dark, smelly cave on the side of the hill.
We were back in our place as the teams came out,
Splashing their colours on the green park.
I think there was another goal
I know we won. But I didn't see.
It wasn't the crowd. No.
I only had eyes for a little boy
As my father had once – for me.

John Cairney

Jonathan Cairney 1977

Chapter Seventeen

Match Report

We have taken all the extra time we can but, regrettably, the final whistle has blown and it's time to leave the pitch. The game has been played, but have all the goals we set ourselves been achieved? Who is to say? We might require to be a long way off yet to attain a proper perspective. Some people will have seen more of the game than others, some will see more in it than the rest might see, but it is a spectator sport, and it is his or her right to see in it what he or she wants to see. We are all partisan in football. Bias is part of our football right. Football. The simple game that is anything but simple in all its ramifications. It is everything and anything the spectator sees in it, from a pleasant picnic in the open air to a cosmic conflict that has the fate of the whole world in its outcome. It all depends on how you see it. It is played out within a confined, prescribed place yet it reaches out beyond its perimeters to touch a part of all who watch in a way that exactly relates to the spectator's involvement. It is a game as elemental as a marathon, as intricate as chess, as exciting as a ski jump, as dangerous as a bullfight and as good as any play. It combines the excesses of grand opera with the cerebral subtlety of a motet but it can move one as deeply as a sonata and lift one like a song. It is point and counterpoint, ballet with a ball. It is football. It is the game that ordinary people have made their own. It doesn't belong exclusively to the clubs, certainly not to the directors, hardly to the players. Nor is it owned – yet – by the multinational global interests that own everything else that we see in the world around us. It is owned by the people who make it what it is by turning up in their dozens, or hundreds, or thousands, or hundreds of thousands to watch a game being played by twenty-two young men on a level piece of ground.

The football athletes of today are a far cry from the whiskered amateurs who romped on the Victorian playing field for healthy exercise. The modern player is a professional, trained to every hair of his shaved head, who has learned to run and run and treat the ball as if it were red hot. Old players loved the ball and hugged it to them but their modern counterpart, except in exceptional cases, is not so sure of it. His instinct is to pass it and run, as if in passing it on to someone else he is also passing on the responsibility for action. The player today knows all about work-rate and the team plan and his commitment is rather to the need not to lose than to the adventure of winning. He has learned all about the furtive spit, the blind-side elbow, the jersey tug, the subterfuge heel-flick and all the other tricks in the professional's armoury, but he has forgotten how to play like a boy. The way he played in the public park, or any open space when nobody could get the ball from him. He loved it so much it was as if it were tied to his boot. The great players still play like boys, and in doing so make us all, as we watch, young again. Over nearly 150 years the expression of football may have changed but its face remains the same and it is always of its own time. It has grown from a casual sporting activity among gentlemen to an international institution that has provoked murder, war and national unrest, and yet at heart it remains what it always was – the pursuit of a goal.

A game of football was once called a goal of football because its whole point was just that – the attaining of a goal. What else is life? A goal is still a goal whether it is flashed on an electronic scoreboard for all the world to see or scrambled home in a hectic scrimmage between two folded jackets on a piece of spare ground. The player is still a player even with his trousers stuck in his stockings enjoying a scratch game with his mates in the park, just as much as any over-paid, prima performer who struts his stuff in the stadium. The Sunday park player has a waistline to watch or a heart attack to worry about, but the other has an image to maintain. Nevertheless, they are both 'merely players'. The scratch player may only have friendly ribbing to deal with, but the professional has to cope with autogenic and assertive coaching methods, press calls and television cameras, not to mention psychological pressures his great-grandfather would never have guessed at, but he is still playing the same game. Yet it is a game that has grown in ways that are not always obvious on the playing field. Football has become a part of show business. The professional player is now recognised as an entertainer, a performer and is as likely to be a member of Actors' Equity as the Players' Union. He has a place in society far beyond mere sporting skills. He is a substitute, a proxy, a stand-in for all that is unattainable for so many. He is young, healthy and rich – what else does anyone want? Except more of it. He is a contemporary clay idol with feet of gold and is worshipped accordingly. Even in circles well removed from football, who has not heard of David Beckham? And for reasons just as much removed from football.

The Jean-Marc Bosman verdict of 1995 changed the status of the footballer forever. The ruling which this modest player won for his better-known colleagues cut them from their bondage to the club and lifted them from the status of mere chattels to being independent properties of some worth in the new, material world of football. He was no longer to be bought and sold as a commodity, but would have the same freedom of movement as any other worker and his contract would now be worth the paper on which it was written. Every contract now would be short-term, and when it was completed, the player could move on from club to club, or country to country, or re-sign as negotiated. George Eastman's court case in 1961 to win a transfer on request was a worthy battle for the player's rights, and with the help of the Professional Footballers' Union, it led to the abolition of the iniquitous maximum wage, but Bosman's victory made it seem no more than a minor court scuffle. The 1995 decision was a big step and it released a whole generation of mercenaries to ply their trade across the whole face of the globe. The original 'Scotch Professors' would have revelled in it. J.J. Lang might have retired early instead of ending his days as a steward at Ibrox. Willie Groves might have been saved from charity, and Mike McKeown from drink. Jim Baxter could have kept his pub.

Essentially, however, football is more than a matter of money. Yes, of course, it exercises the minds of most of us who don't have it, and the love of it is a sin that besets all walks of life, but once a player pulls a jersey over his head and runs onto the park, not all the money in the world will make him play better. Certainly, he will be well aware of bonuses and benefits and all the little extras that abound around the head of a modern footballer, but for the most part that is all dressing-room talk or training-ground gossip. There have been much-publicised incidents of players being paid by the goal but it was noticeable that their scoring rate did not immediately improve. There are more than 12,000 professional players in Britain alone and you can be sure that not one of them is thinking money as he runs out onto the field with his team-mates. Football is a business and clubs are not in the game for the love of it. The players are in it, too, to make a living, but the game is beyond the cash register once the whistle blows.

Football is a global phenomenon but its roots are as English as its first flowering was Scottish. From its establishment it spread around the world and even today it stands as one of Britain's most durable exports, as James Walvin points out in his *People's Game*. Like Mary's little lamb, their sport followed the Brits wherever they went before the end of the nineteenth century, and as a result it flourished in every country in the world, except India, China, Japan, Australasia and North America. It is only getting started in these places now, so watch out for the World Cup in China by 2052. Had it not been for those enterprising soldiers, sailors, public schoolboys, businessmen, wandering footballers and touring teams we might not have had a Puskas or a Pele, a Beckenbauer or a di Stefano, or any of the other majestic players that have sprung from every country visited. Without question it is now the world game, if only for the fact that most of the world plays it. FIFA, the international federation of football clubs, began in a back room in Paris on 21 May 1904 because the Football Association of the time was too high-minded or high-handed to take action that would have kept the international control of football in the country of origin, much as golf is administered from St Andrews and tennis from Wimbledon. Early in 1904, Sir Frederick Wall, the FA secretary, was instructed to sound out the various continental football bodies which had sprung up with a view to a federation, or some measure of control, and suggested a conference of all concerned to be held in London. The continentals agreed and waited for instructions, but all they received was a letter addressed to the Union des Sociétés Françaises de Sports Athlétiques, stating:

> The Council of the Football Association cannot see the advantage
> of such a Federation, but on all matters upon which joint action
> was desirable they would be prepared to confer.

They had obviously discussed it and decided that wogs still began at Calais and they would let them get on with it. So the associations of France, Belgium, Switzerland, Holland, Denmark and Sweden went ahead for themselves and FIFA was born. British insularity had cost the FA its place at the centre of the world, and later it would threaten the very existence of the Scottish, Welsh and Irish Associations, but one can't help feeling that a golden chance was lost in 1904, and it wasn't helped when Britain walked out of FIFA in 1928. It wasn't until the end of the Second World War that England saw the error of its ways and applied to join FIFA in 1952. Scotland followed suit two years later. What a waste of a wonderful football opportunity and what a waste of valuable time too. The Laws of the Game moved to Zurich, but much of its spirit remained in Britain, and to the same extent in Scotland, no matter the changes and the impact of television on attendances. England and Scotland are no longer the mother and father of the sport, the proud parents who could be heard quarrelling in whispers in the bedroom. Rather, they are just another two of its many children, struggling at the rear to keep up. They have been usurped by the Latins and the Teutonics, and the Africans – and the Orientals are coming. The begetters must learn their place. The return of the United Kingdom Associations to FIFA was celebrated by a match at Hampden Park in May 1946 between Britain and The Rest of Europe. One hundred and thirty-five thousand spectators saw Britain, with Scots Billy Steel and Billy Liddell forming the left wing, win 6–1. It was the swan-song of British football supremacy. Such an assertion of superiority could never happen again. The British football Raj is no more. It's another world now.

Similarly, the cigarette manufacturers, once the provider of every schoolboy's dream by giving him a handy and ready – and what was more important, *transferable* – likeness of his football idols, are now in the advertising limbo, and nothing more may be expected from them in a world where a fall in advertising revenue is looked upon as a health hazard. Their place has been taken by the sports clothing manufacturers, in conjunction with the international television interests. The worldwide web of soccer, as they now call the ancient game, is stretched tautly across every screen that can take cable underground or a satellite from outer space. Instead of watching the game wrapped in mufflers, we watch on a wrap-around screen with wrap-around sound. Instead of hearing the crack of the crowd around us on a frosty afternoon we are subjected to the instant punditry of failed or former players who watch on a monitor in a studio. Where once we stamped our feet to keep warm we now flick the remote in order to keep up with the scores on every available channel. It's now almost too easy to watch football. The ritual of dressing for the match, the rite of the walk to the ground, the ceremony of greeting the teams as they come out, the hug of complete strangers when a goal is scored – all that seems pretty remote from the lonely watcher on his couch, sitting patiently through the commercials at every corner kick, a drink in one hand, and – who knows – a cigarette in the other.

And so it goes on, this football story. Even as you are reading this, somebody somewhere is playing football, whether it be on waste ground, on a beach, in a back garden, on a strip of asphalt or inside an echoing gymnasium, the ball is being chased and a goal aimed at. It's something we all strive for – a goal of some kind. What it is, is only important to us, but in that team sport called football there is only one kind, a framed rectangle, draped in nets. Someone, somewhere is kicking towards it now. It might be under a cloudless sky, or in rain or snow – even in a fog – hemmed in by mountains or surrounded by trees. It might be in a city street, but the game is being played out by two, five, or eleven or twenty-a-side as long as there is light and they have breath and they have a ball. Anyone can play. Everyone can watch. Its rules are simple and its place is anywhere where there is space. Its goals are before our eyes. We need to dream to live and the attainment of a goal is the living fulfilment of a dream. We need to worship something and football provides its own icons. The sacrifice offered is a young man's sweat and occasional blood. Its heroes are proved on the field, and its gods are those football greats whose congregation is all the peoples of the world.

Addendum

The *Scottish Athletic Journal* reported in 1882:

> The game was at Annbank. Not more than five hundred people
> were on the field, and a slovenly-looking, petticoated, and
> extremely vulgar section of the crowd had answered to the
> courteous invitation, 'Ladies Free!' The language which came from
> the lips of these ladies was sickening to listen to. The men behaved
> moderately well, and in respect of them, it may be as well to forgive
> the fair sex in the hope that in future they will stay at home.

By 1895, *Scottish Sport* was complaining:

> The members of the new Ladies Football Association, of which we
> have lately heard so much, do not play in fashion's dresses, but in
> knickers and blouses. They actually allow the calves of their legs
> to be seen and wear caps and football boots. The more shame to
> them, is our retort.

All this did was to bring a retort from one lady reader: 'Hands down,
all ye crusaders against knicker-attired females!' Which appeared to be
the last word on the matter of women and football.

That is, until recently.

More than a hundred years later, there have now been moves to
allow the Scottish Women's Football Association to sit on the hitherto
men-only SFA Council, and application has been made to the Sports
Council for funds to appoint a full-time female coach to the women's
national football side. The appointment of a female manager to a club
side in Scotland may yet remain only a possibility in terms of television
fantasy, but there is no doubt that the supposedly weaker sex is
making strong inroads into what has always been a bastion of
maledom. Up till now only Aggie Gray, the tea-lady at St Johnstone's
ground, could be said to have made any impression on the football

scene in Scotland and that was only because she gave Graeme Souness as good as she got. That may only have been a storm over a teacup but it prepared the public for Sally Johnson's co-option on to the Hearts Board, although she herself was reluctant to talk about it.

> It makes it seem as if I'm just some kind of novelty, and I don't think I am. It's almost as if you've got the job because you've got a pair of tits rather than being any good at it.

We have certainly come a long way since those 'knicker-attired females'. Louise Kelly is on the Board of Raith Rovers, but then her husband is the owner. Much is made of her being a wife and mother, and little of the fact that she has a sound business background and the acumen to go with it. She is already well aware that 'some men don't want women here'. Male chauvinism is alive and well within Scottish football, but larger commercial considerations are beginning to make inroads on all the old prejudices. Mary Ann McAdam was financial controller at Celtic Park for six years before moving on to Hibernian. 'I'm a harder person than I was at Celtic Park,' she says. 'Women in football have to fight that little bit harder. When I started, people used to think I worked in catering.' Audrey Bastianelli at Dunfermline Athletic recognises that she works in a male-dominated environment and that it's not going to change overnight. She says, 'The bottom line is that you're here to do a job . . .' Margot McCuaig is curator of the new Celtic Museum and Susan Bonner's job at Tynecastle is to promote football within the female community, but it must be said that even if the efforts of all these clever women do manage to put women into football, it will be a harder task to put football into women. Even if Lee Campbell is Stenhousemuir's approved physio and gets to travel on the team bus, she is saddened by the obscene comments she draws whenever she runs onto the park. Perhaps she could take a leaf out of her Victorian sisters' book and reply in kind. But then, Lee is a lady. That may be the root of the trouble. Football directors are not always gentlemen. They can be relied on to see that it will be a very long time yet before the playing field becomes a level area and women's place in Scottish football attains that star status reached by Michelle Akers and Mia Hamm in the United States. Yet who knows? Julie Fleeting's hat trick for Arsenal's Women's Team in the 2004 FA Cup final may be the start of something. This Kilwinning-born P.E. teacher, who has plied her trade as a professional footballer in the United States, may be the unexpected last word in the Scottish Football story.

A Football Roll of Honour

This book has been concerned with a hundred great footballers who have played for Scotland. Many others have done so – even if only once. Here are their names, with the date of their first cap.

Adams, J.	1889	Baird, A.	1892
Agnew, W.B.	1907	Baird, D.	1890
Aird, J.	1954	Baird, H.	1956
Aitken, A.	1901	Baird, J.C.	1876
Aitken, G.G.	1949	Baird, S.	1957
Aitken, R.	1886	Baird, W.U.	1897
Aitken, R.	1980	Bannon, E.	1980
Aitkenhead, W.A.C.	1912	Barbour, A.	1885
Albiston, A.	1982	Barker, J.B.	1893
Alexander, D.	1894	Barrett, F.	1894
Allan, D.S.	1885	Battles, B.	1901
Allan, G.	1897	Battles, B.	1931
Allan, H.	1902	Baxter, R.D.	1939
Allan, J.	1887	Beattie, A.	1937
Allan, T.	1974	Beattie, R.	1939
Ancell, R.F.D.	1937	Begbie, I.	1890
Anderson, A.	1933	Bell, A.	1912
Anderson, F.	1874	Bell, M.	1901
Anderson, G.	1901	Bell, W.J.	1966
Anderson, H.A.	1914	Bennett, A.	1904
Anderson, J.	1954	Bennie, R.	1925
Anderson, K.	1896	Bernard, P.R.J.	1995
Anderson, W.	1882	Berry, D.	1894
Andrews, P.	1875	Berry, W.H.	1888
Archibald, A.	1921	Bett, J.	1982
Archibald, S.	1980	Beveridge, W.W.	1879
Armstrong, M.W.	1936	Black, A.	1938
Auld, J.R.	1887	Black, D.	1889

Black, E.	1988	Brown, R.	1947
Black, I.H.	1948	Browning, J.	1914
Blackburn, J.E.	1873	Brownlie, J.	1971
Blacklaw, A.S.	1963	Bruce, D.	1890
Blackley, J.	1974	Bruce, R.F.	1934
Blair, D.	1929	Buchan, M.M.	1972
Blair, J.	1920	Buchanan, J.	1889
Blair, J.	1934	Buchanan, J.	1929
Blair, J.A.	1947	Buchanan, P.S.	1938
Blair, W.	1896	Buchanan, R.	1891
Blessington, J.	1894	Buckley, P.	1954
Blyth, J.A.	1978	Burley, C.W.	1995
Bone, J.	1972	Burley, G.	1979
Booth, S.	1993	Burns, F.	1970
Bowie, J.	1920	Burns, K.	1974
Bowie, W.	1891	Burns, T.	1981
Bowman, D.	1992		
Bowman, G.A.	1892	Cairns, T.	1920
Boyd, J.M.	1934	Calderhead, D.	1889
Boyd, R.	1889	Calderwood, C.	1995
Boyd, T.	1991	Calderwood, R.	1885
Boyd, W.G.	1931	Callaghan, P.	1900
Brackenbridge, J.	1888	Callaghan, W.	1970
Bradshaw, T.	1928	Cameron, J.	1886
Brand, R.	1961	Cameron, J.	1896
Branden, T.	1896	Cameron, J.	1904
Brazil, A.	1980	Campbell, C.	1874
Bremner, D.	1976	Campbell, H.	1889
Brennan, F.	1947	Campbell, J.	1880
Breslin, B.	1897	Campbell, J.	1891
Brewster, G.	1921	Campbell, J.	1893
Brogan, J.	1971	Campbell, J.	1899
Brown, A.	1890	Campbell, J.	1913
Brown, A.	1904	Campbell, K.	1920
Brown, A.D.	1950	Campbell, P.	1878
Brown, G.C.P.	1931	Campbell, P.	1898
Brown, H.	1947	Campbell, R.	1947
Brown, J.	1890	Campbell, W.	1947
Brown, J.B.	1939	Carr, W.M.	1970
Brown, J.G.	1975	Cassidy, J.	1921
Brown, R.	1884	Chalmers, S.	1965
Brown, R.	1885	Chalmers, W.	1885

Chalmers, W.S.	1929	Crerand, P.T.	1961
Chambers, T.	1894	Cringan, W.	1920
Chaplin, G.D.	1908	Croal, J.A.	1913
Cheyne, A.D.	1929	Cropley, A.J.	1972
Christie, A.J.	1898	Crosbie, J.A.	1920
Christie, R.M.	1884	Cross, J.H.	1903
Clark, J.	1966	Cruickshank, J.	1964
Clark, R.B.	1968	Crum, J.	1936
Clarke, S.B.	1988	Cullen, M.J.	1956
Cleland, J.	1891	Cumming, D.S.	1938
Clements, R.	1891	Cumming, J.	1955
Clunas, W.L.	1924	Cummings, G.	1935
Collier, W.	1922	Cunningham, W.C.	1954
Collins, J.	1988	Curran, H.P.	1970
Collins, T.	1909		
Colman, D.	1911	Dailly, C.	1997
Colquhoun, E.P.	1972	Davidson, C.	1998
Colquhoun, J.	1988	Davidson, D.	1878
Combe, J.R.	1948	Davidson, J.A.	1954
Conn, A.	1956	Davidson, S.	1921
Conn, A.	1975	Dawson, A.	1980
Connachan, E.	1962	Deans, J.	1975
Connelly, G.	1974	Devine, A.	1910
Connelly, J.	1973	Dewar, G.	1888
Connor, J.	1886	Dewar, N.	1932
Connor, J.	1930	Dick, J.	1959
Connor, R.	1986	Dickie, M.	1897
Cook, W.L.	1934	Dickson, W.	1888
Cormack, P.B.	1966	Dickson, W.	1970
Cowan, W.D.	1924	Divers, J.	1895
Cowie, D.	1953	Divers, J.	1939
Cox, C.J.	1948	Dodds, D.	1984
Cox, S.	1949	Dodds, J.	1914
Craig, A.	1929	Dodds, W.	1997
Craig, J.	1977	Donachie, W.	1972
Craig, J.P.	1968	Donaldson, A.	1914
Craig, T.	1927	Donnachie, J.	1913
Craig, T.B.	1976	Donnelly, S.	1997
Crapnell, J.	1929	Dougall, C.	1947
Crawford, D.	1894	Dougall, J.	1939
Crawford, J.	1932	Dougan, R.	1950
Crawford, S.	1995	Douglas, A.	1911

Douglas, J.	1880	Forrest, J.	1958
Dowds, P.	1892	Forrest, J.	1966
Downie, R.	1892	Forsyth, A.	1972
Doyle, J.	1976	Forsyth, C.	1964
Dunbar, M.	1886	Forsyth, T.	1971
Duncan, A.	1975	Foyers, R.	1893
Duncan, D.M.	1948	Fraser, D.M.	1968
Duncan, J.	1878	Fraser, J.	1891
Duncan, J.	1926	Fraser, J.	1907
Duncanson, J.	1947	Fraser, M.J.E.	1880
Dunlop, J.	1890	Fraser, W.	1955
Dunlop, W.	1906	Fulton, W.	1884
Dunn, J.	1925	Fyfe, J.H.	1895
Durie, G.S.	1988		
Durrant, I.	1988	Gabriel, J.	1961
Dykes, J.	1935	Gallacher, K.W.	1988
		Gallacher, P.	1935
Easson, J.F.	1931	Galloway, M.	1992
Elliott, M.S.	1998	Galt, J.H.	1908
Ellis, J.	1892	Gardiner, I.	1958
Evans, A.	1982	Gardner, D.R.	1897
Ewart, J.	1921	Gardner, R.	1872
Ewing, T.	1958	Gemmell, T.	1955
		Gemmell, T.	1966
Farm, G.N.	1953	Gemmill, S.	1995
Ferguson, B.	1998	Gibb, W.	1873
Ferguson, D.	1988	Gibson, D.W.	1963
Ferguson, D.	1992	Gibson, J.D.	1926
Ferguson, I.	1989	Gilchrist, J.E.	1922
Ferguson, J.	1874	Gilhooley, M.	1922
Ferguson, R.	1966	Gillespie, G.	1880
Fernie, W.	1954	Gillespie, G.T.	1988
Findlay, R.	1898	Gillespie, J.	1896
Fitchie, T.T.	1895	Gillespie, J.	1898
Flavell, R.	1947	Gillespie, R.	1927
Fleck, R.	1990	Gillick, T.	1937
Fleming, C.	1954	Gilmour, J.	1931
Fleming, J.W.	1929	Gilzean, A.J.	1964
Fleming, R.	1886	Glass, S.	1998
Forbes, A.R.	1947	Glavin, R.	1977
Forbes, J.	1884	Glen, A.	1956
Ford, D.	1974	Glen, R.	1895

Goram, A.L.	1986	Harper, J.M.	1973
Gordon, J.E.	1912	Harper, W.	1923
Gossland, J.	1884	Harris, J.	1921
Goudle, J.	1884	Harrower, W.	1882
Gough, C.R.	1983	Hartford, R.A.	1971
Gourlay, J.	1886	Harvey, D.	1974
Govan, J.	1948	Hastings, A.C.	1936
Gow, D.R.	1888	Haughney, M.	1954
Gow, J.J.	1895	Hay, D.	1970
Gow, J.R.	1888	Hay, J.	1905
Graham, A.	1978	Hegarty, P.	1979
Graham, G.	1972	Heggie, C.	1886
Graham, J.	1884	Henderson, G.H.	1904
Graham, J.A.	1921	Henderson, J.G.	1953
Grant, J.	1959	Hendry, E.C.J.	1993
Grant, P.	1989	Hepburn, J.	1891
Gray, A.	1903	Hepburn, R.	1932
Gray, A.M.	1976	Herd, A.C.	1935
Gray, D.	1929	Herd, D.G.	1959
Gray, E.	1969	Herd, G.	1958
Gray, F.T.	1976	Herriot, J.	1969
Gray, W.	1886	Hewie, J.D.	1956
Green, A.	1971	Higgins, A.	1885
Groves, W.	1890	Higgins, A.	1910
Guillieland, W.	1891	Highet, T.C.	1875
Gunn, B.	1990	Hill, D.	1881
		Hill, D.A.	1906
Haddock, H.	1955	Hill, F.R.	1930
Haddow, D.	1894	Hill, J.	1891
Haffey, F.	1960	Hogg, G.	1896
Hamilton, A.	1895	Hogg, J.	1892
Hamilton, A.W.	1892	Hogg, R.M.	1937
Hamilton, G.	1947	Holm, A.H.	1882
Hamilton, G.	1906	Holt, D.D.	1963
Hamilton, J.	1892	Holton, J.A.	1973
Hamilton, J.	1924	Hope, R.	1968
Hamilton, T.	1891	Hopkin, D.	1997
Hamilton, T.	1931	Houliston, W.	1949
Hannah, A.B.	1888	Houston, S.	1976
Hannah, J.	1889	Howden, W.	1905
Hansen, A.D.	1979	Howe, R.	1929
Hansen, J.	1972	Howie, H.	1949

Howie, J.	1905	Kay, J.L.	1880
Howieson, J.	1927	Keillor, A.	1891
Hughes, J.	1965	Keir, L.	1885
Hughes, W.	1975	Kelly, H.T.	1952
Humphries, W.	1972	Kelly, J.C.	1949
Hunter, A.	1972	Kelso, R.	1885
Hunter, J.	1874	Kelso, T.	1914
Hunter, J.	1909	Kennaway, J.	1934
Hunter, R.	1890	Kennedy, A.	1875
Hunter, W.	1960	Kennedy, J.	1897
Husband, J.	1947	Kennedy, J.	1964
Hutchison, T.	1974	Kennedy, S.	1905
Hutton, J.	1897	Kennedy, S.	1975
Hutton, J.	1923	Kennedy, S.	1978
Hyslop, T.	1896	Ker, G.	1880
		Ker, W.	1872
Imlach, J.J.S.	1958	Kerr, A.	1955
Imrie, W.N.	1929	Kerr, P.	1924
Inglis, J.	1883	Key, G.	1902
Inglis, J.	1884	Key, W.	1907
Irons, J.H.	1900	King, A.	1896
Irvine, B.	1991	King, J.	1933
		King, W.S.	1929
Jackson, A.	1886	Kinloch, J.D.	1922
Jackson, C.	1975	Kinnear, D.	1938
Jackson, D.	1995		
Jackson, J.	1931	Lambert, P.	1995
Jackson, T.A.	1904	Lambie, J.A.	1886
Jardine, A.	1971	Lambie, W.A.	1892
Jarvie, A.	1971	Lamont, D.	1885
Jenkinson, T.	1887	Lang, A.	1880
Jess, E.	1993	Latta, A.	1888
Johnston, A.	1998	Law, G.	1910
Johnston, M.	1984	Law, T.	1928
Johnston, W.	1966	Lawrence, J.	1911
Johnstone, D.	1973	Lawrence, T.	1963
Johnstone, J.	1888	Lawson, D.	1923
Johnstone, J.	1894	Leckie, R.	1872
Johnstone, J.A.	1930	Leggat, G.	1956
Johnstone, L.H.	1948	Leighton, J.	1983
Johnstone, R.	1938	Lennie, W.	1908
Johnstone, W.	1887	Lennox, R.	1967

Leslie, L.G.	1961	McCallum, N.	1888
Levein, C.	1990	McCann, N.	1998
Liddle, D.	1931	McCann, R.J.	1959
Lindsay, D.	1903	McCartney, W.	1902
Lindsay, J.	1880	McClair, B.	1987
Lindsay, J.	1888	McClory, A.	1927
Linwood, A.B.	1950	McCloy, P.	1924
Little, R.J.	1953	McCloy, P.	1976
Livingstone, G.T.	1906	McColl, A.	1888
Lochhead, A.	1889	McColl, I.M.	1950
Logan, J.	1891	McColl, W.	1895
Logan, T.	1913	McCombie, A.	1893
Logie, J.T.	1953	McCorkindale, J.	1891
Loney, W.	1910	McCormick, R.	1886
Long, H.	1947	McCrae, D.	1929
Longair, W.	1894	McCreadie, A.	1893
Lorimer, P.	1970	McCreadie, E.G.	1965
Love, A.	1931	McCulloch, D.	1935
Low, A.	1934	MacDonald, A.	1976
Low, W.L.	1911	McDonald, J.	1886
Lowe, J.	1887	McDonald, J.	1956
Lowe, J.	1891	MacDougall, E.J.	1975
Lundie, J.	1886	McDougall, J.	1887
Lyall, J.	1905	McDougall, J.	1926
		McDougall, J.	1931
McAdam, J.	1880	McFadyen, W.	1934
McAllister, B.	1997	Macfarlane, A.	1904
McAllister, G.	1990	McFarlane, R.	1896
McArthur, D.	1895	McFarlane, W.	1947
McAtee, A.	1913	McGarr, E.	1970
Macauley, A.R.	1947	McGarvey, F.P.	1979
McAuley, J.	1892	McGeoch, A.	1876
McAuley, J.	1893	McGhee, J.	1886
McAuley, R.	1932	McGhee, M.	1983
McAvenney, F.	1986	McGinlay, J.	1994
McBain, E.	1894	McGonagle, W.	1933
McBain, N.	1922	McGregor, J.C.	1877
McBride, J.	1967	McGrory, J.	1965
McBride, P.	1904	McGuire, W.	1881
McCall, J.	1886	McGurk, F.	1934
McCall, S.M.	1990	McHardy, H.	1885
McCalliog, J.	1967	McInally, A.	1989

McInally, J.	1987	McMenemy, J.	1934
McInally, T.B.	1927	McMillan, J.	1897
McInnes, T.	1889	McMillan, I.L.	1952
McIntosh, W.	1905	McMillan, T.	1887
McIntyre, A.	1878	McNab, A.	1921
McIntyre, H.	1880	McNab, A.	1937
McIntyre, J.	1884	McNab, C.D.	1931
McKay, D.	1959	McNab, J.S.	1923
Mackay, G.	1988	McNamara, J.	1997
McKay, J.	1924	McNeil, M.	1876
McKay, R.	1928	McPhail, J.	1950
McKean, R.	1976	McPherson, D.	1892
McKenzie, D.	1938	McPherson, D.	1989
Mackenzie, J.A.	1954	McPherson, J.	1875
McKeown, M.	1889	McPherson, J.	1879
McKie, J.	1898	McPherson, J.	1888
McKillop, T.R.	1938	McPherson, J.	1891
McKimmie, S.	1989	McPherson, R.	1892
McKinlay, D.	1932	McQueen, G.	1974
McKinlay, T.	1996	McQueen, M.	1890
McKinlay, W.	1994	McRorie, D.M.	1931
McKinnon, A.	1874	McSpadyen, A.	1939
McKinnon, R.	1966	McStay, W.	1921
McKinnon, W.	1883	McTavish, J.	1910
McLaren, A.	1929	McWhattie,	1901
McLaren, A.	1947	McWilliam, P.	1905.
McLaren, A.	1992	Macari, L.	1972
McLaren, J.	1888	Main, F.R.	1938
McLean, A.	1926	Main, J.	1909
McLean, D.	1896	Maley, W.	1893
McLean, D.	1912	Malpas, M.	1984
McLean, G.	1968	Marshall, G.	1992
McLean, T.	1969	Marshall, H.	1899
McLeish, A.	1980	Marshall, J.	1885
McLeod, D.	1905	Marshall, J.	1921
McLeod, J.	1888	Marshall, J.	1932
MacLeod, J.M.	1961	Marshall, R.W.	1892
MacLeod, M.	1985	Martin, B.	1995
McLeod, W.	1886	Martin, F.	1954
McLintock, A.	1875	Martin, N.	1965
McLintock, F.	1963	Martis, J.	1961
McLuckie, J.S.	1934	Massie, A.	1932

Masson, D.S.	1976	Murray, J.	1958
Mathers, D.	1954	Murray, J.W.	1898
Maxwell, W.S.	1898	Murray, P.	1896
May, J.	1906	Murray, S.	1972
Meechan, P.	1896	Mutch, G.	1938.
Menzies, A.	1906		
Mercer, R.	1912	Napier, C.E.	1932
Middleton, R.	1930	Narey, D.	1977
Millar, A.	1939	Neil, R.G.	1896
Millar, J.	1897	Neil, R.W.	1876
Millar, J.	1973	Neilles, P.	1914
Miller, J.	1931	Nelson, J.	1925
Miller, P.	1882	Nevin, P.K.F.	1986
Miller, T.	1920	Niblo, T.D.	1904
Miller, W.	1876	Nibloe, J.	1929
Miller, W.	1947	Nicol, S.	1985
Miller, W.	1975	Nisbet, J.	1929
Mills, W.	1936	Niven, J.B.	1885.
Milne, J.V.	1938		
Mitchell, D.	1890	O'Donnell, F.	1937
Mitchell, J.	1908	O'Donnell, P.	1994
Mitchell, R.C.	1951	O'Hare, J.	1970
Mochan, N.	1954	O'Neil, B.	1996
Moir, W.	1950	O'Rourke, F.	1907
Moncur, R.	1968	Ogilvie, D.H.	1934
Morgan, H.	1898	Orr, J.	1892
Morgan, W.	1968	Orr, R.	1902
Morris, D.	1923	Orr, T.	1952
Morris, H.	1950	Orr, W.	1900
Morrison, T.	1927	Orrock, R.	1913
Morton, H.A.	1929	Oswald, J.	1889
Mudie, J.K.	1957		
Muir, W.	1907	Parker, A.H.	1955
Muirhead, T.A.	1922	Parlane, D.	1973
Mulhall, G.	1960	Parlane, R.	1878
Munro, A.D.	1937	Paterson, G.D.	1939
Munro, F.M.	1971	Paterson, J.	1920
Munro, I.	1979	Paterson, J.	1931
Munro, N.	1888	Paton, A.	1952
Murdoch, J.	1931	Paton, D.	1896
Murphy, F.	1938	Paton, M.	1883
Murray, J.	1895	Paton, R.	1879

Patrick, J.	1897	Robertson, J.	1931
Paul, H.M.	1909	Robertson, J.	1991
Paul, W.	1888	Robertson, J.G.	1965
Paul, W.	1891	Robertson, P.	1903
Pearson, T.	1947	Robertson, T.	1889
Penman, A.	1966	Robertson, T.	1898
Pettigrew, W.	1976	Robertson, W.	1887
Phillips, J.	1877	Robinson, R.	1974
Plenderleith, J.B.	1961	Rougvie, D.	1984
Porteous, W.	1903	Rowan, A.	1880
Pringle, C.	1921	Russell, D.	1895
Provan, D.	1964	Russell, J.	1890
Provan, D.	1980	Russell, W.F.	1924
Pursell, P.	1914	Rutherford, E.	1948
Quinn, P.	1961	St John, I.	1959
		Sawers, W.	1895
Rae, J.	1889	Scarff, P.	1931
Raeside, J.S.	1906	Schaedler, E.	1974
Rankin, G.	1890	Scott, A.S.	1957
Rankin, R.	1929	Scott, J.	1966
Redpath, W.	1949	Scott, J.	1971
Reid, J.G.	1914	Scott, M.	1898
Reid, R.	1938	Scott, R.	1894
Reid, W.	1911	Scoular, J.	1951
Renny-Tailyour, H.	1873	Sellar, W.	1885
Rhind, A.	1872	Semple, W.	1886
Richmond, A.	1906	Sharp, G.M.	1985
Richmond, J.T.	1877	Sharp, J.	1904
Ring, T.	1953	Shaw, D.	1947
Rioch, B.D.	1975	Shaw, F.W.	1884
Ritchie, A.	1891	Shaw, J.	1947
Ritchie, H.	1923	Shearer, D.	1994
Ritchie, J.	1897	Shearer, R.	1961
Ritchie, W.	1972	Sillars, D.C.	1891
Robb, D.T.	1971	Simpson, J.	1895
Robb, W.	1926	Simpson, N.	1983
Robertson, A.	1975	Sinclair, G.L.	1910
Robertson, D.	1992	Sinclair, J.W.E.	1966
Robertson, G.	1910	Skene, L.H.	1904
Robertson, G.	1938	Sloan, T.	1904
Robertson, H.	1962	Smellie, R.	1887

Smith, D.B.	1966	Thomson, A.	1886
Smith, H.G.	1988	Thomson, A.	1889
Smith, J.	1872	Thomson, A.	1909
Smith, J.	1877	Thomson, A.	1926
Smith, J.	1924	Thomson, C.	1937
Smith, J.	1935	Thomson, D.	1920
Smith, J.E.	1959	Thomson, J.J.	1872
Smith, N.	1879	Thomson, J.R.	1933
Smith, R.	1872	Thomson, R.	1932
Smith, T.M.	1834	Thomson, R.W.	1927
Somers, P.	1905	Thomson, S.	1884
Somers, W.S.	1879	Thomson, W.	1892
Somerville, G.	1886	Thomson, W.	1896
Speedie, D.R.	1985	Thomson, W.	1980
Speedie, F.	1903	Thornton, W.	1947
Speirs, J.H.	1908	Toner, W.	1959
Stanton, P.	1966	Townsley, T.	1926
Stark, J.	1909	Troup, A.	1920
Steele, D.M.	1923	Turnbull, E.	1948
Stein, C.	1969	Turner, T.	1884
Stephen, J.F.	1947	Turner, W.	1885
Stevenson, G.	1928		
Stewart, A.	1888	Ure, J.F.	1962
Stewart, A.	1894	Urquhart, D.	1935
Stewart, D.	1888		
Stewart, D.	1893	Vallance, T.	1877
Stewart, D.S.	1978	Venters, A.	1934
Stewart, G.	1906		
Stewart, J.	1977	Waddell, T.S.	1891
Stewart, R.	1981	Wales, H.M.	1933
Stewart, W.E.	1898	Walker, A.	1988
Storrier, D.	1899	Walker, F.	1922
Sturrock, P.	1981	Walker, G.	1930
Sullivan, N.	1997	Walker, J.	1895
Summers, W.	1926	Walker, J.	1911
Symon, J.S.	1939	Walker, J.N.	1993
Tait, T.S.	1911	Walker, W.	1910
Taylor, J.	1872	Wallace, I.A.	1978
Taylor, J.D.	1892	Wallace, W.S.B.	1965
Taylor, W.	1892	Wardhaugh, J.	1955
Telfer, W.	1933	Wark, J.	1979
Telfer, W.D.	1954	Watson, A.	1881

Watson, J.	1903	Wilson, D.	1913
Watson, J.	1948	Wilson, D.	1961
Watson, J.A.K.	1878	Wilson, G.W.	1904
Watson, P.R.	1934	Wilson, I.A.	1987
Watson, R.	1971	Wilson, J.	1888
Watson, W.	1898	Wilson, P.	1926
Watt, F.	1889	Wilson, P.	1975
Watt, W.W.	1887	Wilson, R.P.	1972
Waugh, W.	1938	Wiseman, W.	1927
Weir, A.	1959	Wood, G.	1979
Weir, D.G.	1997	Wotherspoon, D.N.	1872
Weir, J.	1887	Wright, K.	1992
Weir, J.B.	1872	Wright, S.	1993
Weir, P.	1980	Wright, T.	1953
White, J.	1922	Wylie, T.G.	1890
White, W.	1907		
Whitelaw, A.	1887	Yeats, R.	1965
Whyte, D.	1988	Yorston, B.C.	1931
Wilson, A.	1907	Yorston, H.	1955
Wilson, A.	1954	Young, A.	1905
Wilson, D.	1900	Young, J.	1906

Bibliography

Alcock, Charles W., with Rowland Hill, *Famous Footballers, 1895–96* (Hudson and Cairns, with News of the World, 1897)

Allison, William, *Rangers: The New Era* (Rangers FC, 1967)

Archer, Ian, with Trevor Royle, *We'll Support You Ever More* (Souvenir Press, 1976)

Ball, Peter, with Phil Shaw, *The Book of Football Quotations* (Stanley Paul, 1984)

Bell, Bert, *Still Seeing Red* (Glasgow City Libraries, 1996)

Bold, Alan, *Scotland, Yes: World Cup Football Poems* (Paul Harris, 1978)

Brooking, Trevor, *100 Great British Footballers* (Macdonald/Queen Anne Press, 1988)

Campbell, Tom, with Pat Woods, *The Glory and the Dream: Celtic 1887–1980* (Mainstream Publishing, 1981)

Charlton, Jack, with Peter Byrne, *The Autobiography* (Partridge Press, 1996)

Cosgrove, Stuart, *Hampden Babylon* (Canongate, 1991)

Crampsey, Bob, *The Game for the Game's Sake* (Queen's Park Centenary, 1967)

——— *The Scottish Footballer* (Blackwood, 1978)

——— *Mr Stein* (Mainstream Publishing, 1986)

——— *The First Hundred Years* (The Scottish League, 1990)

Docherty, Tommy, *Call the Doc: An Autobiography* (Hamlyn, 1981)

Forsyth, Roddy, *The Only Game* (Mainstream Publishing, 1990)

Galbraith, Russell, *The Hampden Story* (Mainstream Publishing, 1993)

Gibson, Alfred, and William Pickford, *Association Football & The Men Who Made It* (4 Vols) (Caxton, 1906)

Glanville, Brian, *Soccer: A Panorama* (Eyre and Spottiswoode, 1968)

——— *A Book of Soccer* (Oxford University Press, 1979

——— *100 Great Players of All Time* (The Times, 1997)

Golesworthy, Maurice, *The Encyclopaedia of Association Football*

(Robert Hale, 1956)

——— (with Roger Macdonald) *A, B – Z of World Football* (Pelham Books, 1966)

Green, Geoffrey, *Soccer: The World Game* (Sportsman's Book Club, 1954)

Hamilton, Ian, *The Faber Book of Soccer* (Faber and Faber, 1992)

Hayes, Richard, *The Football Imagination* (Arena Books, 1995)

Henshaw, Richard, *The Encyclopedia of World Soccer* (New Republic Books, USA, 1979)

Hutchison, John, *The Football Industry* (Richard Drew Publishing, 1982)

Inglis, Simon, *The Football Grounds* (Willow Books, Collins, 1985)

Jarvie, Grant, with Graham Walker, *Scottish Sport in the Making of the Nation* (Leicester University Press, 1994)

Joannou, Paul, *Wembley Wizards* (Mainstream Publishing, 1990)

Lamming, Douglas, *A Scottish Internationalists' Who's Who, 1872–1986*, (Hutton Press, 1987)

McAllister, Bill, *Highland Hundred* (The Highland Football League, Inverness 1993)

MacBride, Eugene, and Martin O'Connor with George Sheridan, *An Alphabet of the Celts* (ACL & Polar Publishing (UK) Ltd, 1994)

McCarra, Kevin, *Scottish Football: A Pictorial History* (Third Eye/Polygon, 1984)

MacDonald, Kenny, *Scottish Football Quotations* (Mainstream Publishing, 1994)

McIlvanney, Hugh, *McIlvanney on Football* (Mainstream Publishing, 1993)

McNee, Gerald, *The Story of Celtic: 1888–1978* (Stanley Paul, 1978)

Maley, Willie, *The Story of the Celtic* – original 1939 edition and facsimile, (Desert Island Books, 1996)

Morris, Desmond, *The Soccer Tribe* (Jonathan Cape, 1981)

Murray, Bill, *The Old Firm* (John Donald Publishers, 1984)

——— *Glasgow Giants* (Mainstream Publishing, 1988)

——— *Football: A History of the World Game* (Scolar Press, 1994)

Rafferty, John, *One Hundred Years of Scottish Football* (Pan Books, 1973)

Rollin, Jack, *The Guinness Book of Soccer Facts and Feats* (Guinness Superlatives, 1978)

Soar, Phil, with Martin Tyler, *The Encyclopedia of British Football* (Marshall Cavendish, 1971)

Taylor, Hugh, *Great Masters of Scottish Football* (Stanley Paul, 1967)

Walvin, James, *The People's Game* (Mainstream Publishing, 1994)

Ward, Andrew, *Scotland: The Team* (Breedon Books, 1987)

Watt, Tom, *A Passion for the Game* (Mainstream Publishing, 1993)